UNDER THE RADIANT SUN
AND THE CRESCENT MOON

ANGELA M. JEANNET

Under the Radiant Sun and the Crescent Moon

Italo Calvino's Storytelling

UNIVERSITY OF TORONTO PRESS
Toronto Buffalo London

© University of Toronto Press Incorporated 2000
Toronto Buffalo London
Printed in Canada

ISBN 0-8020-4724-6

Printed on acid-free paper

Toronto Italian Studies

Canadian Cataloguing in Publication Data

Jeannet, Angela M
    Under the radiant sun and the crescent moon : Italo Calvino's storytelling

(Toronto Italian studies)
Includes bibliographical references and index.
ISBN 0-8020-4724-6

1. Calvino, Italo – Criticism and interpretation.   I. Title.   II. Series.

PQ4809.A45Z75 2000   853'.914   C00-930428-4

This volume was published with financial assistance from Franklin & Marshall College.

University of Toronto Press acknowledges the financial assistance to its publishing program of the Canada Council for the Arts and the Ontario Arts Council.

University of Toronto Press acknowledges the financial support for its publishing activities of the Government of Canada through the Book Publishing Industry Development Program (BPIDP).

Contents

The City of Crossed Destinies: A Preface in the Form of a Story   vii

Historical Notes   xi

Introduction   xiii

1 Literature and Doubt   3

2 Surveyors   35

3 Survivors, or The Pastoral Denied   65

4 Telling Stories   101

5 Between Garbage and Cosmos   134

6 Under the Crescent Moon   155

Bibliographical Information   179

Index   191

The City of Crossed Destinies:
A Preface in the Form of a Story

The city was grey under a cold sky. Piles of sandbags stacked geometrically rose to great heights around even taller buildings. Behind them, she was told, there were famous monuments, the Baptistry, palaces, the Cathedral's marble sculptures, bronze and gold doors, the landmarks she imagined only vaguely; they were ghosts of themselves, like the houses and woods that hover in a landscape shrouded by fog. When the alerts sounded mournfully and shrill in mid-morning all over the city (the dark streets batted the sound back and forth, and then let it die away in the mist of the hills), streams of people came out of the buildings to plunge into deep, meandering caves.

She left her classroom with her professor and her schoolmates through the darkened halls teeming with bodies. One of the children vomited once, he was so frightened. But she felt excited, she liked the people's white faces, the noise, the rushing, the civilian guards shepherding people into the shelters, and the loneliness of the streets after the last siren had long ceased to sound. She did not go to the shelter, usually; she liked to find herself alone, to be the last one to say goodbye to the city. Once she saw waves of Flying Fortresses arrive in formation, very high, a geometric grid of steel moving steadily through wisps of clouds. The roar of the engines rumbled through the blue sky, and she looked at the planes with detached curiosity. When the bombs fell, unexpected, the air shrank out of her lungs, and she felt like she was suffocating. That was the time she ran to the shelter, and banged on the locked doors, and someone opened them, as clouds of dust rose, majestic, from the collapsed apartment buildings.

Steps in the street, a marching platoon, at times, a low-pitched song. He despised those moments, and the sadness of the immense distance he felt from the shrouded city, the emaciated people, the frightening singers, and from the other life he had once lived, elsewhere. Years before, so it seemed, in a city where cafés and offices were filled with young journalists and artists, who were his friends. The aroma of coffee enveloped long-ago conversations. The streets, then, shone in the evening; crystal windows and lamps exchanged a myriad of colours with reflected brightness. But now, coffee did not exist any more, unless you could afford the black market price of a few grains, rare dark gems. People he knew were gone. And he could not leave his hiding place, except sometimes at dusk, briefly, in terror.

He returned to his manuscript that performed the magic of making him forget the present; it took him back to another time, to the southern village of his earlier exile, to that light-blinded, courteous, desperate land that Christ had never visited.

He was not going to stay in this city. Too dangerous, now that the war was going into an uncontrollable rampage, like a terrified bull. He thought of his house in San Remo, and the terraced hills, dry and steep above the sea. His parents' place was very near the war zone. Again he tried not to remember his days in conquered France, as a teenage Fascist, months before; he tried to avoid the feeling of shame those days elicited that made him vaguely sick at his stomach.

The university in this city was really not functioning, and he was not going to stay; he was going back to San Remo. The front was approaching, moving up along the entire stretch of the peninsula, destroying everything in its path. Goodbye studies, goodbye natural sciences, botany, forestry. This city was covered by a shroud, the people were tight-lipped, and spoke only to those they knew well. Germans and Fascists were everywhere. What could he do in a city that was waiting for the onslaught as if for a storm, hoping to re-emerge on the other side without being destroyed?

The cafés: that's what he had liked in this city. But now a pall had descended on it. At night, streets and piazzas were dark, lonely, and during the day they were filled with armed men; this was a city gripped by fear. Once, you could sit in the café at the edge of this large square, which actually was one of the dullest in the city, and wait for the group of friends who would invariably arrive, each in his own good time. That's where his life really was. Literature and music and art were the topics of leisurely banter; and how to make ends meet, if one did not have a job because one lacked the party identification card. Poetry still got written and published, and journals still appeared irregularly, keeping jealous guard over the culture they had elaborated through the years of repression. What could one do, now? You had to endure, he thought, you had to wait for the infernal dance to stop, count the wounded and the dead, and go on.

She had to stay put for a while. The rooms her friend had provided for her and her children were cramped, but they were safe. She had changed her name, she was numb and totally concentrated on the survival of her little tribe. Now she was writing a note to a distant friend, after moving north from Rome, to tell her people further up north that she had found a haven, and that she was not going to leave her secret shelter in this beautiful city that looked back at her from under its bandages and shrouds. She was finishing writing the note that she was going to give to a young woman who would be her courier. 'I have lost him,' she was writing her people, 'I am here with our children.' She would not sign her name; once again in her life, she had to deny her existence, she could not say, 'Yours, Natalia.'

One day, that winter, five people crossed, at different times of the day, a vast rectangular space overlooked in the distance by the geometric patterns of a church's marble façade, and by the ever present mountain of grey sandbags: Piazza Santa Croce, in Florence.

In late morning, a young man pedalled a bicycle swiftly in a diagonal line across the square. He observed the pattern his wheels drew, as they cut across the grid of streets reiterated by the pattern of dark-green and pink lines that cut the white marble of the church at straight angles. He looked, then pedalled away, disappearing into a narrow street at the west end of the square.

Around noon, a woman appeared at the corner of a street at the extreme east end of that same square, pulling a little flock of children gently by the hand in an absent-minded way. They moved along slowly, and seemed intent on drawing another set of diagonal lines across the square, which intersected at four different points the two wavy lines left by the wheels of the cyclist, who was by then gone.

In the afternoon, well after the alert was over, a girl of about eleven walked purposefully across the square toward the steps leading to the church that rose high upon them. Her feet followed a line that laid across the six left by the mother, the children, and the cyclist, who were gone, and whom she would never meet in her life. The little girl climbed the steps almost at a run, pushed a small padded door inside the arched portal, and went into the nave, which was very dark but warmer than the outside. She stopped for a very long time in front of each monumental tomb that rose white in the darkness.

Later that afternoon, a plump man strolled slowly across the square, without looking at the church. He went in the direction of the San Niccolò bridge, toward the river. A virtual diagonal, cutting the others on a bias, was all that was left of his passage.

Later yet, but before the curfew fell, a man crossed the square rapidly, close to the walls, and turned a corner into a curved street. His short diagonal path could not intersect the blank traces of the eight previous passers-by. He was gone.

Piazza Santa Croce, in Florence, in the winter season of 1943.

Many more events were to take place in Florence, between that winter and 1945: the mining of the ancient bridges, the passing through of the front, the departures and arrivals of the troops of a hundred countries, with their bartering of goods and flesh, with the despair, shame, exultation, and dull stupor of war. Thousands upon thousands of steps left their mute traces on the stones and dust of Florence. In a celebrated garden that lay softly on the slopes of a hill in view of the city, among throngs of hungry people, a woman was going to cry over the lost pages of her novel, destroyed by the bombs, and was consoled by the artist she had evoked: Artemisia.

Florence in wartime: from all that happened, from the pain and the sorrow, emerge the memories of a childhood, the probabilities of time and place, and the potential web of invisible encounters.

Historical Notes

The preface to this volume presents in a fictional mode some writers who influenced several generations of readers and also were Calvino's mentors or contemporaries. The following notes are meant to serve as a guide. For further information, a most useful tool is the *Dictionary of Italian Literature* edited by Peter Bondanella and Julia Conaway Bondanella (Westport, CT: Greenwood, 1996).

1915–18   Italy fights in the First World War.

1917   The Russian Revolution begins.

1919   Mussolini creates the first nucleus of the Italian Fascist party.

1921   The Italian Communist party is born; Antonio Gramsci is one of its founders.

1922   Mussolini, with a small troop of militiamen, marches on Rome. Victor Emanuel III of Savoy, then king of Italy, accepts the fait accompli and names him to head a new government.

1923   Italo Calvino is born on 15 October.

1925   Eugenio Montale's *Ossi di seppia* (Cuttlefish Bones) is published. Montale will be for a number of years (until his refusal to become a member of the Fascist party) the director of a prestigious library in Florence, the Gabinetto G.P. Vieusseux. He and many other writers and artists are in the habit of gathering at the central café called Giubbe Rosse, which still exists on the Piazza della Repubblica.

1926   'The first memory of my life is that of a Socialist being beaten by a Fascist militiaman'; Calvino, quoted in *Romanzi e racconti* (Novels and Short Stories) I lxiv.

1929	The Lateran Pact is signed by the Vatican State and the Italian Fascist State.
1934	Luigi Pirandello, writer of poems, novels, short stories, and plays, receives the Nobel Prize for Literature.
1935–6	Italy occupies Ethiopia.
1936–9	The Spanish civil war is fought.
1938	Anti-Semitic laws (the so-called racial laws) are promulgated in Italy.
1938–9	Elio Vittorini publishes *Conversazione in Sicilia* (Conversation in Sicily).
1940	Italy enters the Second World War.
1941	Cesare Pavese, who will be Calvino's mentor at the publishing house Einaudi, publishes *Paesi tuoi* (Your Hometown).
1942	Natalia Ginzburg publishes her first novel, *La strada che va in città* (The Road to the City), under an assumed name, Alessandra Tornimparte.
1943	On 25 July the High Council of the Italian Fascist party gives Mussolini a vote of no-confidence.
	On 8 September Italy signs an armistice with the Allies and abandons the alliance Mussolini had forged with Nazi Germany and Japan. Many Italians, men and women, military and civilian, join the Resistance against the Nazis and the reconstituted Fascist party (called Repubblica Sociale Italiana, from which came the term *repubblichino*).
1944	Calvino joins the Resistance. Leone Ginzburg, Natalia Ginzburg's husband, dies at the hands of Fascist torturers.
1945	The Second World War ends.
	Carlo Levi, a physician, painter, and essayist, publishes *Cristo si è fermato a Eboli* (Christ Stopped at Eboli), which he had written while in hiding in Florence.
1946	Calvino publishes his first novel, *Il sentiero dei nidi di ragno* (*The Path to the Nests of Spiders*).
1948	Anna Banti publishes *Artemisia*.
1950s	The 'nouveau roman,' fiction written by a group of innovative young French writers, stirs debate in the literary world.
1953	Stalin dies.
1957	The European Common Market is founded.
1965–74	The Vietnam war is fought.
1985	Calvino dies in Rome.

Introduction

The image [of the Italian writer outside Italy] is different because in Italy you are seen with your entire range of activities, in the context of a culture that is made up of many things and with many points of reference. Abroad, only your books in translation arrive, like meteorites, and readers and critics must reconstruct on that basis the planet from which they broke off. ('L'immagine dello scrittore [italiano fuori d'Italia] cambia perché in Italia uno è visto per tutto l'insieme delle sue attività, nel contesto di una cultura fatta di tante cose, di tanti punti di riferimento, mentre all'estero sono solo i libri tradotti che arrivano come dei meteoriti, attraverso i quali critici e pubblico devono farsi un'idea del pianeta da cui si sono staccati.')

Italo Calvino, *Eremita a Parigi*

As Italo Calvino's death becomes a more distant event, we wonder about the place occupied by his work in what is rapidly becoming 'the past.' The least productive way of answering that question is the one chosen by those critics and historians of literature who have engaged in debate over classification and ranking, arguing whether or not Calvino's fiction can be placed alongside the 'classics'; whether he is first, second, or third on the literary team; and whether he is less exalted than many thought, or greater than some believed.[1]

Certainly the urge to classify once and for all the work of a recently departed artist is very human. Calvino is gone; his cycle is concluded. We have overcome the sense of loss caused by his death, as the events that many of us once shared with him congeal in historical interpretations. Time has moved on since he has grown silent, carrying with it the books he wrote, books that now must be discovered by new generations of readers for whom Calvino never was a physical presence. The temptation to enshrine or forget is strong. And yet our farewell inevitably extends a new welcome to him, as other readings are done, necessarily different from earlier ones. The works left us by a writer named Italo Calvino belong, now more than ever, to a multiplicity of readers.

To speak of those works is not an easy task. Calvino seems to have said everything, controlled everything, foreseen everything about his own writing, with a lucidity and agility that make the critic despair. What is left for the reader to say? This book looks at the core of Calvino's writing practice, from the perspective of a historical moment that has confirmed the collapse of large portions of our culture's edifice and the failure of most experiments that were based on that culture's conceptual foundations. We will attempt to identify some of the voices Calvino listened to, and the 'voices' he created to address the audience he imagined. A constant thread through this volume is the question – explored but never definitively answerable – of Calvino's connections with other practitioners of literature written in Italian. He had very deep roots in the Italian tradition, but he was also a subtle critic and subverter of it, and his profound relationship with it accounts for his ambivalence toward the various -isms that have claimed him. For all readers of Calvino, the leading thread into his fictional labyrinth is his love of storytelling and his faith in its power.

All writers are interpreters of culture, if we take the term 'culture' in its multiple definitions. The term 'interpreter' also must not be used in the traditional sense, as referring to an intermediary between some undecipherable reality and human beings – a function Calvino explicitly refused (although writers' disclaimers should not always be listened to). Interpreting, for Calvino, is what writers do as they elaborate their visions in dialectic exchange with the readers' own. Writers link up with the life experience of their societies in complex ways. They are also nourished by, and in turn nourish, the literary universe from which they issue, whether they do so as representatives of a tradition or as rebels against it. Some writers are placed at a more felicitous junction between those two levels of activity than others, for whatever reason. Readers, particularly those who are attentive to the culture-related dimensions of language, find in them an inclusiveness of concern, a complexity of motif, and an ambiguity of tone that favour a multi-dimensional rapport between reader and text. Through all his writings, in fiction and essays,

Calvino proposed to his readers a variety of literary constructs inviting them to join him in his work at three levels: in bringing their literary heritage to a new kind of fruition, in elaborating new visions of the social experience, and in exploring humanity's changed relationship with its environment (in its widest sense). While it is virtually impossible to separate these three major lines of force in the actual practice of the author, there are ways of analysing, from various points of view, Calvino's profoundly original approach to the questions concerned.

Calvino's fiction emerged from the context of a specific time, a place, and certain existential experiences. It is important to remember that his concept of literature was formed in Modernist environment, but was also challenged at least twice, by those events that caused ruptures in his life and his culture. The first time was when the reality of the Resistance brought to an end the prerogatives of a bourgeois sensibility that had remained anchored, however uncomfortably, in a tradition of Olympian detachment. The second time was when disillusionment with direct political involvement forced him to reflect on who and what he was. Because of those two dramatic moments of coming to awareness, in the passionate times evoked by Paolo Spriano in *Le passioni di un decennio* (The Passions of a Decade), Calvino learned to identify himself as a 'writer,' but at the same time could assert, over and over again, that there is no 'vacanza dalla storia' (*Il menabò* 6, 271; 'we cannot take a vacation from history'). We will see how Calvino himself, in constructing his persona as he elaborated his writings, returned obsessively to four major factors in his formation: a childhood in the ecological paradise of a lost Liguria, the stern rationalism of a secularized Protestantism, his readings of comic strips and travel adventures, and the maturing experience of the Resistance.

His existential path, which included his reading experiences, went from the European twenties to the eighties. His cultural connnections were rich, for he belonged to a portion of the Italian bourgeoisie that was enlightened and intensely devoted to the culture it had elaborated through the centuries, a culture that included concepts of human dignity, justice, and beauty.[2] That intellectual *borghesia*, with its limitations, virtues, and merits, was also only dimly aware of the dispiriting humiliations its culture was suffering and of the major disasters it would have to face; or perhaps it chose to be unaware, first out of incredulity and then out of terror. The ensuing distress, enthusiasm, and disillusionment were that much more profound and determinant for young people, for those who reacted against Fascism, and for those who chose self-immolation in defence of an empty Fascist rhetoric.

Calvino, as he said in autobiographical notes he carefully hid in little-explored texts, had been immunized against the pomposity and sloppiness of Fascist mannerisms by his unconventional upbringing, which was stern, sober, and permeated by dedication to the natural sciences. Most of Calvino's relatives were scientists, including his mother, who was of Sardinian extraction; she was a staunch defender of the purity of the Italian language (*Eremita a Parigi* [A Hermit in Paris] 206) and a Socialist unwavering in her opposition to organized religion. On his father's side, Calvino also belonged to a very small minority in Italy, the Waldenses, whose educational tradition rooted in Protestantism Italo absorbed during his early schooling. Because of their professions, their connections (Calvino's father was a Mason), and their beliefs, the Calvinos maintained a cosmopolitan spiritual and intellectual perspective at a time when Italy was suffocated by isolationist forces emanating from fascist ideology. Calvino, then, inherited a critical attitude toward majority positions, and a mistrust of *all* oppressive systems and all unexamined *parole d'ordine* (passwords). That became clear when he was exposed to the authoritarian ways of Fascism and later of the official Italian Communist party. His vaguely anarchistic secularism would shape even his attention to the pervasive claims of postmodernism – the bourgeois culture's latest (self-)snare. He simply saw in all modes of perception and expression useful tools for discovery. While even postmodernism assumes the existence of a sort of 'progress,' as its use of *post* shows, Calvino insisted on believing only in ambiguity and doubt, and obstinately pursued his explorations of language and reality excluding no means, least of all reason.

In spite of the ex-centric position the Calvinos occupied in Italian society, the young man's life was in most ways prototypical of that of a child of the Italian intellectual middle class: he had a well-regulated and protected existence in a provincial town, his days of happy unawareness were devoted to studies and leisure, and his expectations certainly fit those of his class and time. Both maternal and paternal families were rooted in the lesser landowning class that drew most of its income from inherited wealth and maintained a contradictory relationship to the land, which was dwindling in size and had always been poor in resources. They behaved as owners on the one hand, and as stubborn caretakers on the other, with an aesthetic appreciation of natural phenomena that owed much to the humanistic tradition, but was disciplined, in the Calvinos, by a drive to observe, describe, and catalogue that originated in the tradition of the Enlightenment. The members of that lesser landowning class could not rely on revenues from large estates as the few families of the aristocracy could. Usually, they opted for professional careers that were guaranteed a satisfying development by the *borghesia*'s virtual monopoly on education. The perspective on reality that was the hallmark of that class, therefore, rested not on mythical or religious bases, but on belief in the value of learning, science, and the legitimacy of a generous but stern paternalism.

By the time Calvino was born, the collapse of some classes that had survived the centuries (such as the peasant class) and the shrivelling of an enlightened bourgeois culture were already under way. The young Calvino soon became aware of it, as we can deduce from several short stories, such as 'Pranzo con il pastore' (Dinner with a Shepherd), which is now in the section of *I racconti* (Short Stories) entitled 'Le memorie difficili' (Difficult Memories). He looked with irony at the discomfort created when the symbolic forms of a bourgeois identity (manner of eating, tableware, furnishings) were seen as if for the first time and made absurd by the presence of an alien, in this instance a shepherd from the Ligurian hills. Everything in the well-ordered and innocently self-satisfied bourgeois household assumes new meaning, as it reveals, in the choreography of its conventions, its essential quality as sociopolitical statement. By the 1930s, the idyll of paternalistic ownership, if it ever existed, was over. In the short story just mentioned, while the father of the narrator is blissfully unaware of the awkward situation created by the juxtaposition of two cultures and the shepherd remains enclosed in his silence, the adolescent son of the family, who is the narrator, struggles with feelings of furious impatience and a vague sense of shame. In his first novel, Calvino would make the intellectual Resistance fighter Kim say, 'It was our elders ... who were serene, the great bourgeois fathers who once created wealth' ('Sereni erano i ... padri, i grandi padri borghesi che creavano la ricchezza'; *Il sentiero dei nidi di ragno* [*The Path to the Nests of Spiders*] 149).

Meanwhile, other social realities were taking shape in the newly industrialized world inhabited by Calvino. The late forties and the fifties transformed the Italian social landscape. Later in his career, Calvino mused over his inability to bring into his fiction the universe of the industrial proletariat in a way that he felt was convincing, something he had tried to do. Actually, Calvino wrote perceptive journalistic essays about labour politics in Italy in the new industrial age, and some of those essays found their way into the volume *Una pietra sopra* (Burying the Past). However, the world of labour was a universe that could not be easily analysed or fictionalized by an imagination nurtured on the problematics of a bourgeois cultural tradition that had essentially rural roots. Calvino, with his usual keenness, was aware of that, as we can see from a significant text written in 1977:

> I never believed in the politicization of the students *as a mass* ... The coming to politics of a bourgeois – that particular type of bourgeois that a student *always* is – requires passing through a narrow door, and means separation from the mass of one's peers, individual initiation, isolation, and critique ('Non ho mai creduto alla politicizzazione degli studenti come *massa* ... La politicizzazione del borghese – di quel particolare tipo di borghese che è *sempre* lo studente – è il passaggio per una porta stretta, è separazione dal grosso dei propri simili, è iniziazione individuale, isolamento e critica'; 'I nostri prossimi 500 anni' [Our Next 500 Years], *Saggi* [Essays] II 2297. Calvino's emphasis).

Anyway, the industrial labour class itself was destined to have a very short period of hegemonic glory on the Italian scene, as new configurations of industry and work were to impose their models on a rapidly changing national reality, beginning in the sixties and continuing to the end of the twentieth century.

As we read Calvino's texts, our task will be to reconstruct the profoundly bourgeois dimension of this writer. He was the witness of moments of crisis that were Italian, but not Italian only, when experiences, sensibility, language, and ideals were re-examined, and entire portions of a societal culture sank into oblivion under the impact of swift economic and cultural shifts. The voices that speak in Calvino are the voices of adolescents, poets, and *naïfs* placed in unfamiliar surroundings, who look at their problematic world, and themselves in that world, without self-pity or complaint. They accept that they must live with the contradictions and ambiguities of experience, and they move jauntily among the objects of their universe, using their imagination as a tool to explore an ever deepening doubt.

The primary societal structure privileged by Calvino turned out to be not one of those conventionally studied by sociology or anthropology, but language – first, as a medium with inexhaustible potential, and second as a repository of the historical record, through which the working out of a culture's self-definition is most evident. His formation was at the origin of his choice and of his trust in the written language and in literature. Reflecting on his 'masters,' he had discovered a failed integration ('un'integrazione mancata') between literature and culture, and felt the need to avoid their failure. Ultimately, it was the written word that he saw as the supremely flexible medium, through which all that is written and unwritten is filtered and finds its expression. As many twentieth-century authors did before him, he believed that from language as a societal tool, through poetics in its varied manifestations linked to the conventions of human societies, one could reach the universe of doing that is synonymous with moral integrity and with politics in the wide sense.

Calvino's curiosity and versatility make his works a valuable textual resource for scholars, because he provides examples that enrich all sides of the debate over changing concepts of literature and language. He confirmed the views of those who held that the poetic effect consists in the ambiguity of the message. He mastered the surprise effect caused by a writer's evasion of expectations, when he or she uses a linguistic code system in which readers are constantly, repetitiously, and boringly immersed. Calvino seemed too conventionally Italian to the sixties' avant-garde, because of his adherence to supposedly stale linguistic, stylistic, and cultural norms. Yet paradoxically it was Calvino who produced paragons of the self-reflexive text, and forced readers to re-evaluate the standards that serve the needs of everyday communication and of literature. On the other hand, the playfulness and richness of Calvino's fiction make it attractive to less scholarly readers. His texts shift between styles and modes, from 'modernist' to 'postmodernist' positions, from the meditative posture of the Enlightenment to the twentieth century's obsessive fear of loss of self in an uncharted void, and in the end they stubbornly confirm their author's refusal of despair.

Chapter 1 of this book explores Italo Calvino's literary affinities with some of the Italian writers active between the two wars, especially during the period that encompassed his formation.

In chapters 2 and 3, the focus is on Calvino's dilemma-filled vision of reality and writing practice, in which perplexity mixes with playfulness and humour, and language reflects the condition of *dimidiamento*, of 'halved' selves. The efforts made by Calvino's characters to overcome the rift, which turns out to be both internal and external, infuse the narrative with comic energy and with melancholy. At this point, we see how Calvino's texts re-examine and bring to closure the elaboration of several thematic and stylistic models that were his inheritance from the Italian poetic and cultural tradition.

Chapter 4 looks at the magic of fiction as Calvino interpreted it. It discusses his views about the function of storytelling in literature and society, and his intellectual and poetic bequests.

Chapter 5 follows the transformations in Calvino's images of the human community, and examines the roots and expression of his evolving social concerns.

Finally, chapter 6 focuses on the elaboration of the feminine in Calvino's works, not only as a thematic element but as an essential component of his stylistic and theoretical universe.

Titles of books by Calvino and others are given in Italian, but they are translated the first time they appear in the volume.

1   On this topic, the best example is a publication that appeared well after this manuscript was completed. Carla Benedetti has contrasted Calvino, a 'bloodless' author ('l'autore immagine'), with Pier Paolo Pasolini ('l'autore in carne ed ossa,' a 'flesh-and-blood author'), and called for 'an impure literature.' Her volume has been followed by heated polemical articles in various Italian dailies and journals, as was to be expected.

2   Gobetti's act of accusation against a 'non-bourgeoisie' in *La rivoluzione liberale* accentuates the importance of the slight minority, cosmopolitan and thoughtful, that was decimated by various agencies and social shifts between 1930 and 1950. The Calvinos belonged to that minority. For a treatment of these concepts, see the essay by Paolo Flores d'Arcais that serves as a preface to the 1995 edition of Gobetti's book.

UNDER THE RADIANT SUN
AND THE CRESCENT MOON

1

Literature and Doubt

Born in 1923, as in the heavens the radiant Sun and gloomy Saturn were guests of the harmonious Libra ... ('Nato nel 1923 sotto un cielo in cui il Sole raggiante e il cupo Saturno erano ospiti dell'armoniosa Bilancia ...')

Italo Calvino, *Tarocchi*, biographical note

Two Generations, Two Lives

For a young man of the well-to-do, well-educated middle class, who was in his teens in the thirties and living in a small town in Italy, evidence of the contradictions that filled daily life must have been fraught with mystery. On the one hand, there was the obvious comfort and sense of safety provided by a culture deeply rooted in the past; on the other, there was growing repression, which was silencing some of the best and brightest critics of the regime, throwing a pall over all intellectual life, and causing anxiety and confusion. Books were forbidden, people were being forced into exile or confinement, and a dull tension was building up everywhere. The drafting of young people into Fascist paramilitary organizations provided them with excitement and promised adventure; but disenchantment and pessimism grew among their elders, as they saw with alarm that wars kept breaking out year after year. Young people lived their time of innocence and dawning awareness surrounded by a population that was in part co-opted and in part silent, in the midst of uncertainty, fear, and, ultimately, mounting resistance.

Reading was the primary component of learning and leisure for that generation of young Italians, even though films also, powerfully but too briefly, made an impact on them. And all the contradictions of those times and that society found intensified expression in some of the texts that appealed to those same young people. For Italo Calvino, once he had traversed the worlds of *Pinocchio*, Stevenson, and Kipling and had absorbed the lessons of his beloved comic strips, one author loomed large in his formation: Eugenio Montale.

Montale's poetry could have been a paralysing ideal for young readers-writers, as it rose solitary against the background of a shabby official culture. The seduction of its essentiality and of the poet's refusal to 'obey' was undeniable, in the face of a regime that was at the same time crude and pretentious, and whose motto was Believe, Obey, Fight. For the young Calvino, the statement made by the Montalean voice was immediately and profoundly congenial, as he asserted years later in one of the first, and perhaps most famous, of his essays, 'Il midollo del leone' (The Lion's Marrow, 1955). He evoked with evident rhetorical impetus a Montalean 'uomo ermetico,' autonomous, unsentimental, and elusive, a man 'who seemed to have been created expressly to weather unpropitious times ... with a minimum of contamination and also a minimum of risk' ('che sembrava costruito apposta per passare attraverso tempi infausti ... con un minimo di contaminazione e insieme con un minimo di rischio'; *Una pietra sopra* 4). The period of intense social and political activity of the early 1900s was over by the time Montale started publishing, and the impact of the First World War and its aftermath were causing widespread sociopolitical retrenchment. Soon, entire societies had to learn to negotiate the various forms of totalitarianism that emerged from the rubble of the previous half century. For Montale, the function of literature was not to be consolatory but rather to encourage disengagement, to serve as a warning about the fallacies of existence, and to suggest a radical doubt about the 'real' as well as about the language that attempted to capture it. His poetry spoke of distance and solitude, and yet, by its very being, was stubbornly present. It was also important that Montale's voice, although powerful and deep, privileged understatement and a discretion that had explicit musical affinities: it spoke *in sordina*, in falsetto, refusing the oratorical heroics and the loudness that were then in vogue. It prized a personal sort of involvement, as it addressed without emphasis an elusive interlocutor, using the intimate *tu* in dialogues as spare as those 'cuttlefish bones' that gave his first published volume its title. Montale's voice had drawn richness and sensibility from D'Annunzio's flamboyant example,[1] but had chosen a direction antithetical to that taken by the earlier poet.

It has been said that Italo Calvino is not an 'Italian' writer,[2] for a variety of reasons. To the contrary, he is *very* Italian, if that attribute means to have been nourished by a literary tradition that includes continuous attention to the French- and English-language cultures, and if it means to believe that only the very controlled linguistic medium used by literature can adequately express a fundamental doubt, and by expressing it hope to dominate it. On close analysis, the similarities between the beginnings of Montale and Calvino, both very Italian but also very cosmopolitan writers, are striking. First of all, they developed a distinctive persona, in their respective milieux: a young man 'timid, thoughtful, and perplexed' ('timido, pensieroso, perplesso'; Luperini 10), whose experience of reality as a 'history of defeat and frustration' ('vicenda di scacco e di frustrazione'; Luperini 20) was counterbalanced by trust in literature as the realm of integrity and meaningfulness. A feeling of existential and social failure, due to a *diversità* that was also a source of pride, found solace in what Luperini calls 'aesthetic compensation' ('risarcimento estetico'; 7). And yet Montale and Calvino moved along dissimilar lines, as they belonged to very different family environments and entirely different epochs.

Montale was the last son of a prosperous middle-class family, and his youth was evenly divided between contempt for middle-class aspirations, and dandyism. Twice he witnessed the collapse of the world he knew, as the First and then the Second World War transformed the landscape of his life. He focused on the individual experience of loss, wilfully closing his universe to the outside, burrowing into a bruised conscience, and placing a certain distance between poetry and current events, while not refusing compassion. Because of artistic congeniality, he chose to be a disciple of those late nineteenth-century and early twentieth-century literary figures who are variously listed under the Symbolist or Modernist headings. It is important to remember, at this point, that, while the term 'Symbolism' was more clearly and consistently defined across the various linguistic areas of Western literature, 'Modernism' was, and still is, used to denote very different phenomena, as any specialized reference text will show (under *Modernism* in English, *modernismo* in Italian, *modernismo* in Spanish, etc.).[3] No matter what term we may wish to use, it is clear that Montale had affinities with writers such as Baudelaire, Flaubert, Verlaine, Keats, Mallarmé, Eliot, and Valéry. If he felt in 'total disharmony with the reality that surrounded [him]' ('una totale disarmonia con la realtà che [lo] circondava'; *Sulla poesia* [On Poetry] 570), he found his solace in art, 'the form of life of those who do not truly live, a compensation, or *ersatz* ('la forma di vita di chi veramente non vive: un compenso o un surrogato'; 562). He found his sense of belonging in a tradition that 'wrung eloquence's neck' – in Verlaine's words, which he quoted – and concentrated on the play of images that took place inside an exact and taut web of language. Lyric poetry was for him, as for his elders, 'a fruit that was meant to hold its reasons inside, and not reveal them' ('un frutto che dovesse contenere i suoi motivi senza rivelarli'; 566–7).

It was through Montale, without doubt, that the richness of Symbolist and Modernist literature reached the adolescent Calvino and left an indelible mark on him. Even later generations of readers, such as those who came of age in the late forties, followed the same path. But the world around the younger man was a very different place from Montale's. The Calvinos' rationalistic secularism, their lack of roots in Catholicism, and their allegiance to a scientific vision of the universe contrasted with Montale's more common Italian formative pattern, with its mixture of mistrust for religious institutions and profound attachment to the emotional and spectacular dimensions of all aspects of life. The coincidences of history also paradoxically and brutally underlined the epochal change in atmosphere: Piero Gobetti was the editor who first published Montale's poetry, in 1925. It was Gobetti, a martyr of Fascist repression at twenty-four years of age, who was to have a major influence on the younger generation of which Calvino was a member, through the political inheritance he left behind.[4]

Above all, it was the Resistance that played a determinant role in Calvino's life, as it effected for him a radical break with the past.[5] Montale's poetry had cultivated distance, closure, and negation of all action as postures enabling one to survive the 'tempi infausti,' but for Calvino and his contemporaries action and human contact were an inescapable choice. The guerrilla actions that bloodied Italy between 1943 and 1945 were the traumatic but energy-laden reinstatement of an entire people in the sociopolitical arena. The 'ethical commitment' ('volontarismo etico'; Luperini 24) that had been for some a passive exercise for over twenty years found its outcome in the choice of a side in the struggle, with the Resistance or with the Fascists, as one became a *partigiano* or a *repubblichino*. A few were granted the luxury of a place in the middle, which in any case could be the most dangerous choice of all, but all Italians – with no exception – discovered what bound one person to all others, because individual survival became impossible.

Existential choices and discoveries meant new perspectives for literate young people, too. In the fervour of political and military action, they also learned to appreciate anew the quality of sharedness in artistic and literary experience, for better or for worse. Even within Fascism, someone like Elio Vittorini had represented a critical and populist wing in politics and literature. And, like Vittorini, the new generation of writers came to privilege storytelling, placing new value on the communally shared pleasure of *raccontare:* 'We found ourselves face to face, filled with tales to be told ... We moved in a multicoloured universe of stories' ('si era faccia a faccia, carichi di storie da raccontare ... ci muovevamo in un multicolore universo di storie'; *Il sentiero dei nidi di ragno* 7–8). Italian history had become autobiography, and literature knew again the excitement of adventure and the sense of community.

Other Voices

Montale's naysaying and his practice of simplicity and clarity were accompanied by the exaltation of 'aridità' (dryness) and the speaker's retreat from the world of action. He claimed the necessity of choosing a posture not of indifference but of refusal. He looked upon historical events as phenomena of a superficial and transitory nature, and therefore preferred to focus on what he saw as essential, a human condition that was inevitably and unchangeably made of solitude and disillusionment. A deterministic universe allowed the Montalean persona no alternatives. Even in the late forties and the fifties, times that were not as 'infausti' (unpropitious, a term often used to refer to those years) as the thirties had been, the poetic voice's rejection of all certainties counselled against any dynamic interaction with the new political, emotional, and literary epoch. However, the changed historical milieu meant that other readings, in addition to those rooted in turn-of-the-century culture, had also become influential for Italian readers: Gramsci for instance, Moravia, and above all Pavese and Vittorini.

Although Calvino insisted throughout his career that the new generation of Italians was looking at the world 'as if for the first time,' and then turned that statement into an image of his ideal for literature and a component of his poetics, there is no doubt that his elaboration of a personal existential experience and literary expression was filtered through numerous screens.

A new mode of writing had been announced shortly after the end of the First World War by Alberto Moravia's early fiction, from *Gli indifferenti* (The Indifferent) of 1929 to *La mascherata* (The Masquerade) of 1941, whose impact on the Italian literary scene was immediate. As Alberto Arbasino inimitably put it in *L'anonimo lombardo* (Anonymous from Lombardy), 'He evokes the most ambivalent and curious feelings in our literature; Moravia, or my heart belongs to daddy' ('suscita i sentimenti più ambivalenti e curiosi della nostra letteratura, Moravia cioè my heart belongs to daddy'; 89–90). The gelid pessimism of Moravia's texts, the malignant vitality of his universe, and his dispassionate observation of the human scene foretold the arrival of the French 'littérature du refus.' Most important for Italian readers, Moravia's non-rhetorical writing and technical skill provided an antidote to bad writerly habits and was a school for the new generation of writers. As for his language, it adhered to the standard of the middle class, free of preciosities and dialectal limitations, and was most apt to record the chronicle of a *borghesia* that was by then becoming aware of its claustrophobic situation.

Moravia had especially mastered the writing of short fiction, the pride of the Italian tradition. Contained in a prescribed narrow space that lent intensity to scenes, episodes, and entire life histories, his short texts focused on prototypical existential moments with uncannily convincing verisimilitude. Each story caught characters of a recognizable low, middle, and high bourgeoisie in their daily compromises and least flattering positions. Several of Calvino's early short stories, such as 'Visti alla mensa' (At the Cafeteria), 'Dollari e vecchie mondane' (Dollars and Old Ladies of the Night), 'Un letto di passaggio' (A Temporary Bed), and 'Furto in una pasticceria' (Thieves in the Pastry Shop), were patterned on Moravia's. Moravia's voice can be heard in Calvino's evocation of urban settings and raw action, underlined by a modern vocabulary and a quickened narrative pace. It can be detected in the descriptions of port cities, with their cafés and bars, soldiers and prostitutes, bodies and clothes. Calvino's focusing on the poorer strata of society and on the vulgarity of petty human preoccupations, be they economic problems in their most humble, yet painful, forms or the strategies used by small-time crooks to survive in the urban jungle in the aftermath of a world war, are recognizably Moravian. It is true that the expressionistic techniques appropriated by Calvino, although skilfully used, seem marginal to his fictional universe: they insist on the physical grotesque, on marionette-like behaviour, and on the raw economic motives of people's emotional interactions. However, those short stories were largely experiments, a way of playing with different possibilities, and they served to focus on, and define, a truly Calvinian domain. Occasionally, Calvino's writing, even then, veered away from the model. The proliferation of words singing the praises of abundance, sensuousness, and joyful abandon tells readers that they are indeed reading Calvino.

In Calvino's words, 'the exit from the climate of Hermeticism' ('la sortita dal clima ermetico'; *Una pietra sopra* 5) was enacted precisely by those who moved on to, and at least temporarily were identified with, Neorealist poetics.[6] The new style of literature appealed to him because it had an epic and adventurous charge that suggested physical and moral energy ('la carica epica e avventurosa, di energia fisica e morale'; *Una pietra sopra* 56). Always sensitive to the concrete dimensions of literary phenomena, he pointed out that the move involved even a change in geographic location, a fact that visibly highlighted the shift in cultural balance that took place when Italy emerged from the Second World War: Turin and Milan, instead of Florence and Rome, became intensely active literary spaces in the late forties and the fifties, confirming their growing importance in several domains of life. Already in the late thirties and early forties, shortly after Moravia had started giving the Italian public the well-structured texts of European quality that it craved, a new influential dyad had begun operating between those two cities, Elio Vittorini and Cesare Pavese. Also, Turin and the Italian Communist party were the places where a large number of young and less young intellectuals clustered after 1944. 'We had drawn for ourselves a line of departure, or rather a sort of triangle, each of us on the basis of a local lexicon and landscape: *The House by the Medlar Tree*, *Conversation in Sicily*, and *Your Hometown*' ('Ci eravamo fatti una linea ossia una specie di triangolo: *I Malavoglia, Conversazione in Sicilia, Paesi tuoi* da cui partire, ognuno sulla base del proprio lessico locale e del proprio paesaggio'; *Il sentiero dei nidi di ragno* 9). Verga's lesson, though, seems to have been overshadowed for Calvino by the influence of the two more recent authors, through whom European and American voices reached the Italian reading public.

Vittorini's *Conversazione in Sicilia* (Conversation in Sicily) appeared in 1938–9, and it is hard today to appreciate fully its impact in those dark years. Here was a narrative whose intense language echoed at the same time American voices, everyday Italian speech, and the obsessive rhythms of mythic tales. The sense of despondency and fury that open the novel found an echo among the young; it provided a new prototype for the most turbulent and passionate recounting of journeys. No matter what the interpretation of that text may be today, after so many years, it offered then a concrete example of the wealth of possibilities available to future literature in Italian. The first Calvino short story to reach the public, 'Andato al comando' (Sent to Headquarters), is an exercise in Vittorini's footsteps, down to the impersonal names of the protagonists, 'the Armed Man' and 'the Unarmed Man,' the 'voi' address used by the characters, and the tautological, singsong quality of the dialogue. Yet Calvino finds a little side path of his own while following Vittorini's example: the conversational quality of the lexicon and the idiomatic expressions, which he uses sparingly, show his familiarity with Tuscan texts and his cautious incorporation in his own writing of the flavours of regional Italian. Also very significant, in Calvino the setting is the woods, *il bosco*, with its magic aura that will continue to impart a most distinctive quality to Calvinian prose. Above all, the world is quietly called 'ambiguous' ('un mondo ambiguo'; *I racconti* 50), and even the image of death is striking not because of its dramatic quality, but because of the precision of its homely and yet macabre details: 'And so he remained, a corpse in the depths of the woods, with his mouth full of pine needles. Two hours later, he was already black with ants' ('Cosí rimase, cadavere nel fondo del bosco, con la bocca piena d'aghi di pino. Due ore dopo era già nero di formiche'; *I racconti* 51). The Vittorini model, rather stiffly followed in the first part of the story, allows the sound of a more harmonious rhythm, sparingly quickened by familiar speech, to come through at the story's closure. The sober tone of the ending makes the reader aware of the astonishing ordinariness of all life cycles.

Pavese, speaking in 1946 of F.O. Matthiesen, and of his own quest for an authentic voice, indirectly expressed the importance of what Vittorini had achieved with *Conversazione*: he had used a language so concrete that he had succeeded in eliminating all barriers between the ordinary reader and the most profound reality of symbols and myths ('Maturità americana' [American Ripeness], *La letteratura americana ed altre cose* [American Literature and Other Essays] 180). As Pavese reflected on literary history in the making, he served as an intermediary between the other two writers, Vittorini and Calvino, and his mediation was determinant in Calvino's development as a writer. First of all, there was Pavese's search for a standard language actually spoken by everyone, that could also be a tool for the writer. He aimed at giving Italians what the Americans supposedly had: a national literature, common to the entire country, and a 'local written style' ('scrittura provinciale') rich with all the juices and nuances of a regional but not dialectal universe, and accessible to the majority. Pavese also gave the young Calvino the example of a writer open to the voices of foreign literatures, a writer who was an attentive reader and a fine critic, an intellectual with solid roots in the soil of his origins, and a student of disciplines (ethnology in Pavese's case) with insights and hypotheses that enriched his writing. The breadth of Pavese's interests underscored his search for meaning; what he achieved, and Calvino valued, was the sort of clear-eyed, dry detachment that is appropriate to an observer who will not indulge in nurturing illusions. When it comes to the more specific, technical aspects of the writing practice, there is no doubt that Calvino experimented along Pavesian lines. A group of short stories, 'Le memorie difficili' (Difficult Memories), conveys a Pavesian feeling even by its title, foregrounding the pain involved in the evocation of an adolescence tormented by curiosity, self-doubt, and a deep-seated sense of guilt. One can cite as an example the Pavese-like opening of a short story from that group. Written in the first person, the story is entitled 'I fratelli Bagnasco' (The Bagnasco Brothers), and the brothers referred to are two happy-go-lucky small landowner's sons. The story is set in a rural area, the hills of a Northern Italian region reminiscent of Pavese's Langhe. The theme also is familiar to readers of Pavese, the return of aimless men from long journeys. A static countryside and an old house embody the narrator's nostalgia for his own childhood, with its lack of responsibilities:

> I am away from home for months on end, sometimes for years. Once in a while I go back, and my house is still there, on top of the hill, with its reddish old stucco that you can glimpse from far away, behind the olive trees thick as smoke ... In the house there is my brother, who is always roaming the world like me; but he returns home more often than I do, and when I go back I always find him there ... ('Io sto via da casa mesi e mesi, talvolta anni. Torno ogni tanto e la mia casa è sempre in cima alla collina, rossiccia per un vecchio intonaco che la fa intravedere da lontano tra gli olivi fitti come il fumo ... In casa c'è mio fratello, che è sempre in giro per il mondo anche lui, ma torna a casa più spesso di me e io tornando ce lo ritrovo sempre'; *I racconti* 210).

Suddenly the evocative, melancholy tone is broken by vivacious exclamations and Tuscanisms (here marked by italic type): 'Hey! – he goes when I arrive, and perhaps we haven't seen each other in years and he didn't expect me at all' (' – Oh, – *mi fa* quando arrivo, e magari sono anni che *non ci si vede* e lui non s'aspettava che arrivassi ...,' etc.).

The examples of Pavesean and Vittorinian patterns in the early Calvino could be multiplied, and the evolution of a Calvinian model could be further documented; but what is most important is that Vittorini and Pavese – no matter what their differences might have been – were of one mind in assigning a fundamental importance to the act of writing, which is a persistent characteristic of the Italian literary ethos. On that basis, they made an almost puritanical commitment to the writer's trade. For them, the craft's practice required an integrity that crossed over into the personal realm and defined individual ethics. Nowhere did Calvino's appreciation of that posture become more evident than in the pages he wrote after Pavese's suicide, when he evoked his mentor's 'extraordinary, stubborn, devouring love of work' ('straordinario testardo divorante amore per il lavoro'; *Una pietra sopra* 8).

From the practical point of view, where actual writing was concerned, Italian narrative achieved its most effective realization, with Vittorini and Pavese as well as with Moravia, not in massive novels but in novellas or texts composed of recognizable episodes. One could debate the extent to which the mechanics of the publishing world influenced the pace of some of their works and those of many other writers whom Calvino recognized as influential (*Conversazione*, for instance, first appeared serially in the journal *Letteratura*), or the extent to which that choice was due to their authors' having found a congenial rhythm, almost their breathing cadence. What is important here is that Calvino's 'masters' did most of their writing, and their best, in the realm of short fiction. They refused totalizing structures, illusions, and consolation, and they kept their faith in the written word.

The Montalean imprint, through all this, remained the primary one for Calvino, almost as a subconscious presence. For a person who had come of age reading Montale's *Ossi di seppia* (Cuttlefish Bones), inevitably 'rhythm and ethics [were] already seen as interdependent' ('ritmo ed etica appaion già correlativi'; Contini 6). Later, in 1953, Calvino would assert, 'If Turin attracted me, it was because of its moral and civic, and not literary, aura' ('è stata un'immagine morale e civile, e non letteraria, di Torino, ad attrarmi' *Saggi* II 2705), collapsing in a very Calvinian way concepts of literature, ethics, and the presence of a city. And in a statement dated 1959, he again emphatically acknowledged the importance he attributed to the connection between ethos and poiesis:

> The poet of our youth was Eugenio Montale. His poems, tight, hard, difficult, with no connection to a story except individual and interior, were our point of departure. His universe, stony, dry, glacial, negative, without illusions, was for us the only solid ground in which to set roots ... He taught us to stay close to the bone in everything; he taught us that the things of which

we can feel certain are very few, and must be painfully felt deep within us; he taught us the lesson of stoicism ('Il poeta della nostra giovinezza è stato Eugenio Montale: le sue poesie chiuse, dure, difficili, senza alcun appiglio a una storia se non individuale e interiore, erano il nostro punto di partenza: il suo universo pietroso, secco, glaciale, negativo, senza illusioni, è stato per noi l'unica terra solida in cui potevamo affondare le radici ... ci ha[nno] insegnato in ogni cosa a tenerci all'osso, ci ha[nno] insegnato che ciò di cui possiamo essere sicuri è pochissimo e va sofferto fino in fondo dentro di noi: una lezione di stoicismo'; 'Tre correnti del romanzo italiano d'oggi' [Three Currents in the Contemporary Italian Novel] *Una pietra sopra* 48–9).

The conviction that style is an indivisible quality of life and literature became a Calvinian tenet never to be repudiated; it marked the various phases through which, right from the beginning of his writing career, Calvino constructed his universe.[7]

Between Neorealism and Perplexity

Reading and writing were vital and connected activities for Calvino, as is true for any writer, even those vociferously given to the praises of orality. In autobiographical notes that seem to have been more important to him than he wanted others to believe, Calvino drew his self-portrait as a man of few words, whose communicative and expressive needs very soon found their exclusive medium in the written word (*Eremita a Parigi* 206). He was always careful to keep oral expression, particularly dialectal, at a safe distance: 'The language in which I write no longer has anything to do with any spoken idiom, except through the filter of memory' ('la lingua in cui scrivo non ha più nulla a che fare con alcun parlato tranne che attraverso la memoria'; *Eremita a Parigi* 207). No less could be expected from a writer who made his characters find ways to communicate through all sorts of unconventional media, such as tarots and chess, after they had been struck by mysterious aphasias.

As suggested earlier, Calvino's first short stories, those written between 1943 and 1949, were often experiments, forays into different kinds of writing and narrative modes that reflected the variety of his readings. They ranged from the apologue to the *tranche de vie*. But in his best pieces, those in which his voice is more self-assured, his prose insistently echoes the Montalean rhythms of *Ossi di seppia* (Cuttlefish Bones, 1925) and *Le occasioni* (Occasional Poems, 1939). That rhythm had been committed deeply to memory and was to remain audible in the Calvinian texts until at least the mid-sixties. If Montale's poems had a narrative quality that tempered the traditionally inaccessible heights of Italian lyric poetry, Calvino's prose incorporated poetic modes in his own distinctive diction, which was plain and elegant. The classical seven-syllable and eleven-syllable lines (*settenàri* and *endecasillabi*) appear frequently in Calvino's descriptive passages; at other times, they give musical lightness to the opening of a story, or bring a story to closure with dreamlike suspense. The examples one could provide are innumerable, as even an incomplete list taken from *I racconti* will show. Those lines, with their very effective pattern of stresses and rhythms, reveal the skill of a poet. They often include various rhetorical devices, synaesthetic touches, and triads of adjectives, and very frequently discreet alliterations:[8] 'Muoveva attento intorno gli occhi ansiosi' (10; 'He watched anxiously with mobile eyes'), and 'Ombre di pietra chiara / circondavano il fondo tutt'intorno' (10; 'The shadows of clear stones surrounded the bottom'); 'ed un lento veliero vi passava' (24; 'and a slow sailing ship was crossing it'); 'in mezzo all'acqua ferma e densa d'alghe' (13; 'in the middle of the water thick with algae'); 'e sporgevano gli occhi senza sguardo' (27; 'and they looked out with their blind eyes'); 's'alzò un volo di passeri con gridi. / Poi ritornò silenzio. / Era forse un giardino abbandonato?' (31; 'sparrows flew up screeching. Then silence returned. Was it an abandoned garden?'); 'Ne raggiunsero i margini: / era a piastrelle azzurre / ricolma d'acqua chiara fino all'orlo' (31; 'They reached the edge. It was made of blue tiles and was filled to the brim with clear water'); 'infreddolito, candido e belante' (39; 'chilled, pure white, and bleating); 'Mai nessuno degli uomini lo seppe' (40; 'No man ever knew it'); 'Crede d'avermi ucciso, invece vivo' (51; 'He thinks he killed me, but I am alive'); 'il lampeggiare / del dorso di una trota / che riaffiorava subito a zig zag' (52; 'the flash of a trout's back that came fluttering to the surface'); 'C'era un'aria / timida e tersa, da mattina presto' (53; 'The air was mild and polished as of early morning'); 'forse un galletto di marzo. Uno sparo / e cadde' (55; 'perhaps it was a March cockerel. A shot, and it fell'); 'Il corvo s'abbassava lentamente / a giri' (56; 'The crow was circling down, slowly'); 'quinte di uno scenario spaesato' (57; 'wings of an odd stage'); 'prati minati gravidi di morte' (58; 'mined meadows bearing death'); 'le pareti di roccia nuda e ripida' (71; 'the walls of bare, steep rock'); 'una lunghissima e stretta caverna' (72; 'a long, narrow cave'); and, later, 'l'acqua calma batteva senza spuma' (314; 'the waves came ashore quietly without foam'); 'Così arrivammo al porto e c'era il mare' (384; 'So we reached the port, and there was the

sea'). Quite logically, there are no poetic rhythms in any of the 'neorealist' short stories, those patterned on Moravia's model, but they return in
'Il gatto e il poliziotto' (The Cat and the Policeman) and become very
frequent in the stories that have the character Marcovaldo as a protagonist. Some of the titles of the early period are particularly striking: 'Un
pomeriggio, Adamo' (Adam, an Afternoon); 'Mai nessuno degli uomini
lo seppe' (No One Ever Knew It), which is echoed by the last sentence of
the story; and 'Ultimo viene il corvo' (The Crow Comes Last). One of the
clearest examples of the rhythm Calvino impressed on his prose comes
from the ending of *Il barone rampante* (*The Baron in the Trees*). The phrasing vibrates with tension, and the paragraph becomes poem:

> Il cielo è vuoto / e a noi vecchi d'Ombrosa / abituati a vivere / sotto quelle
> verdi cupole / fa male agli occhi guardarlo ... Ombrosa non c'è più.
> Guardando il cielo / sgombro / mi domando / se davvero è esistita / ... e
> tutto il resto è palme / coi loro ciuffi scarmigliati / alberi inospitali del
> deserto' (87; 'The sky is empty, and for us, the old people of Ombrosa, who
> were accustomed to living under those green canopies, it hurts our eyes to
> look at it ... Ombrosa is no more. When I look at the clean sky, I wonder if it
> really once existed ... and all the rest is palms with their dishevelled tops,
> those inhospitable trees from the desert).

Rhythm taken by itself would be an empty shell; it cannot be
abstracted from the context of lexicon, images, and themes, to which it is
intimately bound. As far as that context was concerned, Calvino showed
no interest in engaging in avant-garde experiments, a choice that was
certainly not universal during his period of Italian literary life. The components of his expression are invariably standard, although by no
means dull, flat, or banal. In fact, Calvino waged an increasingly intense
battle against the flattening and devitalizing of the Italian language by
incapable users in bureaucracy and the media. The adjectives he used
to characterize the writing by authors he prized remained constant
through the years and were borrowed from the Montalean vocabulary:
'hard, difficult, rocklike, dry' ('duro, difficile, pietroso, secco'). The same
can be said about the substantives he selected to define metaphorically a
literature of value: bone, earth, rock, cliff, roots, dryness, stoicism.

It is not surprising, then, that the lexical constants in most of Calvino's
own short stories would cluster around key words of the early Montalean lexicon: stone, rock, crag, cliff, seaweed, agaves (*sasso, pietra, roccia, scogliera, alghe, agavi*). Very early in his career, Calvino even played

with borrowing from the world of images of his favourite poet. An echo from Montale's 'Marezzo,' for instance, appeared in 'Ultimo viene il corvo' and acquired more than a hint of preciosity in the hands of the youthful imitator. Montale's classic hendecasyllable 'e il cristallo dell'acque si smeriglia' (*Ossi di seppia*; 'and the crystal of the water is troubled as if brushed by emery') became 'the flowing of the stream brushed the silence, as if with emery' ('lo scorrere del ruscello smerigliava il silenzio'; *Ultimo viene il corvo* 30). The image obviously fascinated Calvino, who continued working with it until the end of his life. In 'Il nome, il naso' (A Name, the Nose), he wrote again, more aptly and with greater ease, 'half of the letters have been erased by the emery of the sand-laden wind' ('metà delle lettere [sono] state cancellate dallo smeriglio del vento carico di sabbia'; *Sotto il sole giaguaro* [*Under the Jaguar Sun*] 7).

With practice and experience, the loans became more subtle and complex. In the titles cited earlier, the metric pattern of *settenari* and hendecasyllables, along with a variety of stresses, served to foreground settings, symbolic presences, and a sense of mystery that clearly evoked a Montalean aura. Living beings and images familiar to readers of Montale return: molluscs clinging to sea rocks, sunny afternoons in an arid landscape overlooking the sea, Mediterranean gardens in the heat of midday, the craggy line of the Ligurian coast, and animals of a domestic world (crickets, frogs, crabs, fish, cicadas, and spiders). Two images most clearly filter from the Modernist tradition into Calvino's world through the elaboration effected by Montale's poetry: that of children intent on their games on streets and near water (rain puddles, streams, or the sea) and the occasional presence of a clownlike adult, whose grip on reality is usually tentative. The clown figure, in twentieth-century Italian poetry and fiction outside the avant-garde, had already acquired more understated and universal characteristics: from circus or stage character he had become a clumsy, perplexed individual pulled in opposite directions by contradictory impulses; and such he remains in Calvino.

Those images, which in Montale were 'occasions' for a deceptively plain narrative poetry firmly anchored in the observation of life's phenomena, found a congenial environment in Calvino's poetic narration. As a matter of fact, the natural image that was Montale's favourite metaphor for describing the very essence and mechanics of writing returns quite often in Calvino, playfully developed and elaborated, most probably in unconscious emulation. Montale said:

I will have before me a land of untouched snows ...
... happily will I read on their whiteness
the branches' black markings
like a basic alphabet

('Avrò di contro un paese d'intatte nevi ...
... lieto leggerò i neri
segni dei rami sul bianco
come un essenziale alfabeto')

'Quasi una fantasia' (Almost a Fantasy), *Ossi di seppia*,
in *L'opera in versi* (Poems) 18

In several Calvinian texts, also, writing acquires an organic quality, becomes thicket (see the end of *Il barone rampante*, and 'L'avventura di un poeta' [The Adventure of a Poet] – in *I racconti*), ball of thread ('La penna in prima persona' [The Pen in the First Person] in *Una pietra sopra*), or hare's footprints ('I figli di Babbo Natale' [Santa's Children] in *Marcovaldo*); a maze of black hieroglyphics against a white background creates whimsical variations on the conventional image of writing as a pattern of black on white. The temptation of calligraphy, inevitable product of the writers' love for the miraculous power of the 'technology' that is writing, turns into a play of concrete images in Calvino's texts, and in doing so reconnects literature with the life of the senses.

The first manifest indication of the impact of the Montalean world-view on the younger author goes back to a 1943 creative piece in which Calvino actually did a sort of prose translation of a 1923 poem by Montale. The choice of text is important, not only because of its theme and the obvious fascination it held for Calvino but because in 1976 he returned to it and gave a second and more skilfully elaborated 'reading' of it. That rereading is a valuable indication for Calvino's readers of the importance the poem had for his artistic consciousness and of the constancy of his poetic vision, but it also confirms the emergence of a new dimension in the Calvinian universe as distinct from the Montalean. This is the complete poem by Montale:

Forse un mattino andando in un'aria di vetro
arida, rivolgendomi, vedrò compirsi il miracolo:

il nulla alle mie spalle, il vuoto dietro
di me, con un terrore di ubriaco.

Poi come s'uno schermo, s'accamperanno di gitto
alberi case colli per l'inganno consueto.
Ma sarà troppo tardi; ed io me n'andrò zitto
tra gli uomini che non si voltano, col mio segreto.

'Forse un mattino andando ...,' *Ossi di seppia*, in *L'opera in versi* 40

('Perhaps, one morning, moving in a dry crystal air, I will turn around and
will see the miracle accomplished, in drunklike terror: nothingness in back
of me, emptiness behind me. Then, as if on a screen, trees houses hills will
flash back to their places, for the familiar illusion. But it will be too late; and
I will walk on, without a word, among the men who do not turn around,
with my secret').

All three texts, the one by Montale and the two by Calvino, are reflections on a founding experience told in the first person. Montale's is pro-
jected into a probable future, while Calvino's 1943 'transcription' takes
place in a definite past, and his 1976 analysis is the retelling of a crucial
encounter in Calvino's artistic autobiography. The terror-inspiring revelation of something that other men do not see has a Magritte-like quality
in Montale. The prodigy will perhaps take place when the poet's persona looks back, as silent men march in the distance along parallel lines,
without turning around. The entire lightning-swift episode will take
place in the 'dry crystal' light of the morning, which lends fixity and
precision but also an air of surreality to the vision. Hence the fright,
inspired by that lucidity, and the speaker's staggering. The return to the
daily spectacle of trees, houses, and hills will do nothing to erase the terror and sense of solitude caused by the awareness of that void, that
nothingness.

Calvino's 1943 text is perceptively entitled 'Flash of Lightning' ('Il
lampo,' *Prima che tu dica pronto* [*Numbers in the Dark*] 18–19) and introduces some significant variations. Although the Montalean 'forse' ('perhaps'), an expression of perplexity and doubt (see Savoca's Montalean
concordances, and West 57–66), was going to be a significant and frequent presence in the texts of the mature Calvino, it is left aside here.
The beginning of the Calvino piece has a simpler narrative function, as it
distances the experience by placing it in the past, like a fable or a short

film sequence: '*Once*, it happened to me ...' ('Mi capitò *una volta* ...'
Emphasis added). Also, the narrator's discovery has to do with the
absurdity of the world, in an existentialist vein; and the character,
instead of adopting a silent and decorous demeanour like Montale's,
behaves in a manner reminiscent of a Pirandello anti-hero, laughing,
shouting, and gesticulating to attract the attention of the bystanders. In
Montale, the crowd was indifferent, as if the protagonist were invisible,
and the experience remained entirely and disturbingly personal. In
Calvino, the crowd is communicative even if hostile, and the protagonist ends up apologizing for his 'error.' Very Calvinian in all ways, the
man struck by the revelation of the world's basic flaw wants to have a
dialogue with the crowd; he wants to explain what has happened, but
he can no longer speak. His silence comes not from a Montalean reserve
induced by the magnitude of the experience, mixed with a sort of pride
for its uniqueness and pity for his unwary fellow human beings, but
from clumsiness – 'The great revelation had been sort of swallowed up'
('la grande rivelazione m'era stata come ringhiottita'; 19) – and has mys-
teriously vanished. The ending of Calvino's piece indicates an important shift in world-vision. Everything, just as in Montale's poem, 'has
returned to its customary place ... and yet from it came not quiet but torment to me' ('tutto era tornato al suo posto ... e pure non me ne veniva
tranquillità ma tormento'; 19). However, the narrator, in curiously self-
deprecating mode, views his experience as something to be prized. He
looks forward to recapturing the frightening but worthy revelation of a
different 'wisdom': 'Even now, *every time I don't understand something
(which is often) ... I have a hope that ... I will again understand nothing, in
order to reclaim that other wisdom I found and lost in the very same instant*'
('anche adesso, *ogni volta* [*spesso*] *che mi accade di non capire qualcosa* ... mi
prende la speranza *che ... io torni a non capire più niente, a impossessarmi di
quella saggezza diversa, trovata e perduta nel medesimo istante*'; 19. Emphasis
added).

What does the mature Calvino do to honour Montale's eightieth
birthday, in 1976? He returns to that same poem, placing it at the beginning of his 'libro della memoria' ('book of my memory'), to borrow
Dante's expression. As an eighteen-year-old, he says, he had memorized
Montale's poems, in addition to the classic ones he learned in school,
and they had become part of his consciousness and his unconscious.
Calvino's emphasis, in 1976, is on the Montalean lexicon: he pays homage to the poet by borrowing his expressions and minutely analysing his
word choices, tonic accents, and rhymes. The text he has chosen to

reread brings him not nostalgia but the freshness of yet a first reading. He interprets very perceptively the fact that in his memorization the line 'alberi, case, colli' ('trees, houses, hills') had become 'uomini, case, strade' ('people, houses, streets'), with the same 'error' that is visible in the 1943 transposition. For Calvino, the experience was not a solitary one, it had an urban landscape as a background, and there were people, however hostile, in potential dialogue with the narrator. To him, 'the presence of the men "who do not look back" suggests the coming and going of passers-by ... [and] the disappearance of the world ... a disappearance of the city rather than the disappearance of nature' ('la presenza degli "uomini che non si voltano" mi suggerisce un viavai di passanti ... [e] la scomparsa del mondo ... come scomparsa della città piuttosto che come scomparsa della natura'; *Perché leggere i classici* [Why Read Canonical Authors?] 259).

Calvino's remarks about Merleau-Ponty's pages on the subjective experience of space detached from objective data, and his observations on the multiple, linear, and uniform movement that closes Montale's poem, deserve further attention. But for our purpose now, only one additional comment must be made: Montale saw the invisible barrier that is always in place between the poet and the world as a protective shield, a sort of glass bell that guaranteed a detached but clear vision. Above all, Montale said, that crystal surface was not to be shattered, under penalty of decreeing the end of humankind's illusion and of erasing a reality that is pure representation (*Sulla poesia* 88). Calvino, on the other hand, reasserts that, while the 'miracle' is an experience akin to that of terror-provoking vertigo, it is also the discovery and first glimpse of a truth that is to be desired, exactly because it destroys the 'lie' of customary perception (*Perché leggere i classici* 262).

The lexicon used by Calvino in his lengthy analysis of Montale's expression, 'aria di vetro,' is a condensation of Montalean and Calvinian motifs. Dryness, clarity, lightness, transparency, magic, self-sufficient solidity, and concreteness define the Montalean air as a medium which, with its precision, conveys a sense of tension and balance, a sense of 'being suspended in the void' ('d'essere sospesi nel vuoto'; 260). It is in the appropriation of this poetic theme that the genesis of Calvino's hunting for the 'invisible' is to be found; but for him the invisible multiplicity is inextricably bound to the 'visible.' The dialectic of those terms underlines the fact that Calvino's writing had taken a path that diverged significantly from Montale's, in the years of *Le cosmicomiche* (*Cosmicomics*, early sixties), *Il castello dei destini incrociati* (*The Castle of Crossed Desti-*

nies, 1969), and *Le città invisibili* (*Invisible Cities*, 1972). Qfwfq, the tarot players, and Marco Polo were torn between their admiration for the qualities of light and hardness that crystals possess, on the one hand, and their fear for the crystal world's immobility, on the other. The world appeared to them as a precarious construct, rife with contradictions and ambiguities. What Calvino's stubbornly optimistic narrators ultimately discovered, and by discovering were enabled to become more human, was that 'true order is what carries within itself impurities and destruction' ('l'ordine vero è quello che porta dentro di sé l'impurità, la distruzione'; 'I cristalli' [Crystals], *Ti con zero* [*t-zero*] 45). That is why Calvino's fiction tends to privilege as its location the urban community and its exquisite blend of all human qualities, rather than a solitary, retrenched, and more generic 'world.'

The continuation of Calvino's 1976 article chronicles the evolution of his preoccupations. He speaks of the characteristics of humankind's vision with a small Montalean quotation, as he is beginning to write his Palomar pieces:

> Actually, the image we see is not something that the eye records, nor something that has its origin in the eye, but something that happens entirely in the brain ... [and] only in a region of the brain acquires form and meaning. That region is *the screen on which images are flashed* ('In realtà, l'immagine che vediamo non è qualcosa che l'occhio registra né qualcosa che ha sede nell'occhio: è qualcosa che avviene interamente nel cervello ... che solo in una zona del cervello acquista una forma e un senso. È quella zona *lo 'schermo' su cui s'accampano le immagini*'; *Perché leggere i classici* 267. Emphasis added).

He reminds us of the impact exerted on writing by changing technologies that have caused the shift from theatrical to cinematic metaphors. He also stresses the importance of meditation, which he feels Montale's poem suggests by the subtle change of rhythm of its ending, and which, I would argue, would be paralleled by Calvino's own evolution toward the pages of *Palomar* (*Mr. Palomar*). If we wanted evidence of the coherence of Calvino's artistic journey, the sort of coherence that is at the heart of all major artistic universes, these 'Montalean' texts would serve as prime supporting material.

The miracle ('prodigio') of an unexpected encounter in the midst of everyday life and the revelation, as sudden as it is brief, of a chasm and a solitude necessarily create suspense, give rise to a doubt about the reliability of the world's appearances,[9] and also cause a sort of estrangement from the 'real,' a posture that is ideally suited to detached observation. One of Calvino's characters calls it 'a cautious, restrained relationship with the world' ('un cauto, avaro rapporto con il mondo'; *I racconti* 350). That distancing is the necessary root of an image that is central in both authors. If we go back to Montale's 'Marezzo,' we discover that the sea bottom harbouring disturbing matter is a world observed through limpid water: 'He looks at the world that can be glimpsed on the bottom, its outlines *distorted as if by a lens*' ('Guarda il mondo del fondo che si profila / *come sformato da una lente*'; *Ossi di seppia*. Emphasis added). Calvino used again and again that Montalean metaphor of the lens that distorts in spite of its making one's vision clearer; but he manipulated it and transformed it. Speaking with approval of Chekov's fiction, he used a subtly polemic tone, when he wrote that literature is supposed to look at the world through 'a clear lens that does not hide from us any of the world's negative aspects, but does not induce in us the feeling of being defeated by them' ('una limpida lente che non ci nasconde nulla della negatività del mondo ma non ci persuade a sentircene vinti'; *Una pietra sopra* 27–8). In fact, that same image of the lens often performed a symbolic function for Calvino, underlining the world's ambiguity and providing his narrative with a variety of closures. Some instances are found in 'Pesci grossi, pesci piccoli' (Big Fish, Little Fish), 'La formica argentina' (The Argentine Ant), 'L'avventura di una bagnante' (The Adventure of a Swimmer), and 'L'avventura di un poeta,' just to mention a few early texts, and reserving for another chapter some consideration of later writings such as *Palomar*. One may say that Calvino's keen understanding of the world's negatives did not erase from his consciousness the memory of the vitality and sense of humour he had found in the epic poems, tales of chivalry, adventures, and travel narratives belonging to an earlier literary tradition, which had charmed him as a young reader.

Thus grounded in recurring rhythms, lexical choices, and images, some major thematic patterns of Montale's poetry find a transformed existence and a critique in Calvino's works. One of those themes offers an ideal example of the complex relationship that bound the two writers: the theme of immobility. Its icon is the agave in Montale ('L'agave su lo scoglio' ['The Agave on the Sea Rock], *Ossi di seppia*). In a richly contradictory manner, immobility is the source of a tormented yearning for movement, but also the assurance of enduring. It is the choice of those 'who remain earth-bound' ('di chi rimane a terra'; 'Falsetto,' *Ossi di seppia*), and also a symbol of resistance to the blandishments of a universe that has revealed its indifference and emptiness. The immobility of a plant or an animal in the harsh habitat of a rocky sea coast is the signifier of the text's refusal of illusions, in Montale, and unquestionably lends dignity to the poetic voice that speaks of it. Those same icons appear in Calvino's fiction, but his world of plants and animals is richer, more crowded and whimsical.[10] Where in Montale a solitary individual (bird, plant, flower, insect, or fish) was the focus of the poem, in Calvino the natural world is teeming with creatures at the same time rigorously placed within scientific categories and sensuously described with their characteristics of colour, shape, sound, and smell. First based on images, the Calvinian theme then expands its range of expression along narrative lines. Cosimo di Rondò is 'rooted' in the trees in *Il barone rampante*, and the simple image of a static situation in an immobile realm is developed through the complex construct that is the novel. That 'rootedness' serves to elaborate a paradox: Cosimo's life actually becomes an example of utter mobility and intense communal concern. The characterization of some noble Spaniards, who are also bound to a life in the trees in that same novel, provides the needed contrast; they, unlike Cosimo, are unable to transform their confinement into freedom, but rather conform to the strictures of their forced stasis.

The drama elaborated poetically by Montale through his early volumes had to do with the conflict between a yearning for action and the stasis caused by incompatibility with the world and a refusal of contamination. That theme was the starting-point for a very Calvinian variation when, in 1959, at the end of a long but fruitful period of crisis, Calvino wrote *Il cavaliere inesistente* (*The Nonexistent Knight*). The knight Agilulf is torn between his obsessive desire to exist, even though he is disgusted by everything that is imperfect and changing, and his conviction that an unchangeable state – even that of non-existence – is superior to any other. Agilulf may be a humorous, parodic characterization of the 'hermetic man,' who is disdainful of life's messiness and who fears (even while longing for it) the contaminating nearness of human beings. Calvino's text mocks, while understanding it, the human desire for order, unambiguousness, and permanence. On the other hand, existential chaos and becoming are embodied in the youthful Raimbaut; he is an aspiring knight perennially mobile and enthusiastic, but also perennially betrayed by his own desires and the world's chaotic sluggishness. The novel becomes the playful battleground of a dyadic vision that is reinforced by the one-dimensional and fleshy presence of Agilulf's squire, Gurduloo. Ultimately, in appropriate fictional manner, the text and its narrator, the nun/warrior Dorothea/Bradamant, give the victory to Raimbaut, who may be imperfect but who is a very human mixture of love and lust, coherence and incoherence, passion and determination. As Calvino said in a reflective moment, 'Action has always been more congenial to me than immobility, wilfulness more congenial than resignation, and the exceptional more congenial than the routine' ('l'azione mi è sempre piaciuta più dell'immobilità, la volontà più della rassegnazione, l'eccezionalità più della consuetudine'; *Una pietra sopra* 56). That statement was clearly accurate on the creative plane, which is what concerns us here.

From Dialogue to Subtext

There is no doubt that for Montale literature was a means to knowledge. Even the unexpected discovery of a void that, until its discovery, had been hidden from the speaker's awareness, the discovery of the emptiness that lurked behind the illusory scenery of the world, prompted 'not a vague feeling of dissolution, but rather the construction of a cognitive model' ('non ... un' indeterminata sensazione di dissoluzione [ma] la costruzione di un modello conoscitivo'; *Perché leggere i classici* 263). Gianfranco Contini has focused on a technique used by Montale, as a clue to understanding the poet's relationship to the knowable: 'Naming things, truly a frenzy of naming ... that impression of overcrowding ... are the manifestation of a desire to put one's knowledge of the world into practice' ('il nominare le cose, un vero delirio di nominare ... quell' impressione di gremito ... corrispondono a una velleità di esercitare la conoscenza del mondo'; Contini 11–12). The same rhetorical device of naming is very familiar to Calvino's readers,[11] even in his early texts (in 'L'avventura di una bagnante,' 'L'avventura di un poeta,' and various stories in *Le cosmicomiche*). But in Calvino there is not the feeling that possession of the world is fated to be only potential; impetus, rather than a sense of disheartened frustration, accompanies the attempt to grasp knowledge of the world.

When Montale's *La bufera* (The Storm) was published, in 1956, the 'feeling of perennial descent, of the splintering apart of physical reality, of disappearance and wastage' (Almansi 46), which was already present in the early Montale, intensified. Most dramatically, 'Piccolo testamento' and 'Il sogno del prigioniero' (Brief Testament, and The Dream of the Prisoner) told the reader what depths of despair had been reached, and what a puny light poetry seemed to shed in the darkness of history and life. The yearning for knowledge did persist: 'To know, that is what counts, even if the why of representation escapes us ... a profound *everyday* lesson, the hardest of virtues' ('*sapere*, ecco ciò che conta, anche se il perché della rappresentazione ci sfugge ... alta lezione *quotidiana* la più difficile delle virtù'; 'Visita a Fadin' [A Visit to Fadin], *L'opera in versi* 217. Montale's emphasis). However, the effort expended was immense, and – what is more important – the fruits of that effort ended up by belonging only to an individual consciousness: 'the gift I dreamed of / not for myself but for all / belongs to me only' ('il dono che sognavo / non per me ma per tutti / appartiene a me solo'; 'Anniversario' [Anniversary], *L'opera in versi* 264). A reading of Calvino's texts of those same years and then of his later ones, undertaken to measure the widening distance between the world-visions of the two writers, will remind readers of Calvino's sensuous and playful embracing of the ambiguity of the world, and his stubborn pursuit of our common sharing in the life of that world.

In the same decade, the fifties, Calvino created one of his most significant characters, Marcovaldo, a lovable anti-hero whom a hostile environment forced into enacting elaborate strategies for survival, however passive and self-defensive (Biasin 1985, 79). Marcovaldo's refusal to be defeated once and for all is set against the text's lack of consoling illusions. Doubt and obstinacy coexist. The 'ordine scordato' ('forgotten order') of a lost natural perfection that haunted the Montalean memory (see 'Dissipa tu se lo vuoi' [Dissolve, if you so wish ...] 59) is said by the Calvinian voice never to have existed. Marcovaldo's nostalgia for a benign natural order is the humorous and somewhat pathetic nostalgia of the urban dweller that takes the form of an idolization of literary commonplaces. Precisely with the Marcovaldo stories, which elaborate the theme of the all-inclusiveness of the mazelike city, Calvino began to develop a new metaphor for human existence. That metaphor, the labyrinth, would inform his fiction and his essays for years to come. It was a major shift from the Montalean and Calvinian metaphors of collapses and cave-ins (for the frequencies of terms such as *crollare, crollo, frana, franamento*, and *sfacelo* in Montale, see Savoca). While these terms evoke chaos and elicit an emotional response, the labyrinth is an intellectual construct. It can be analysed, and is a challenge to the obstinacy of the prisoner who envisions escaping. Precisely because it is designed to prevent escape, the labyrinth suggests it, in a glaring paradox. Montale also had spoken insistently of imprisonment and yearning for flight (see

Avalle 103–4), but in Calvino's universe there is no Montalean 'miracle' a prisoner can hope for. In Calvino's works, the human mind exerts itself alone against the negativity and heaviness of the real, to make space for lightness in all its forms. Escape can most especially take place along the thread of an arabesque traced by the pen, since the activities of writing and storytelling are a combination of game, geometry, and probability.[12] The time was ripe for Calvino's cosmicomic tales, his combinations of opposites, and the full deployment of his paradoxes.

Meanwhile, Montale's poetry of the sixties and seventies went on to explore the farthest boundaries of scepticism and nihilism. The poem entitled 'Arsenio,' in *Ossi di seppia*, had already defined with an oxymoron the desperate struggle against an immobility that suggested death. Montale's lines evoked the Mallarméan image of the swan trapped in ice, singing his death song: 'immobile going / oh! too familiar / delirium … of immobility' ('immoto andare, oh troppo noto / delirio … d'immobilità'). *Satura*, published in 1971, contains an even bleaker disawoval of history,[13] again entrusted to oxymorons: 'You alone knew that motion / is not different from stasis, / that emptiness is fullness, and a clear sky / the most expansive of clouds' ('Tu sola sapevi che il moto/ non è diverso dalla stasi, / che il vuoto è il pieno e il sereno / è la più diffusa delle nubi' ('Xenia' 14, *L'opera in versi* 294).

The interlocutor's nickname, Mosca, is already a metaphor for the tiresome, terrible dailiness of living, a familiar theme for a poet Montale knew, Emily Dickinson. Beyond the private sphere, the poet sees only universal decay and the spreading of an industrial wasteland encrusted with objects (Avalle 105). In addition, the disappointment with the political scene suggests to Montale's persona expressions of a sacrificial despair that leads to disgruntled self-isolation. Knowledge of the world is defeated, corroded by the assertion of the absolute impenetrability of the real (Luperini 192; Mengaldo *La tradizione* 1975, 28; West 113). Closed again in the world of a poetry of which only the happy few can partake, Montale's memories of a beginning can be only returns to a lost childhood paradise.

And yet, Montale's 'calcolo dei dadi' ('throw of the dice'), with its capriciousness, can be inscribed by other voices in other universes that are light-years away from the Montalean. While chance can be the harbinger of loss, a source of frustration and dejection, it can also contain a promise of surprising encounters and serendipity. In 1970, presenting a new edition of *Gli amori difficili* (Difficult Loves), Calvino defined his own short fiction as an exploration of a fundamental 'core of silence' ('nucleo di silenzio'; ix) and of the 'pain of living' ('male di vivere'; xi). The citations from Montale are even too explicit, but Calvino's comment pointedly modifies with a polemic assertion the paradigm that Montale had drawn for his poetic universe: 'It must be said that for Calvino this core of silence is not only a negative part that cannot be eliminated from any human relationship; it also carries within a precious and absolute value' ('Va detto che per Calvino questo nucleo di silenzio non è soltanto un passivo ineliminabile in ogni rapporto umano: racchiude pure un valore prezioso, assoluto'; ix). It is clear that at this point Calvino's dialogue with Montale has become a subtext: the Montalean text is at the same time an essential presence and the hidden object of critique.

Two thematic constants are evidence of that subtext: the sea and the city. If the coast of Liguria provides a background and a cluster of metaphors for the writings of both Montale and Calvino, it also embodies their two different perspectives. In Montale, the coast has 'a lean, harsh, hallucination-inducing beauty' ('una bellezza scarna, scabra, allucinante'; *Sulla poesia* 88). The poet looks out to the stormy or becalmed waters from a point that is sheltered by the dry slopes of Ligurian rocks overhanging the sea. The Mediterranean, at once paternal and maternal, is the focus of the poet's gaze. But for Calvino's characters the Mediterranean is a third dimension, that 'terzo lato' that defines the human landscape and provides it with depth; it is the warrantor of a geometry of desire, it opens the way to voyage, which the Montalean persona refused, and marks the path of return to one's city.[14] In fact, Calvino's characters are often out at sea, they are even faced with the revelation of the presence of monsters in the depths, but their eye stubbornly turns inland, toward fields, woods, villages, and cities. For Calvino, there is coexistence, however conflicted, between Montale's ideal city, 'city of glass within the sharp sky-blue' ('città di vetro dentro l'azzurro netto'; 'Mediterraneo,' *L'opera in versi* 54), and the real city, the industrial city of the present. The two cities are connected in experience and fantasy, they are the unavoidable reverse of each other, and they are the human race's sole habitat and unique achievement, as he makes clear in texts such as *La giornata d'uno scrutatore* (A Day in the Life of a Watcher), *Marcovaldo*, *Ti con zero*, and, most abundantly, *Le città invisibili*.

The Paradox of Literature

When Calvino analysed the poem in which the Montalean man looks back and discovers the void behind him, he was responding with profound empathy to its sense of 'stress and dismay' ('una vibrazione sgomenta'; *Perché leggere i classici* 261), a 'dizziness caused by the disappearance of all points of reference' ('un barcollare senza punti di riferimento'; 262), and a need to construct a cognitive model against a double danger: the appearance of 'vain images and nothingness' ('schermo d'inganni ... e ... vuoto'; 264). What already made memorable for him his reading of the Montalean poem, however, were those characteristics of writing that he would list meticulously at a much later date, as chapter headings of his *Lezioni americane* (*Six Memos for the Next Millennium*): lightness, quickness, exactitude, visibility, multiplicity, in carefully studied balance (*Letture montaliane* [Reading Montale] 38).

However, a paradox haunted him. In 1969, as he was writing *Le città invisibili*, he wrote a review of the Italian translation of Northrop Frye's *Anatomy of Criticism*, which he asserted he had read earlier, we must assume in the English original. As he said, 'We extract from each book the book that serves us' ('ognuno scava da ogni libro il libro che gli serve'; *Una pietra sopra* 195). He was particularly struck by Frye's definition of the city as a symbol and as a human translation of the fixity of the mineral world (Fry *Anatomy* 1971, 141). He speculated on the changes that have taken place in the values and syntax that structure the relationship between human beings and the world. Civilization as a total imitation of nature by human beings was a concept that intrigued Calvino, but much more was involved in his reflections on Frye's text. On the one hand, he found in the scholar's text a welcome attention to rhetorical elements, to the inevitable connections between literary and scientific discourse, and to the inherent value of literature: 'All structures in words are partly rhetorical, and hence literary, and ... the notion of a scientific or philosophical verbal structure free of rhetorical elements is an illusion' (Frye *Anatomy*, 1971, 350). On the other hand, Frye's search, like Calvino's, was the search for a theory of criticism that would account for the major phenomena of literary experience, while at the same time defining the place of literature within civilization as a whole (Frye *Critical Path* 1971, 14). Calvino's formation as a person and a writer required more than the achievement of technical and rhetorical skills as ends in themselves.

> From being accustomed to a 'historicistic' view that insured the integration of literature in the context of human activities ... I have gone to searching for ways of reading literature that are internal to their object ... but they do not fill the emptiness left in the place of that integration ('Dalle abitudini

d'una lettura 'storicistica' che mi garantiva l'inserimento della letteratura nel contesto dell'attività umana ... sono passato a cercare modi di leggere la letteratura più interni al loro oggetto ... ma essi non coprono il vuoto che è rimasto al posto di quell'inserimento'; *Una pietra sopra* 196).

Frye's emphasis on the complexity of the relationship between literature and life meant that he assigned value to both parts of the writer's experience, even though his concern was more clearly with literature's intrinsic value: 'Literature also proceeds by hypothetical possibilities, and though literature, like mathematics, is constantly useful ... having a continuing relationship to the common field of experience – pure literature, like pure mathematics, contains its own meaning' (Frye *Anatomy* 1971, 351). For Calvino, Italian politics and the future of the entire planet remained at the basis of his personal concern, perplexity, and disillusionment. As he matured as a writer, he saw that what bound his texts to the world, and to the audience that had replaced the tribe of preliterate times, was still their quality as storytelling, the weaving of that thread of narration that materialized in the ink trace left on the paper. His inheritance from the past was still the lesson he had learned in the crucial decade 1945–55:[15] not the recapturing of a lost paradise or a childhood myth, but the rediscovery of community and of the pleasure of sharing fictions. Defining such a paradox of literature and attempting to resolve it are the concerns we find at the core of Calvino's writings from the sixties on. In 1976, returning to some earlier debates, Calvino wrote, 'What the writer is asked to do is to guarantee the survival of what we call *human* in a world where everything appears inhuman ... the survival of a discourse that is *human*' ('Ciò che si chiede allo scrittore è di garantire la sopravvivenza di quel che si chiama *umano* in un mondo dove tutto si presenta inumano ... la sopravvivenza di un discorso *umano*'; *Una pietra sopra* 290. Calvino's emphasis). One may argue about the viability of such concerns in times that are called postmodern. As a matter of fact, Calvino brilliantly paid his dues to the postmodern sensibility, with the elaborate virtuoso displays of *Il castello dei destini incrociati* and *Se una notte d'inverno un viaggiatore* (*If on a Winter's Night a Traveller*). Within a supposedly collapsing culture and an offended universe, the Calvinian persona explored in those works an ever growing doubt about the ability of the human race to provide for the survival of the planet and attain knowledge of the world. But he did so using the tools in which that persona fiercely believed, reason, language, and *mestiere* (skilled work), all placed in the service of storytelling.

One may argue, and it has been done, that Calvino ended up by engaging in a rearguard action, attempting to rescue what no longer matters, that which Calvino called 'human,' and that his definition of style as an ethical and linguistic construct was hopelessly dated. But even postmodern *bricoleurs* do not need to explain where they found the materials for their operations. Calvino's last personae were more perplexed than ever and anguished by doubt, yet they used the *astuzia della ragione* (the wiliness of human reason) to acquire the first elements that would provide them with leverage as they reached for knowledge of their problematical universe. The writer did not reject old techniques, as he constructed well-wrought artefacts in order to attain his goal. He returned first of all to the classic 'clean slate'; then he resorted to bestowing on his characters imperfect sensorial qualities and various lenses, from glasses to binoculars to the rear-view mirror of the automobile age (*Letture montaliane* 42–3), for their forays into the knowable; and he used many well-tested rhetorical devices to convey what they were bringing back for further meditation in their everyday existences.

If we follow a chronological sequence, the character called 'Mr Palomar' continues the search that was the motor of all of Calvino's production. He is a *sui generis* dandy, who aspires to move from the dyadic games of our culture to a world of connectedness and cosmic continuity. Vittorini's and Pavese's models had long been left behind, and Montale was only subterraneously present as the other term of a dialectic. Now readers could detect more clearly an affinity between Calvino's anti-hero and the aging middle-class male characters of another Italian writer of European stature, Luigi Pirandello. Pirandello had written a curious page, in the novel entitled *Uno, nessuno e centomila* (*One, No One, and One Hundred Thousand*),[16] relating an episode from the adolescence of his protagonist:

> As I walked, deep in thought, in the countryside, I found myself lost, beyond all paths, in a lonely faraway place made gloomy in its stillness by a blinding sun. The fright I experienced ... was this: the horror of perhaps having something revealed to me alone, away from the sight of all other human beings ('andando sopra pensiero per la campagna m'ero visto a un tratto smarrito, fuori di ogni traccia, in una remota solitudine tetra di sole e attonita; lo sgomento che ne avevo avuto ... era questo: l'orrore di qualche cosa che da un momento all'altro potesse scoprirsi a me solo, fuori della vista degli altri'; 125).

Pirandello stopped short of revealing the actual discovery, and his text veered in a clearly existentialist direction, but his character's reactions to the fear he experienced are close to those of Calvino's early hero and of Mr Palomar: their reactions are self-deprecating and manifested in comically incongruous ways. In effect, we realize that Calvino's characters, like most if not all the Pirandellian middle-class anti-heroes, are plagued by incompetence, clumsiness, and the sense that they hold a displaced position in the universe. They contemplate with horror the puzzle of their own death, and hold the conviction that a man's appropriate posture before it all is defiant argumentation and clownish misbehaviour. Mr Palomar's slyness and elegant discoursing, then, rather than indicating coldness and calculation, are the masks of a distress that refuses metaphysical temptations, however limited (*Perché leggere i classici* 273). However, instead of becoming (melo)dramatic as they do in Pirandello, his reflections are playful, ironic, and open to infinite possibilities.

In sum, Calvino's very secular intelligence, faced with the emergence of mass culture, the imperialism of consumerism, and existential anguish, insisted on trusting the potential of human intellect and the pleasures of invention. In his maturity, he looked upon T.S. Eliot as the greatest poet of the twentieth century 'precisely because of the persistent impalpable irony in which he veils those things, often not at all humorous, that he has to tell us' ('proprio per la continua impalpabile ironia di cui avvolge le cose che ha da dirci, spesso in sé nient'affatto amene'; *Saggi* II 1684).

Last Wills and Testaments

Trusting in *words*, particularly written words, is possible only in epochs whose belief in universal truths has been shaken. In Calvino, the paradox of a necessary coexistence between the concepts of the 'usefulness' of language and literature and the autonomy of literary activity is redefined: 'The critical reading I am looking for does not point directly to the "external," but by exploring what is "internal" to the text manages to find an opening unto what is "external"' ('l'analisi critica che cerco è quella che non punta sul "fuori" direttamente, ma esplorando il "dentro" del testo riesce ad aprir[si] ... sul "fuori"'; *Una pietra sopra* 201). Literature is autonomous but rooted in a culture, and the writer, as a person and a citizen, is not irresponsible.

In 1977, a public controversy erupted in the Italian newspapers. It had to do with whether and to what extent a citizen has a moral obligation to agree to perform public service when doing so may be dangerous to that citizen's safety. At issue in the particular instance was the performance of jury duty in the trials of some members of the Red Brigades. Montale declared publicly that fear was a valid justification for a refusal to serve, and cited in support of his views the famous words of Don Abbondio, a character in Alessandro Manzoni's *I promessi sposi* (The Betrothed): 'Courage, you cannot force yourself to have it' ('Il coraggio, uno non se lo può dare'; 433). Calvino, also publicly, expressed dismay at that statement: 'I see as dangerous the fact that our greatest poet, indeed a man who deserves our respect for the positions he has always taken publicly, would encourage us to follow the ethics of Don Abbondio' ('sento come un pericolo il fatto che il nostro massimo poeta [e per di più un uomo che merita rispetto anche per la linea che ha sempre tenuto nella vita civile] ci esorti a far nostra la morale di Don Abbondio' (*Coraggio e viltà degli intellettuali* [The Courage and Cowardice of the Intellectuals] 8). On the issue of civic duty, the old poet and the mature writer – both of whom had experienced profound disappointment with the political and social situation in Italy – regretfully parted ways. The writer's work, Calvino asserted again, has meaning within a context, and writers, like all other human beings, cannot avoid a messy contact with history, whatever form that contact may take. In 1970, in his introduction to *Gli amori difficili*, he had stated, quoting from a critic:

> One must ... notice here how, almost in a Brechtian way, useless agitation is contrasted with real action, the fishermen's work. As for the poet, he still can find meaning only in looking. That gives us the story's marvellous last page, a mesmerizing tracking-shot in writing, where the southern village, crushed under the sun's glare, is displayed and utters its scream. A *lesson* emerges here that is beyond mere *dénonciation* ('Si noti ... qui (e in un modo quasi brechtiano) all'agitazione inutile è chiaramente opposta l'azione reale: il lavoro dei pescatori. Ma il poeta, lui, non può fare ancora altro che rifugiarsi nello sguardo: il che vale a darci quella mirabile pagina finale, stupefacente "carrellata" letteraria in cui il villaggio del sud schiacciato dal sole offre il suo spettacolo e il suo grido ... qui la *lezione* s'affaccia al di là della *denuncia*'; xvi. Emphasis in the original).[17]

In spite of their disagreements, which had been brought about by a concrete confrontation with events, there was something Calvino had yet to say about Montale's poetry. In 1981, on the occasion of Montale's death,

Calvino returned to his never ending praise of the poet's 'exactitude ... [that] deliberate choice of vocabulary, of terminological precision used to pin down the uniqueness of an experience' (*The Uses of Literature* 286). What Calvino remembered again at that time was the image of the Montalean unheroic hero, who spoke 'of a spinning world driven by a wind of destruction, with no solid ground to stand on, where we have no help but that of an individual morality hanging on the edge of the abyss' (286). And the last writerly homage Calvino paid Montale was the impetuous text of 'Un re in ascolto' (A King Listening), in which the cloistered king addresses an elusive 'tu': 'Leave! Flee! Wander!' ('Esci! Scappa! Spazia!'; *Sotto il sole giaguaro* 78).[18] The anguish of loneliness, the effort toward understanding and connection, and the poetic intensity of expression all place Calvino's 'king' in the company of Montale's and Samuel Beckett's personae, with the added charm of a very Calvinian sensual longing.

Calvino's own death loomed. His *Lezioni americane*, devoid of comicity but astonishingly filled with youthful passion, remains as the last will and testament that Montale, grown enclosed and arid, had refused to leave. At that edge from which literature peers toward what is as yet unsaid, a message of hope and encouragement – not petty, but endowed with the slightly comical nobility of desperate endeavours – was written not by Montale but by Calvino. The *Lezioni* speaks of a never abandoned project, of the writer's human concern for the future, and of literature as the supreme form of resistance, communication, and joy.

1 For the connections between Montale and D'Annunzio, see Mengaldo *La tradizione* 1975.
2 See Pasolini 1960, 288, and also Mengaldo 1991.
3 For the etymology and the history of the words 'modernism,' 'modernity,' etc., see Calinescu.
4 His essay, entitled *La rivoluzione liberale. Saggio sulla lotta politica in Italia*, was first published by Cappelli (Bologna, 1924).
5 See Calvino's autobiographical writings in the many volumes published after his death, and Falaschi 1972.
6 For an extensive exploration of Neorealism and Calvino's connections with it, see Re's study, which focuses on Calvino's first novel, *Il sentiero dei nidi di ragno*.
7 On this topic, see Eugenia Paulicelli's keen remarks on another twentieth-century author, Natalia Ginzburg.

8 The quotations here are given first in Italian, because the emphasis is on Italian prosody, metrics, and rhetorical devices.

9 West has elegantly analysed the expression of an all-enveloping doubt in Montalean poetry, at every point of the poet's production.

10 Only 'Dall'opaco' (From the Shady Side) is utterly spare.

11 De Lauretis, in an early article (de Lauretis 'Narrative Discourse' 1975), spoke of a Borges-like *enumeración caótica*, but Calvino's passion for lists and enumerations had earlier, and multiple, origins.

12 See the last page of the story 'I figli di Babbo Natale' (Santa's Children) in *Marcovaldo*.

13 For this topic, see Carpi and Bàrberi-Squarotti in *Letture montaliane*, 165 and 283–96 respectively.

14 See the essay entitled 'Il terzo lato è il mare' (The Sea Is the Third Dimension).

15 For this assertion, see Corti's interview (1985).

16 The novel was published in 1925, but Pirandello had been working on it since at least 1914 (see *Tutti i romanzi* II 1057).

17 He is quoting from François Wahl, 'one among the few foreign readers who have established a true rapport of collaborative criticism with the Italian writer' ('uno dei pochi osservatori stranieri che abbiano stabilito con lo scrittore italiano un vero rapporto di collaborazione critica').

18 See the poem quoted in chapter 2, p. 39.

2

Surveyors[1]

The eye searches around,
the mind investigates, matches, disjoins ...

(Lo sguardo fruga d'intorno,
la mente indaga, accorda, disunisce ...)

Eugenio Montale, 'I limoni,' *Ossi di seppia*

Watcher of a World Divided

The Italian title of one of the most controversial[2] of Calvino's books, *La giornata d'uno scrutatore*, plays on the ambivalence inherent in the second substantive. 'Scrutatore' refers here to a poll watcher, but may also indicate someone who intensely focuses the eye on the object of interest.[3] Although the term entered the Calvinian lexicon for the first time with that slim volume, the action it described, *scrutare*, had already been a major feature of Calvino's fiction and essays, and would remain so until his very last writings. His protagonists are usually searchers who inspect and watch intently the world around them in order to understand themselves and it. Pin, in *Il sentiero dei nidi di ragno*, was searching for something whose identity escaped him, observed intently what was happening around him, and found the nests of spiders; the Baron Cosimo di Rondò, in *Il barone rampante*, was a watcher in the trees; Amerigo the Explorer, in *La giornata d'uno scrutatore*, silently observed the many manifestations of what some writers had rather pompously named 'the human condition'; Qfwfq, the essential consciousness that inhabits the universe in *Le cosmicomiche*, 'saw' with his penetrating gaze every cosmicomic event; and Mr Palomar would patiently begin anew the task of scrutinizing and reordering everything, texts and universe.

It all started, that penchant for intense watching, with the discovery, made early in the game by Calvino's characters, of an incompleteness that was inherent in everything, a condition of being 'divided in half' that first manifested itself in the external world, in what was observed, and then revealed its presence and origin within the observer. That discovery and the subsequent effort to negotiate it were the origin of a puzzlement, a curiosity that led to a distinguishing characteristic of the Calvinian text: its view and construction of reality as a complex of dilemmas.[4] Dualism is a challenge, and antithesis mirrors it, becoming a favourite rhetorical device. The authorial voice speaks at the same time with perplexity and humour, playfulness and melancholy, pessimism and optimism.

One of the first situations of incompletenesss to appear in Calvino's work had to do with the inequities of social status. A fictional alter ego, the adolescent son of a well-to-do family in the 1948 short story entitled 'Pranzo con un pastore' (Dinner with a Shepherd), had the feeling that some injustice had been perpetrated, but was only vaguely aware of the political implications of that feeling. He mused over his embarrassment, which paralleled the discomfort of the clearly out-of-place dinner guest, the shepherd: 'I felt at that time that the things I had not had, so that I could be him, and those he had not had, so that he could be me, were evidence of an injustice. *They made me and him two incomplete human beings* ... mistrustful and ashamed' (Le cose ch'eran mancate a me per essere lui, e quelle che eran mancate a lui per esser me, io le sentivo allora come un'ingiustizia, che *faceva me e lui due esseri incompleti* ... diffidenti e vergognosi'; *I racconti* 228–9. Emphasis added). Speaking of himself in retrospect, the narrator pointedly says that his feelings belonged to a particular moment in his life and in history. Yet the sense of incompleteness widens in later texts, becoming a fundamental part of the experiences of many other Calvinian characters, an existential rift that mirrors the gap between themselves and their environment. So profound is the phenomenon that it appears to be 'natural.'

But the most disheartening discovery of the world's hidden face is often entrusted to female characters. In 1950, in 'Pesci grossi, pesci piccoli' (Big Fish, Little Fish), an unmarried woman afflicted by love sorrows finds an echo to her pain in the evidence of universal suffering that mars even the beauty of a little boy's marine paradise. He, called with Arcadian lightness Zeffirino, is unaware (with a Leopardian adjective, 'ignaro'), and revels in the excitement of successful underwater fishing. She, on the other hand, can only feel the cruelty of living, and cannot stop crying, even when the boy proudly brings her his catch. She sees proof of the world's misery, hidden under the shimmering surface of the sea, on the bodies of Zeffirino's marvellous prey: 'There, she saw the beautiful silver body pockmarked by innumerable almost invisible holes' ('ecco vedeva aprirsi, nel bel corpo d'argento, mille fori minutissimi'; *I racconti* 13). Every victim of the boy's underwater gun is a witness to the discrepancy between the boy's and the woman's visions of the world: 'At the same moment, in the same place, two intense passions coexisted, so opposed and irreconcilable. Zeffirino could not think of both of them together, nor could he abandon himself to one or the other' ('Nello stesso momento, nello stesso posto esistevano insieme due struggimenti cosí opposti e inconciliabili. Zeffirino non riusciva a pensarli entrambi insieme; né a lasciarsi andare all'uno o all'altro'; 12). Such is the story's dilemma, experienced, one could say, in the flesh, by the two paradigmatic faces of human consciousness in Calvino, a child's and a woman's. Only an octopus, pink, sensuous, and ominously immobile, 'alone among the creatures caught, seemed to her free of blemishes and pain' ('unico tra gli esseri pescati, a lei sembrava senza macchia né tormento'; 13). But that creature is meditating an aggression; the octopus is precisely the embodiment of the world's treacherous duplicity, and with its unexpected attack causes the woman to remain frozen in a classical pose of horror, 'standing on the rock, as if fleeing from her own arm that was imprisoned' ('in piedi sullo scoglio, come fuggendo dal suo stesso braccio prigioniero'; 15). As in a fairy tale, a sort of latter-day Little Red Riding Hood story, it takes the intervention of a wise and taciturn fisherman to free the woman from the nightmare in which even she, in spite of her scepticism regarding the beauty of the world, has managed to be caught. The complexity and significance of this short story, whose echoes would be found throughout Calvino's production, prompted the author to place it at the opening of one of his richest volumes, *I racconti*, when he collected what he considered to be the best of his short fiction.

The protagonist of 'L'avventura di una bagnante' ('The Adventure of a Swimmer,' 1951) also fathoms the 'duality' that is at the core of the world, its 'duplice essenza,' which ordinary life has previously kept hidden from her. The story's backdrop is again the sea, a familiar stretch of the Mediterranean, with its seductive surface that seems to be 'unbroken.' The world's two faces are mirrored by her own double perception of the world; that parallelism is revealed during an unexpected and apparently minor crisis, her loss of the bottom of her bathing suit while she is swimming far from shore. The new, ambiguous experience of her own body, now naked, reveals to her the opening up of a chasm, a 'distance' that cannot be bridged, since she cannot simply come out of the water and return to the beach. Her first realization is that there is a dichotomy in the world due to gender, that there is a dimension of experience open to men and another open to women – which is a theme that could be analysed at length. But she is immediately overwhelmed by a wider sense of estrangement, something that remains inexplicable to her, an astonishment at the impenetrability of a material reality that is apparently benign but harbours unfathomable depths.

The suggestion that there is another side to what we call the 'real,' a side fearsome and unrevealed, is confirmed by a multitude of other phenomena in Calvino's fiction. None is more disconcerting than the scene revisited several times in his early writings, for instance in 'L'entrata in guerra' (The War's Beginning): the peculiar spectacle of impaired, monstrous, or demented human beings suddenly thrust into public view because of some dramatic event, flood, fire, or war. A world fenced off from what seemed to be the 'norm' is forced to show itself in the open in moments of crisis. An 'ancient secret' of the poorest country villages is revealed (*I racconti* 237), and the fascinated repulsion the text makes evident at its unveiling has to do with the discovery of how tenuous a hold the human mind has even on everyday life. The anguish of incompleteness goes beyond social and existential flaws. It is a blemish that can mar the very source not of our certainties, which Calvino excluded from his fiction right from the beginning, but of the possibility of pursuing knowledge and completeness. Nothing can undermine a conception of the world in which the fundamental premise is the power of the subject (I, eye) to look, organize, and interpret, more than the loss of intellectual lucidity. Even the mere reminder that such a loss exists somewhere in the human community is frightening. Only a detached and playful posture can negotiate such discoveries, and avoid a shift of the text in the direction of drama. The lightness and whimsy of Calvino's pen in attacking such an issue was revealed by *Il visconte dimezzato* (*The Cloven Viscount*), published in 1952, which surprised some critics with its unexpected fable-like quality. The story used paradoxes to address the existence of a chasm within the Calvinian universe. Inexhaustible and light-hearted absurdities result from the invention of a literal clovenness in the protagonist,[5] and from the descriptions of his ways of mutilating the world around him in order to turn it into a mirror of his own deformity. This was the main road that would be taken by Calvino's fiction, a highly entertaining mixture of naïvety and sophistication, since images and events live a double life: they exist in the memory of a narrator who is an adult, but was a child when he witnessed and committed to memory their happening.

The happy ending of the cloven viscount's story, complete with an ingenious healing of the monstrous wound and a wedding, tells us that we are reading a fable. But when Calvino, shortly after publishing *Il visconte dimezzato*, started a long fictional piece that confronted the same dilemma in a reflective mode, its writing required ten years of elaboration: *La giornata d'uno scrutatore* bears the dates 1953–63. The chronicle of the days Amerigo Ormea spent as a poll watcher within the walls of an institution for incurables, the famous Cottolengo in Turin, brings together the various strands of the writer's reflection about the world's deceptive appearances. The ambivalence experienced by the young bourgeois Communist party member in the performance of his civic duty takes several forms: at first, he feels a mixture of enthusiasm for the democratic process, which was evidence of change in post-Fascist Italy, and irritation for its shabby implementation and the political manipulations of it. That feeling gives way to disillusionment and puzzlement, disdain and surprise, as Amerigo Ormea successively becomes aware of the gulf that separates political ideals from the world's opaqueness, the innumerable faces of love (after all, his family name, Ormea, is an anagram of *amore*), and the conflicted quality of his relationship with a woman, Lia. After the day-long struggle with new and conflicting feelings, the novella closes with the discovery that there exists another humanity, not defined by power of mind and self-reflection but guided by its own logic and feelings, that is to say, the universe of the Cottolengo. Those inhabitants of a hidden world end up by representing for the protagonist a mysterious human dimension that puts into question his own identity, while at the same time reasserting for him the value of human constructs: cooperation, game playing, and the building of the city.

Triangles

'Look for a broken link in the net / that binds us / you leap out, flee!' ('Cerca una maglia rotta nella rete / che ci stringe, / tu, balza fuori, fuggi!'; 'In limine,' *L'opera in versi* 5). Such was Montale's exhortation to an elusive listener. There are indeed ways to escape entrapment, and over the years Calvino's characters adopted a variety of approaches and techniques to deal with the anxiety caused by the double-faced world in which they lived, and the pain experienced because of their cloven selves.

The first technique was to turn surprise and anguish into something comical. Calvino's characters become more humorous as they turn clumsier and clumsier and develop tics. In 'La speculazione edilizia' (Building for Profit, 1956), the protagonist is aware of the illusory social superiority that is an important component of his bourgeois identity. In fact, he is incapable of dealing with his brother's accounting for some construction expenses, and with the ensuing discussions with a building contractor. His contribution to the 'business' talks is 'an idiotic screech' ('un gridolino da demente'; *I racconti* 407), as he nervously makes small piles of 'toothpicks shaped by his hands and teeth in zigzag or straight angles' ('stecchini tutti contorti a zig-zag o a greca dalle mani e dai denti'; 405). Such gestures and demeanour are clearly coping devices that seem to have been borrowed from a straight-faced clown, and several other Calvinian protagonists, for instance Marcovaldo, display similar behaviours.[6] The characters are stumped by an unmanageable reality and troubled by their lack of success in life, but they never give up. In order to overcome their bewilderment and unease, they develop another ingenious way of coping, by becoming absorbed in the 'geometric' obsession that had already made its appearance in early Calvino stories.[7] The making or drawing of straight lines and right angles that combine to form a plane geometric figure, the triangle, haunts the Calvinian text. In *Il visconte dimezzato*, where Medardo's halved body and double personality foreshadow the threat of universal *dimidiamento*, curious triangular situations abound: goats stop 'in a strange pattern of straight angles' ('in uno strano disegno d'angoli retti'; 22); the viscount advances on his crutch 'with a calipers-like movement' ('con un movimento a compasso'; 22 and 97), and he sports an 'icy triangular smile' ('gelido sorriso triangolare'; 33).

It is perhaps superfluous to recall that the triangle has a long history in the culture that nurtured Calvino's writing. It was a privileged geometric entity in philosophic-mystical circles, from the Pythagoreans to the biblical tradition, and in modern secret societies such as the Masons. As a matter of fact, in one of Calvino's most polished and autobiographical texts, the narrator evokes the Masonic symbols, a triangle and an open pair of compasses, inscribed or sculpted at the entrance of his ancestral home: 'the ancient dwelling at Cadorso ... still bearing above its doorway the faded traces of the Masonic symbol that the old Calvi-nos used to place on their houses' ('l'antico casolare di Cadorso ... con ancora la traccia sbiadita, sopra la porta, del simbolo massonico che i vecchi Calvino mettevano sulle loro case'; *Romanzi e racconti* [Novels and Short Stories] III 24). The pivotal element of the triangle is the num-ber three, which is connected with magic, but at the same time the trian-gle is tied to the most rational and pragmatic way of measuring. In surveyors' practice, triangulation is the basis for gauging the relative distances of points in space. In short, the triangle sums up two contra-dictory aspects of human reflection: the emotional and metaphysical drive and the search for rational certainty. In Calvino, too, the triangle, which at times is an emblem of control, possession, and the creative game, is often also a manifestation of neurotic defence. Later in the Cal-vinian production, other sources of anguish based on geometry will emerge: the complexity of the labyrinth, the solidity of crystals, and the formless aggregates of glass or sand.

In the practice of surveying, the crucial elements are, first, the choice of point of view or of the location of the surveyor's eye, and, second, precision in taking measurements. Almost as a confirmation of the met-aphor of triangulation, Calvino's narrative, right from its beginning, gave a large space to his characters' reliance on sharpness of vision, and privileged the action of the eye that measures rather than that of the eye that penetrates. Renato Barilli, in a perceptive but hostile article, declared that the Calvinian way of looking was 'a gesture of intermittent engagement ... that [moves] from one object to the other with an unsteady and restless curiosity' ('atto d'impegno saltuario ... che [passa] da un oggetto all'altro con curiosità instabile ed irrequieta'; Barilli 214). Those were the years of the *nouveau roman*, or 'new novel,' in which Bar-illi saw authentic innovation on the epistemological plane, and it was tempting to make comparisons between a Robbe-Grillet and a Calvino. Barilli thought that what he called the Italian 'common sense' translated into timidity about any sort of radical change. Therefore, he saw in Calvino's 'measure,' in his 'cheerful and witty' ('ilare e arguto') style, a form of scandalous light-heartedness. The criticism had to do mostly with pursuing a literary polemic. Today it is interesting to contrast the praise of lightness drafted by Calvino many years later in his *Lezioni americane*. In any event, it was obvious that Calvino's order was neither a given nor a conquest, but rather the contradictory other face of a disor-der within which he searched the point of encounter between the world and language. Calvino acknowledged that he was not inclined toward the tragic, the pathetic, or the darker emotions; he was little interested in the psychological factor, and did not believe in the myth of childhood as an irretrievable paradise, as Barilli himself rightly remarked in a vaguely reproachful tone. At the centre of Calvino's writing is a sense of the impossibility of bringing order to the world, accompanied by a drive to do so. In 1976, Calvino wrote in a letter to Sandro Briosi[8] that the crucial point for him was an antinomy that found no outlet in anguish or in a problematical concept of freedom or in existentialist *néant*, but remained as a condition that is not accepted and from which there is no exit. His theme was the obstinate effort to live, in spite of everything, with that knowledge and that contradiction.

There are many instances of the surveying eye holding a position of central importance in the first period of Calvinian writing. In the short story written in 1946 that gave the title to a collection Calvino reworked several times, 'Ultimo viene il corvo' (The Crow Comes Last), the young protagonist is presented as an infallible shot. A country boy, he wonders about the distance that separates him from his gun's targets, a distance that suggests to his naïve vision of the world a gap, a disquieting void. The entire short story revolves around the question he asks himself as he is taking aim: 'Why that empty space between him and the objects?' ('Perché quella distanza tra lui e le cose?'; *I racconti* 8). The answer, if answer it is, comes from the act of shooting: 'If he pointed the gun ... *the air was a straight and invisible line, stretching from the tip of the gun to the thing* ... It was easy to see that the empty space was a trick' ('Se puntava il fucile ... *l'aria era una linea diritta ed invisibile, tesa dalla bocca del fucile alla cosa* ... la distanza vuota si capiva che era un trucco'; 8. Emphasis added). The boy's gesture erases the distance while underscoring it, since the Resistance fighters in the story know how difficult it is to hit a target. It negates the void and becomes the cruel assertion of a presence, that of the boy who knows nothing else but his target, while the target becomes such because of the infallible precision of his marksman's eye. The boy's lightning-quick and exact triangulation leaves its mark; the contact becomes a mysterious touch of death.[9]

However, the recourse to geometric exactness designed to exercise control over the real and to set anchor in the world by asserting one's presence in it, soon reveals its ambiguity in the Calvinian universe. Tracing lines, rather than a gesture of dominion and self-definition, becomes obsessive activity aimed at gaining the conviction that what is hostile and uncontrollable in the world can be kept at bay. In 'La formica argentina' (The Argentine Ant, 1952), a Captain Bruni, who is convinced that 'everything must be done scientifically' ('tutto va fatto con criteri scientifici'; *I racconti* 374), untiringly measures a terrain infested with ants, and builds contraptions in the shape of a V in which the open side, covered with a flimsy top, works as a trap for the insects. The invasion of ants continues, however, like a nightmare that cannot be stopped, while the captain-surveyor obstinately persists in his measuring and constructing.

The sense of defeat deepens when Calvino, creating his comic-ironic alter ego Agilulf, further defines the exorcising function of measuring and its geometric outcomes. In *Il cavaliere inesistente*, the inexperienced young knight Raimbaut, who is impatient for action of any sort, looks for Agilulf and finds him

> under a pine tree ... arranging small pine cones, which had fallen on the ground, according to a regular pattern, an isosceles triangle. At that time of dawn, Agilulf always had to apply himself in an exercise of precision: counting objects, ordering them in geometric shapes, and solving mathematical problems ('sotto un pino ... disponeva le piccole pigne cadute al suolo secondo un disegno regolare, un triangolo isoscele. A quell'ora dell'alba, Agilulfo aveva sempre bisogno d'applicarsi a un esercizio d'esattezza: contare oggetti, ordinarli in figure geometriche, risolvere problemi d'aritmetica'; *Il cavaliere inesistente* 29).

The lack of certainty about his own existence may be assuaged for Agilulf by his having recourse to the abstract and precise forms devised by the intellect. The word 'obstinacy' returns twice in a few lines and becomes 'a tense obstinacy' ('una tesa ostinazione'; 31); the gestures made by the knight with rapidity and concentration reveal an imperious need. He has chosen his weapon in the struggle against non-existence, as the poor rich little boy Giancarlo will do, a few years later, to overcome boredom (*Marcovaldo* 136). Agilulf is trying to keep afloat in what Calvino will call the world's 'magma,' the realm of the squire Gurduloo.[10] To be precise, we must note that Agilulf's triangle is not only isosceles, but also rectangular. He 'was then placing [the pine cones] in squares on the sides of the triangle, and obstinately added up the pine cones of the squares of the sides, comparing them with the square of the hypotenuse' ('disponeva poi [le pigne] in quadrati sui lati del triangolo e sommava con ostinazione le pigne dei quadrati dei cateti confrontandole a quelle del quadrato dell'ipotenusa'; 30). When added to its complementary image, the isosceles rectangular triangle produces the square, the geometric symbol of perfection and of self-sufficient closure in Pythagorean thought. It is precisely Pythagoras's theorem (known even to people who have mastered little or no geometry) that Calvino evokes in this episode. Faced with Agilulf's obsessive activity, it's Raimbaut who starts feeling lost, as he wonders what truth lies under all rituals, conventions, and formulas. His doubt widens to the point that even action begins to seem questionable to him. Action may be just 'a ritual to avoid sinking into nothingness' ('un rituale per non sprofondare nel nulla').[11] Raimbaut is not the only one fascinated by Agilulf's false appearance of self-confidence. Bradamant also sees in him the only one who, in the mess that is life, 'knew its secret geometry, the order, the rules for understanding its beginning and its end' ('ne sapeva la geometria segreta, l'ordine, la regola per capirne il principio e la fine'; 101). Such is the form that desire takes in the Calvinian universe.

When Calvino's narrative entered urban space, the function of triangular forms became more ambiguous, the supposed rationality of human constructs more problematical, and the texture of writing more complex. Some stories have a fairy-tale quality, for instance 'Il gatto e il poliziotto' ('The Cat and the Policeman,' 1948). The young protagonist, a policeman who gets lost during a search in a maze of working-class apartment buildings, has a sudden revelation of the contrast between human beings and a geometrically built environment. He contemplates, from high on a roof, what he believes to be enemy territory: 'the sprawling city ... [where] geometric iron structures rose beyond factory fences' ('l'enorme città ... [dove] costruzioni di ferro geometriche s'alzavano dentro i recinti delle fabbriche'; I racconti 132). However, he finds out that the geometric city with its buildings and fences hides only families at the dinner table, elderly people, frightened housewives, mischievous cats, and young girls who read romance novels.

The contradiction the young policeman saw at the heart of that particular city was the sort of urban double image that, by the sixties, readers were accustomed to find in Calvino's texts. In 1960, he described Turin as a paradoxical place, 'a city that suggests vigour, linearity, style. It counsels logic, and through logic opens the road to madness' ('una città che invita al vigore, alla linearità, allo stile. Invita alla logica, attraverso la logica apre la via alla follia'; Eremita a Parigi 16). To confirm the fundamental importance of the city's duplicity, Calvino's later texts not only returned more than once to a description of Turin, but rewrote a peculiar episode against the backdrop of the urban scenery. The autobiographical note placed in an appendix to the 1969 edition of Tarocchi

(Tarots)[12] reads: 'Then Turin, industrious and rational, held me, a city where the danger of going mad ... is not lesser than elsewhere. I arrived there in years when *the streets opened free and interminable* because of *the rarity of cars* ... I moved through it *drawing invisibile hypotenuses* between *the grey sides of triangles*' ('Poi mi tenne Torino operosa e razionale, dove il rischio d'impazzire ... non è minore che altrove. Vi arrivai in anni in cui *le strade s'aprivano deserte e interminabili per la rarità delle auto* ... avanzavo *tracciando invisibili ipotenuse tra grigi cateti*'; 161–2. Emphasis added). The walker in the city, a familiar character in European and especially French literature around mid-century, has acquired here special connotations that need analysing. First of all, antithesis rules the subject's experience:[13] he was born under the signs of Sun and Saturn housed in Libra, poised between light and gloom; the city where he grew up, San Remo, was green and luxuriant, while the streets of Turin are grey; and madness hides in the rational city. The narrator is 'held' by the city in a neurotic game of entrapment and contradictions, but he has managed to confront the dilemma, in the deserted streets that imprison him, by resorting to the exorcising power of geometry. In fact, his action of drawing lines by walking mimics and extends the writing function. He keeps making marks on a wider blank surface beyond the page made of paper, and by doing so inserts himself in the city's topography and its problematical rationality. The lines he draws complete the geometric figure of a triangle, and more specifically a rectangular triangle, because only in that case can one speak of hypotenuse and sides. At the same time, however, the concrete gesture of the walker in the city reminds us of the invisibility of those same signs. This writing turns out to be also erasure, so that, paradoxically, a breach is opened in the geometry without exit created by the streets.

The theme recurs, widens, and becomes more and more varied in the second series of Marcovaldo stories.[14] The rigidity of the city's structures is challenged by images of the protagonist's zigzagging path along 'the endless and deserted streets and avenues' ('le vie e i corsi ... sterminate e deserte' [sic]; *Marcovaldo* 25). The inscription of Marcovaldo in the cityscape is accompanied by the possibility of liberation. '*The grey walls* ... the things of every day, *angular and hostile*' ('i grigi muri ... le cose di tutti i giorni *spigolose e ostili*'; Emphasis added), suddenly disappear when the cityscape is erased by a snowfall, and Marcovaldo can give free rein to his imagination.[15] It is clear that Marcovaldo's proceeding in zigzag fashion denotes at times an ambiguous freedom that hinges on his discovery, neither joyous nor sad, of the duplicity and opaque resistance of the world. Again in 'La fermata sbagliata' (The Wrong Stop; 75), Marcovaldo's walk follows an irregular pattern. In 'Marcovaldo al supermarket' (Marcovaldo at the Supermarket; 100), he goes in zigzag fashion through the aisles. And the autobiographical concept we noticed earlier is anticipated in full in *Marcovaldo*, worded in almost the identical way it would appear more than five years later in *Tarocchi*. In the wide and deserted streets, coloured by a touch of grey, the promise of Marcovaldo's escape is couched in geometric terms: '*The streets opened in all their wide, endless expanse, empty of cars and deserted ... the grey hedge* of iron roll-up shutters ... Now he could ... *cross the streets diagonally* and stop in the centre of the squares' ('*S'aprivano larghe e interminabili le vie, vuote di macchine e deserte ... la siepe grigia* delle saracinesche abbassate ... ora poteva ... *attraversare in diagonale*, e fermarsi nel centro delle piazze'; 113–14. Emphasis added). For Calvino's watcher, the gesture of physically drawing those lines opening and closing around him becomes the chance to see differently and to construct a world of his own ('The City All to Himself' – 'La città tutta per lui' – is the title of the Marcovaldo story just quoted). Soon a more capricious horde of protagonists, 'i gatti ostinati' ('the stubborn cats'), would stride along the paths hidden at the core of the city, bringing out its invisible reverse, a sort of urban blueprint, and the first pattern for Calvino's invisible cities.

Other Geometries

Even in 1964, when Calvino evoked a bygone Liguria, the image of the triangle returned, with its clean-cut precision. But one side of that geometric form, rather than defining the point of vision, escaped measurement and receded in the distance, like a mirage: 'The sea is there, in a triangular cleft of the V-shaped valley, but it is as if it were miles and miles away' ('il mare è lí, in uno spacco triangolare della valle a vu; ma è come se fosse miglia e miglia lontano;' *Romanzi e racconti* III 26). As the years went by, the threads of geometric lines criss-crossed in Calvino's writing, and the patterns became more elaborate. The plane or linear figures of the early times, nostalgic connections to the landscape of youthful experience, gave way to the nightmare of the labyrinth and the four-dimensional vertigo of spirals. Qfwfq was still, in Calvino's own words, 'a voice, a point of view, an eye' ('una voce, un punto di vista, un occhio'; *La memoria del mondo* [The Memory of the World] 7), but his habitat was the space/time of geological eras. Calvino's interest in scientific discourse and imagery became more methodical. He adopted a scientific language in order to explore the resources of exact discourse (Bernardini Napolitano 853–9), with a view to constructing more powerful geometric models and thus continuing the search for order and freedom begun earlier by various counters and measurers. As Francesca Bernardini Napolitano says, the Calvinian text pursues the possibility of an opening, and Calvino's characters trust in an ability to draw the plan of the enclosures in which they are held. Solid geometry offers the tools to overcome the perspective in which the world is made up of indistinct masses, sand and glass. The mind gazes upon a world that has the configuration of 'an indestructible, gelid blossoming of quartz' ('un' indistruttibile gelida primavera di quarzo'; *Ti con zero* 40); but the *esprit de géométrie* that tends toward equilibrium is also a passion with fiery impetus, and it privileges at the same time crystals and fire. Equilibrium is found in the celebration of the wealth of variants present in the forms of the world, so that order is not 'the sign of a character submissive to an interior discipline, a repression of instincts ... The idea of a world that would be absolutely regular, symmetrical, and methodical is bound to this first impulse and luxuriance of nature, to amorous tension' ('non è il segno di un carattere sottomesso a una disciplina interiore, a una repressione degli istinti ... l'idea d'un mondo assolutamente regolare, simmetrico, metodico s'associa a questo primo impeto e rigoglio della natura, alla tensione amorosa' (*Ti con zero* 40–1).[16]

Unfortunately, the world actually is 'a corroded, tarnished, and impure crystal' ('un cristallo corroso, macchiato, mescolato'; *Ti con zero* 45). The chaos of disintegration advances, leaving behind only grains of sand, atomized and uncontrollable (*Ti con zero* 44). Salvation remains the possible outcome only if the mind increases its efforts to measure more and more complex structures, and the draughtsman manages to extend the lines on the page and beyond. In 'Il conte di Montecristo' (The Count of Monte Cristo), the probability of success in escaping from the castle/prison is not entrusted to Abbot Faria's desperate attempts, but to Dantès's probabilistic calculations:

> Beginning with the disorder of these data, I see in each isolated obstacle *the evidence of a system* of obstacles; *I develop each segment into a geometric figure,* connect those figures *to form the faces of a solid form* ... inscribe those polyhedra in spheres or hyperspheres, and by doing so *the more I enclose the shape of the fortress the more I simplify it, defining it through a mathematical relationship,* or an algebraic formula ('partendo dal disordine di questi dati, vedo in ogni ostacolo isolato *l'indizio d'un sistema* d'ostacoli, sviluppo *ogni segmento*

in una figura regolare, saldo queste figure come facce d'un solido ... iscrivo questi poliedri in sfere o in ipersfere, e così *più chiudo la forma della fortezza più la semplifico, definendola in un rapporto numerico o in una formula algebrica*'; *Ti con zero* 157. Emphasis added).

When the need to universalize is identified explicitly with sphericity, globality, and the self-reflexiveness of discourse in *Le cosmicomiche* and *Ti con zero*, as Gian Paolo Biasin has said (1978, 860–72), the act of measuring is more closely attuned to recent scientific views; but at that very moment, it also becomes more *angst*-producing, the source of ever more laborious attempts to find certainty. The dihedra, cuspids, and prisms we find in the 1967 short story entitled 'I cristalli' (Crystals) are illusions. It is the magma of glass that has overcome, and the world's apparent order hides in fact a profound disorder. The infallible marksman of 'Ultimo viene il corvo' has become the archer of 'Ti con zero,' for whom arrow and target, instead of meeting triumphantly, forever miss each other. The moment of suspense that is incessantly repeated delays the ultimate target, death, but builds a virtual prison. What to do? It turns out that the problem to be solved is not spatial, but temporal: 'The lines of possible futures depart in a cone-shaped sheaf from this second ... [and] the very same lines follow oblique paths from a past that is also a sheaf of infinite possibilities' ('da questo secondo si dipartono a cono linee di possibili futuri ... [e] ... le stesse linee provengono oblique da un passato che è anch'esso un cono di possibilità infinite'; *Ti con zero* 113). Time, then, not space, is the void that Agilulf and Raimbaut were trying to fill. To see clearly, and to establish a fixed point in the oscillations of the phases of the universe (*Ti con zero* 109 and 111) – that is the actual goal, or what another Calvino, the essayist, called the 'project.' The conclusion reached by the fictional text is hardly satisfying: 'In order to find a steady point in time I must move with time, to become objective I must remain subjective' ('per fermarmi nel tempo devo muovermi col tempo, per diventare oggettivo devo mantenermi soggettivo'; *Ti con zero* 118). And the situation does not change with the adoption of solutions with opposite signs. The zigzagging line of *The Count of Monte Cristo* by Dumas, the line that should lead out of the prison, is mirrored by the phantomatic spiral of a novel in the negative (*Ti con zero* 163). Abbot Faria's digging for an escape route from the prison-fortress is the negative image of the 'thinking the fortress' by Dantès. Only if the fortress constructed by the mind does not coincide with the real fortress will there be a hope of fleeing from it.

Breaking out of a prison implies drawing either physical or mental itineraries inside it, in the heart of the labyrinth, but there is no telling where the broken lines of those paths may lead. In 1969, a narrator who is a structuralist/semiologist places at the end of his own path the all-encompassing square formed by tarots which, continually placed, moved, displaced, and replaced, tell all the tales of the world. We have arrived at the castle not of If but of crossed destinies, or crossing paths; we have reached the seat of a double origin at 'the heart of chaos [and] ... the point of intersection of all the potential orders' ('il cuore caotico delle cose ... [il] punto d'intersezione di tutti gli ordini possibili'; *Il castello dei destini incrociati* 33).

A comment inserted in a preface Calvino wrote for one of his collections of short stories insists that 'the geometric pattern is what counts' ('Quel che conta è il disegno geometrico'; *Gli amori difficili*). It is not clear if this is meant to be an exorcism of an obscure fear, or a return to felicitous constructs. The Calvinian character is not content with one option; he is attracted by multiplicity, and plays on all the boards. In the most self-reflexive short story Calvino wrote, entitled 'Dall'opaco' (From the Shady Side, 1971), he experimented with a new approach. The narrating voice has only intratextual referents, and wavers between the effort to grasp what is mutable and the contemplation of a linear world: 'To describe the world's form, the first step is to pinpoint my position' ('per descrivere la forma del mondo la prima cosa è fissare in quale posizione mi trovo'; *Romanzi e racconti* III 90). A background of rocky hills, a thirsty vegetation in the wings, and the 'luminous stage of the horizon' ('la ribalta luminosa dell'orizzonte') place the protagonist I/Eye at the cusp of a triangle that is on the verge of metamorphosis. The world stretches and writhes like a lizard ('s'allunga e contorce come una lucertola'; 98). We are back on the Ligurian coast, from which vertigos push human beings toward all kinds of elsewheres. The elsewheres perhaps converge, and thanks to that convergence the eye can return to gaze upon the familiar lines of a congenial landscape. The triangle may simply be the shape of sea-inspired contemplations that sum up and placate all pulsions. In 1973, the Ligurian coast returned once again, not as a surface but as a line from which one could draw compensation for a lost felicity ('l'indennizzo d'un bene perduto'; 'Liguria' 9 and 14). And in 1975, the marine portion of Genoa, the Ligurian city *par excellence*, is described in this way: 'Piazza Caricamento has the shape of a triangle with only two sides ... without the invisible side the two visible ones would never have emerged, and the piazza would not exist' ('Piazza

Caricamento ha la forma d'un triangolo con due soli lati ... senza il lato invisibile non sarebbero mai sorti i due lati visibili e non esisterebbe la piazza'; 'Le piazze' 84). That is how the prototype of the city is built according to the character named Calvino, who is no less anchored to a cityscape than his Marco Polo. The invisible, desired and elusive, structures the visible. Piazzas and cities hold a mesmerizing attraction precisely because they fulfil the dream of overcoming *dimidiamento*, by dissolving the two into the magical three. In fact, the title of this virtuoso piece is 'The Sea Is the Third Dimension' ('Il terzo lato è il mare'), which underlines the presence/absence of the one element, the sea, that ties faraway places and times, while separating them.

The Invisible that inhabited the Calvinian texts right from the beginning finally found a form precisely in those years, through the writing of the Cities, where men pursue not only the shadow of Woman (de Lauretis 1978) but all their phantom constructs. It was precisely the protagonist of the autobiographical note of 1969 who, afflicted with a geographical neurosis, having escaped the severe triangles of a grey network of streets, had landed in the concentric City, source of all the knowable, 'Paris, a city surrounded by forests ... surrounding in turn the Bibliothèque Nationale' ('Parigi, città circondata da foreste ... e circondante a sua volta la Bibliothèque nationale'; *Tarocchi*), where he consulted rare books containing the inexhaustible patrimony of the stories of the world. Now, a multiplicity of cities erupts out of the singularity and concreteness of the City, Cottolengo or Paris, Turin or New York. Whether they are perceptions in a field of vision (Frasson-Marin) or a system of binary structures (Almansi 1971) or a model of sestinas (Mengaldo 1975), the Invisible Cities bear within them, like a watermark, the traces of the old geometric forms that have become mobile and therefore generative.[17] The two patterns according to which the chapters of *Le città invisibili* can be arranged[18] confirm this assessment. There is a first pattern in which two rectangular triangles enclose a rectangle; in the second and more analytical pattern, two rectangular and isosceles triangles enclose a square, the perfect magical square in which all the factors of specularity triumph. It is traversed by what Carlo Ossola calls the axis of central symmetry, 'so that, bisected by this ideal hypotenuse, the square is divided into two more triangles' ('cosí che bipartitó da questa ideale ipotenusa il quadro si divide in altri due triangoli'; Ossola 246). The same diagram also permits the drawing of two large isosceles triangles equivalent to two squares. This may seem an excessive manipulation of geometric suggestions, but Calvino did provide an elaborate puzzle, enticing the reader to share in his game, with important repetitions and recalls. The game of chess between Marco Polo and Kublai Khan also ends with the geometric enclosure of a square, black or white, after checkmate. Anything can be read in the flat surface of that simple form in which two inverted triangles meet. Calvino will call it 'an emblem of nothingness' ('un emblema del nulla'; *Lezioni americane* 71), but we know that it contains *en abîme* many other things: an atlas with no borders, an infinite catalogue of shapes, the document of a living form, and a spiral that tries to draw us down toward the infernal city. There seemed to be a pause, perhaps a hint of stagnation, in the elaboration of that aspect of the Calvinian project. The classical geometric forms that were sought earlier as the basis for certainty seemed to have dissolved, like Agilulf, and writing tentatively entered the tangle of a forest/root/labyrinth, hoping to discover the secret path toward what is not the abyss. A danger loomed, of which the storyteller was well aware: 'The harmonious intellectual geometry borders, at its limit, on a paranoid obsession' ('l'armoniosa geometria intellettuale sfiora al limite l'ossessione paranoica'; *Il castello dei destini incrociati* 107). A new start was needed.

Hypervision

In 1980, Calvino published *Una pietra sopra*, a selection of essays written from 1955 to 1978, with the explicit intervention of an observer who was in charge of the selection, the preface containing the instructions for the reader, and the commentaries accompanying each text. The disenchanted posture of the editor contradicts the linearity of the sequence of the texts selected, its supposed inevitability, and the passionate tension that inhabits the essays. The observer's name as well as the name of the essayist is Italo Calvino; the function of the former is to frame the selected essays within a perspective that distances the latter's youthful project and relegates it to a past of almost mythical quality. The metaphor of the thread, discursive and calligraphic, which had informed Calvino's earlier fictions, has yielded to the metaphor of the gravestone, dramatic and final. As was to be expected, though, the metaphorical burial was part of a strategy: the old projects needed to be classified, organized, and set aside. At the same time, this effort was a preview of what Calvino was going to write, and why, and how. Out of the *tabula rasa* something new could emerge, and did. A Mr Palomar began anew the laborious, stubborn process of observing, measuring, and comprehending the real, as if for the first time.

The waves of the sea, the scales of reptiles, and the blades of grass in a lawn provide the field of observation for Mr Palomar, who devotes his reflexive tercets to those objects in the 1980s.[19] The text is written in a poetic-fantastic key, and its totally controlled writing makes it a perfect mechanism, as self-enclosed as an egg. To follow Calvino's progress in this venture, we must keep our eyes open and carefully inspect the inside of the inspecting mechanism. The title itself is a gentle trap, obviously allusive, saying and not saying that the discourse is duplicitous, and that the layers of the narration are many more than are apparent. Calvino himself spoke of a double and opposite character, named Mr Mohole, who was supposed to appear in the same fictional space as Mr Palomar; but his appearance was continually delayed, until the Palomar cycle was concluded and no space remained. As concerned with the depths as Mr Palomar was concerned with the surface of the world, Mr Mohole was supposed to be the negative pole of a duality, the other term of an antithesis. Having been excluded from the work in progress, the absent character was then going to have his own space; but the second book was never written, partly because of the author's fatigue, and partly because the narrator decided that Mr Palomar already included his antithetical character – in other words, that 'Palomar was also Mohole' ('Palomar era anche Mohole'; *Romanzi e racconti* II 1403). We may add that Calvino was not fond of focusing on the depths, by temperament and because he had found enough with which to keep his character busy in the inexhaustible surface of the world.

And besides, things may have been even more complex than Calvino's voice suggested. The narrative space is actually inhabited by three presences. First, the text harbours a wily handler of codices, unnamed, self-effacing, who foresees everything, plans everything, guides us by the hand, and entraps us with the clarity of his language. As in *Una pietra sopra*, an observer (Italo Calvino?) lends his voice to the protagonist, creating in this manner a double, his own, in a narrative fabric with no visible seam. As a corollary, the reader's path is traced by the writing hand with simplicity and self-assurance. Thus, although Mr Palomar is at the centre of this fiction, it is the narrator who relates the character's experiences as *he* sees them, and the reader is inexorably drawn in by the narrative vortex disguised as an innocuous sequence of episodes. Distance from the text is made possible by the absence of first-person interference, by the oblique presence of an irony that hides the imposition of a forced symbiosis, and by an inescapable tripartite involvement. The eye is the ruling metaphor, three is the cardinal number, and the discourse is rational, masculine, and singular. The book, to all appearances, belongs to the dominant current of Western written culture, and owes to that connection its power as an efficient and devious artefact, its generous and blind obstinacy. But there is more to it. Something is hidden in this project designed to redefine and undermine all dualisms; there is a restlessness, a nervousness, a sense of probable inadequacy, and also a determination to overcome it. *Palomar* is a pitiless exploration of the ultimate points of arrival of a proud culture that is endowed with (ironically) limited vision. Rather than a revisitation of ground already covered and of familiar techniques, however seductive such a revisitation might have been for some readers, *Palomar* has turned into an original, but not ponderous, meditation on fundamental matters.

The Eye is not naked. As a matter of fact, the early and classic Calvinian image of a man who inspects the world 'training [on it] his spectacled gaze' ('appuntando il suo sguardo occhialuto'; *I racconti* 15) aptly occupies centre stage in this text. The Eye is technologically enhanced, reinforced by lenses of various types, so that it never actually tackles the act of 'seeing' without the filter of another eye. The character whose name proclaims the triumphs of astronomy and optical technology is continually frustrated in the exercise of his visual functions. Whether excessively near-sighted or far-sighted, astigmatic or simply distracted, the watcher ends up by feeling uncertain, frustrated, or confused. On the other side of the lens, the world also resists; it refuses to reveal itself with clarity and stays out of focus, ironically accentuating the limitations of all watchers, who are faced with the impenetrability of the world. Mr Palomar is therefore the lens, or to put it less nobly, the minimal transparent surface through which things wink at each other and the world looks at itself. In addition, the technological prosthesis reveals the dangers of experimentation, because a somewhat keener vision leads to a greater fear, not the fear of discovering the Montalean void, but the fear of man's disappearance. Obstinacy would seem vain, in these circumstances, and the otherness of the 'real' seems reconfirmed. The lack of focus should also lead to a sense of defeat, a weakening of the voice, and ultimately to the silence of the text. To the contrary, it is precisely at the edge of this potential fall into silence that writing blossoms and rules. The narrator retrieves the ancient tricks of discourse, from the lyrical to the comical levels, at the expense of Mr Palomar. Once again, writing means that the narrating voice posits its existence, in a universe as indifferent as Leopardi's. It is not by accident that material Objects, 'les Choses, les innomables,' as Sartre wrote in *La nausée* (177–91), reappear: 'From the mute expanse of things must come a sign, a call, a wink. Some thing stands out from among the others meaning to signify something ... but what? Itself ... nothing else, among other things that mean themselves and nothing else' ('Dalla muta distesa delle cose deve partire un segno, un richiamo, un ammicco: una cosa si stacca dalle altre con l'intenzione di significare qualcosa ... che cosa? se stessa ... nient'altro, in mezzo alle cose che significano se stesse e nient'altro'; *Palomar* 117). The beckoning of Objects, which made Roquentin sick with nausea, that viscous relationship between human beings and the world that the 'école du regard' rejected, returns here exorcised, and even sought as a basis on which to understand the world. Mr Palomar calls on all his senses, limited and treacherous as they are. Calvino is far from subscribing to a postmodern vision of the new approach to knowledge, according to which 'the referent ... has ended up by breaking away from the real, and being substituted for by simulation models' ('il referente ... ha finito per sganciarsi dal reale, sostituito dai modelli di simulazione'; Alinovi 112).

The volume ostensibly privileges order and coherence. After all, the narrator had said elsewhere that Mr Palomar still trusted in a possible epiphany: 'It is not to be excluded, thinks the ever trusting Mr Palomar, that, when one least expects it, the secret pattern, the Form toward which blindly tends all our culture, may spring forth from these arbitrary and messy visions' ('Non è escluso, pensa il sempre fiducioso signor Palomar, che quando meno ci s'aspetta da queste visioni arbitrarie e scomposte scaturisca il disegno segreto, la Forma a cui inconsapevolmente tende tutta la nostra civiltà'; *Saggi* II 1992–93). Mr Palomar's 'adventures,' then, prepare the ground for that order, almost as in a propitiatory gesture. Agilulf's and Giancarlo's arithmetic and geometry return, raised to a more sophisticated level. The volume is structured in three parts, of which the first is anchored in rationality, the second in semiotics, and the third in existential meditation. Each part is in turn subdivided into three sections, and the writing is done at three degrees, description (a sort of degree zero), story, and metanarrative. There is no space for reader misunderstanding or undue speculation: numbers and patterns are explicitly identified by Calvino in an appendix, and mark a return to the very origins of observation, symbology, and Western thought. This meditated immersion is the (strictly intellectual) analogue of a deep-sea diver's exploration, and Calvino confirms that, in selecting the title of the volume, he thought, among other more obvious references, of the assonance between Mr Palomar's name and the Italian *palombaro* ('deep-sea diver'; see *Romanzi e racconti* II 1405).

The first section of the volume is a cosmogony centred on the metaphor of the eye, and takes its point of departure from the classic place delegated to that function, at least in the Mediteranean tradition, the sea. The effort consists in attempting to fix the object, arrest it, define it, and give it limits. The eye, again, is not contemplative, but rather searches and delimits; it does not sweep the vastness of the sea, but rather attempts to isolate a single wave, the discrete object to be measured and therefore defined. The emphasis is placed on the watcher. As he swims, Mr Palomar states, 'I am swimming in my mind' ('sto nuotando nella mia mente'; *Palomar* 16). He is at the cusp of the golden triangle that shimmers between sky and sea, he is like a sun of the system of space/time. The universe first found its order when the material world and light-receptive matter met, gave each other life, and became the source of the original creation: 'One day, an eye came out of the sea' ('Un giorno un occhio uscì dal mare'; 20). In a didactic moment Calvino had said more explicitly, 'In short, the brain begins in the eye' ('insomma il cervello comincia nell'occhio'; *Collezione di sabbia* [A Collection of Sand] 125); and the illustration taken from *L'enciclopedia d'un visionario* (The Encyclopedia of a Visionary) by Luigi Serafini, which accompanies that statement, shows many pairs of semi-submerged eyes floating on an imaginary sea (149–53). What does it matter that the sea is covered with detritus produced by decay and pollution? 'This is my habitat ... I can exist only in its midst' ('Questo è il mio habitat ... solo qua in mezzo posso esistere'; *Palomar* 19). In the second section, the subject attempts to penetrate inside the object, observing the lovemaking of turtles, the whistling of a blackbird, and the blades of grass in that population called 'lawn,' but a doubt remains as to whether what is observed is 'a regulated and orderly cosmos, or chaotic proliferation' ('cosmo regolare e ordinato o proliferazione caotica'; 34). In the third section, the act of focusing on the world is crucial, because Mr Palomar confronts the unknown that had once been the object of Pascal's meditation. Like Leopardi's personae, he does so through the mediation of the senses, and in fact he carefully limits his scope: 'The first rule I must give myself is this: to limit myself to what I see' ('la prima regola che devo pormi è questa: attenermi a ciò che vedo'; 40). To the luxuriant splendour of a starry sky, he opposes the discipline of self-imposed modesty, in search of a clarity that eludes him. In the second part, with its own three sections, Mr Palomar goes through the exploration of the structure of the object, the relationship between senses and languages, and what may be the line of separation between human and non-human. The torment of disharmony permeates these pages, a fear that the presence of the Other may be only a hypothesis of the mind.

The environment in the first part of the volume evokes Mr Palomar's solitary vacations by the seaside, a bourgeois concept of contact with Nature. The second part takes place in an urban landscape, where a balcony, stores, and a zoo mark and define the area of the human versus the non-human, and contacts with other people are reduced to a glimpse of a solicitous wife. The third part makes explicit what has not been obvious, Mr Palomar's silence. His silence is audible when Mr Palomar is among crowds, and the narration abounds in images of things innumerable: grains of sand, the stones of ancient ruins invaded by tourists, and found objects in a crowded bazaar.

The formless, moving, and seemingly infinite mass of sand appears often in Calvino. It has a magically distancing and soothing effect in 'La formica argentina.' In a 1974 autobiographical piece, 'Ricordo di una battaglia' (Memories of a Battle),[20] it was a metaphor for memory: 'My memories are still there, hidden in the grey bundle of the brain, in the humid bed of sand deposited at the bottom of the stream of thoughts' ('i ricordi sono ancora là, nascosti nel grigio gomitolo del cervello, nell'umido letto di sabbia che si deposita nel fondo del torrente dei pensieri'; *Romanzi e racconti* III 50). In *Collezione di sabbia*, it becomes the object of observation, but beyond the expanse of sand, beyond the burial site of memories, there is a silence that grows and invades the entire scene in the last section of this book. The world looks at itself through a window, Mr Palomar, an incorporeal and anonymous point in the universe, who no longer knows where his I can be found ('il suo se stesso ... non sa più dove si trova'; *Palomar* 120). The theme is now how to be out of the game, to disappear. And yet that 'blur of disquiet that is our presence in the world' ('macchia d'inquietudine che è la nostra presenza'; 124) can contemplate the moment when 'it will be Time that will become worn and extinct in an empty sky' ('sarà il tempo a logorarsi ed estinguersi in un cielo vuoto'; 128). The narration, at this point, having reached the ineffable anti-vision, dissolves not in Dantean ecstasy, but like a soap bubble: 'At that moment, he dies' ('In quel momento muore'; 128). The eye has closed and matter has frozen; focusing was either a miss or a perfect shot, but either way its conclusion is death. The closure of the text contradicts the driving metaphor, and gives the reader a key to *Palomar*'s universe.

Whether we see it as an encyclopaedia or a discourse on writing, *Palo-mar* refines a storyteller's effort to reconcile opposites by inventing shift-ing triads. Antithesis, which is made possible by a third term, the presence of the narrator, is central to this text, and is the origin of its irony, which alone can keep at bay the *angst* caused by doubt. Roquen-tin had his nausea, and Robbe-Grillet's *voyeur* had his (rather too obvi-ous) surveyor's slide-rule. Mr Palomar, the eye/window on the world, has a shadow, the author, who can manipulate rhetorical devices. By definition, antithesis is a figure of rhetoric based on logic's principle of non-contradiction, whereby something cannot be at the same time its opposite. However, this technique paradoxically evokes and brings face to face opposite elements, binding them in the contiguity of their oppo-sition, and bringing to light their covert, ambiguous relationship. Antithesis is rhetoric's analogue to the discovery of a gaping void, and of the attempt to go beyond it. That may be the reason why it is favoured by those authors who live in tormented historical times, whose discourse attempts to impose order on chaos, through the accen-tuation and classification of opposites.[21]

The evidence of an antithesis mediated by the narrator's intervention is present everywhere. First of all at the level of language, which is a *koiné* with archaic and learned nuances interspersed with poetic rhythms and vernacular expressions, from 'gadget' ('trappola'; 17) and 'playing dead' ('fare il morto'; 18), to 'shitting' ('scacazzanti'; 68).[22] Antithesis is even more potent, in the sense that it is obvious and serves an essential function, at the level of metaphor. The desire to watch, to observe in the closest and most precise way, is constantly impeded, or prevented, or accompanied by the blurring of the image, a frustration that causes the humorous and almost farcical asides of the narrative voice. The eye, though enriched by a variety of lenses, turns out to be structurally inept. The desired immersion finds its antithesis in the con-tinuous surveying of an elusive surface. To the immobility of the eye focusing on its object corresponds the unceasing flowing of the visible. And the latter does not even have the orderly direction of the Hera-clitean river, in whose waters one cannot bathe twice. It is a motion in place that eludes the grasp and remains irritatingly active. At the struc-tural level also, antithesis triumphs. *Palomar* is a monologue with three voices, and its conclusion is a discourse made of silence. The method for reaching knowledge proposed by each part of the text is anchored in the most prestigious traditions of Western thought – rigour, rationality, and empirical observation – but it does not inspire trust, with its vain agitation. In fact, it suggests an impaired intellect ('demenza'; 49), a certain comical weakness of mind ('debolezza di mente'; 76). The voice says, 'I must,' and another voice, sounding silently through the text, says, 'I cannot,' or 'I am not able to.' The precision of the philosophic-poetic lexicon ends up in the numerous instances of 'perhaps' and 'who knows' ('forse' and 'mah!'), characteristic of the perplexed and the inarticulate. The antithetical pattern exists even within the character: on the one hand, he is definitely enlightened and intellectually astute, and his eye is open to possible discoveries, but on the other hand he is 'slow' ('uomo tardivo'; 15), a 'diligent and bookish person' ('persona diligente e libresca'; 41) who is foiled by his physical limitations, his slightly neurotic habits, his bizarre ideas, and his grotesque, at times even unintentionally animal-like, gestures. His imagination is the antithesis of his eyesight, which is as weak as the former is youthful and lively. His behaviour is akin to that of a clown full of dignity, with the straight face of the best comics.

Antithesis is the basis of self-irony. As in previous works by Calvino, the writer's adventure ends up in failure, if one is to look at results. What is knowable and how one can speak of it remain unanswered questions, and the solitary search of the watcher risks remaining sterile. While the world of the knowable becomes richer and more varied, the text becomes antithetically leaner. Writing, which appeared to be one with life, is perhaps only a delayer of death. Poetic richness turns into aridity, the cosmic into the comic, and the comic into the rictus of the corpse of Pirandellian memory. There is no doubt that Pirandello was an important presence in the construction of Mr Palomar, more determinant than the Monsieur Teste mentioned several times by Calvino. Mr Palomar is as earnest, humorous, and self-deprecating as Valéry's alter ego was fastidious, haughty, and inhuman. Most important, the world of the senses in all their seductiveness is Mr Palomar's realm, whereas Monsieur Teste barricaded himself in the rarefied atmosphere of an icy intellect. As for the Pirandello connection, it has to do with two factors. Pirandello's characters often appear divided in two, on stage or in fiction, as they are accompanied by the antithetical presence of their opposite halves. Also, death looms ominous and grotesque, with its ever present mockery of human beings' desire for logic and intelligibility, in both authors' oeuvres. The orneriness of Pirandello's dead, so distressing for the living and so subversive for the ideal of an orderly universe, is the final resource of the serious, concerned, and slightly comical man that inhabits Calvino's last fiction. Mr Palomar says he will be 'a cantankerous corpse' ('un morto scorbutico'; 127), with Pirandellian relish.[23] And the narrator comments wryly, 'It is in this lack of responsibility that the dead find their gaiety' ('è in questa irresponsabilità che i morti trovano la loro allegria'; *Palomar* 125). Death is the ultimate contradiction, the definitive word written, not by Mr Palomar but his invisible watcher/scribe.

Mr Palomar is the inheritor of 'the old mariners and the nomadic shepherds' (*Palomar* 45), but his eye comes from the optician, and his most clearly visible stars are those that are marked on maps. The narrator speaks of 'Mr Palomar' as if he were inside his creature, but refuses any identification, even fictional, with him; he looks with fascination at his tics and gestures, registers all his most intimate emotions, and chuckles about them. Writing is the equivalent of putting in focus, a metaphorical triangulation that measures the dizzying distance between desire and attainment. The text's courage consists in speaking the stubbornness of an ancient project that by now is undermined from the outside and the inside. From the poetic/proletarian Marcovaldo, we have returned to the sort of character that was dear to the writers of a Europe poised at the edge of the abyss – to Gide's anchorless intellectual and Svevo's Zeno Cosini, to Kafka's bewildered protagonists and Sartre's Roquentin.

There is an intriguing contrast between the English term *to freeze*, which indicates the act of stopping the flowing of images, and the one that describes, in Italian, the operation that precedes it: *mettere a fuoco* ambiguously may refer to 'setting on fire' or to 'focusing.' The Calvinian text contemplates the vanity of the protagonist's efforts to refine an instrument that seems to be inoperative. That is at the narrative's core, the fact that it is a perfect mechanism undermined by gnawing doubt. There is no alternative to the situation, and the subtle, self-ironic game is seductive precisely because at the same time it admits and refuses its defeat, making of it the source of its humour while dissecting it with cool passion. What attracts us in the acrobats' exercises is the daring, the moment of stillness before the void, and the stubborn concentration on an invisible trajectory. Mr Palomar's ambition is to find 'the norm hidden in the depths of what exists' ('la norma nascosta nel fondo di ciò che esiste'; *Palomar* 87), the non-homogeneous harmony of human and non-human; but ironically he may be backing into a dead end. The 'lesson' may be that we are all complicitous in our imprisonment in the labyrinth of cultural illusions, because the challenge of the labyrinth, at the same time an intellectual and a symbolic construct, has attracted us. The culture we share (or used to share), with its modes and tenets, from the

Greeks to the Romantics, from Aristotle to Galileo, from Stendhal to Leopardi, was our idol.

The illustration on the cover of the Einaudi edition of *Palomar*, with its exquisite appropriateness, parallels the volume's conclusion. It is an Albrecht Dürer drawing: a wise man focuses his gaze on a reclining woman who is framed by the lines of a grid that makes possible a three-dimensional perspective. She is softly abandoned in a sleep that turns her into a docile object. The designer's gaze, his most abstract and 'purest' sense, envelops her, and he can draw her thanks to her immobility and distance. Behind them, who are absorbed and bound in their web, there is a landscape also rigorously framed by rectangular windows, rigidly patterned by small trees well pruned and potted. The illustration is a vision of stillness and serenity; and yet it is a fallacy, or rather a confirmation of the antithetical quality of the text. Actually, there is no certainty or quiet in Mr Palomar's universe, the images are out of focus, and the lines and grids of a geometric perspective devised by the Renaissance artist's mind frame only details of a world that opens onto emptiness. The geometric obsession demands stillness, it freezes the surface of 'reality' and is unable to reach its living core. New instruments and other routes of escape must be imagined, and found elsewhere. The human eye must keep searching from its shore for that third side, that third dimension, that marks the boundary between visible and invisible and opens a passage to flight.[24]

That is what Calvino explored in the two posthumously published collections, one made up of essays and the other of fiction, which parallel each other. The grains of sand shine under the jaguar sun in the exotic places where silence is a web of signs. The world is a hypothesis ('The Written and the Unwritten Wor[l]d') that, in spite of everything, an obstinate watcher must repropose without cease. Down to his last words, a voice asserted,

> The universe may be dissolving in a cloud of heat, may be sinking down the vortex of entropy, but inside this irreversible process there is *the possibility of areas of order*, portions of an existent *straining to achieve a form*, and *privileged points* from which *it seems that one can glimpse a design, a perspective* ('L'universo si disfa in una nube di calore, precipita senza scampo in un vortice d'entropia, ma all'interno di questo processo irreversibile *possono darsi zone d'ordine*, porzioni d'esistente *che tendono verso una forma*, *punti privilegiati* da cui sembra di *scorgere un disegno, una prospettiva*'; *Lezioni americane* 68. Emphasis added).

The eye and the world are not separate entities, and perhaps antitheses and triangles have been superseded by the magic of mutual and reciprocal construction.

1 This chapter is a re-elaboration of concepts that I have presented at several professional meetings.

2 Its realism displeased the avant-garde critics, and its reflection on petty electoral politics displeased the critics on both sides of the political spectrum.

3 In 1996, after this manuscript was completed, a significant book by Marco Belpoliti entitled *L'occhio di Calvino* (Calvino's Eye) was published. The author's preface states, 'Questo libro vorrebbe raccontare la storia dell'occhio-mente di Calvino, il suo irrefrenabile desiderio di leggere il mondo come "superficie inesauribile"' (xii; 'This book would like to tell the story of Calvino's mind-eye, his irrepressible desire to read the world as an "inexhaustible surface"'). My essay focuses instead on an analysis of Calvino's characters.

4 I have drawn suggestions about the question of the dilemma-driven approach in a writer's conception and representation of reality from Marietti's article.

5 Calvino must have been deeply struck by the image that appears in I.10 of *Don Quixote*, where a miraculous balsam heals a knight who had been severed in two during a battle. From that image he spun a whole story, in which he used nicknames patterned on Cervantes's own (lo Stracciato, il Beltenebroso) and resorted to almost the same words as Cervantes to describe the miraculous healing.

6 But 'in every neurosis there is method, and in every method a neurosis' ('in ogni nevrosi c'è del metodo e in ogni metodo, nevrosi'; *Il castello dei destini incrociati* 116).

7 'A certain type of geometric and rather abstract imagination is a permanent part of my taste and personality; that allows me to work with greater method, even though I must be watchful not to fall into a mechanical performance' ('un certo tipo di immaginazione geometrica e un po' astratta fa parte stabilmente del mio gusto e del mio carattere e questo mi permette di svolgere un lavoro più metodico, anche se devo guardarmi dal cadere nella meccanicità'; *I libri degli altri* [Other People's Books] 526–7).

8 *Inventario* 25: 19 (January–March 1987): 7.

9 For the concept of 'pathos della distanza' in Calvino, see the much cited article by Cesare Cases (1958), now in *Patrie lettere* 160–6.

10 The pages mentioned (29–30) house two semantic populations, one denoting

uncertainty, ambiguity, and malaise, and the other solidity, will-power, and certainty, from which I have made the following lexical selection:

limbo incerto	di fronte
sfiorate	muro massiccio delle cose
quasi alonate	tensione delia volontà
insicurezza	sicura coscienza di sé
sfumare	pensiero distinto
ambiguo	scatto di decisione
annegare	puntiglio
morbida penombra	sforzo estremo
vuoto	contare
star male	mettere in fila
venir meno	ordinare
dissolversi	esatte occupazioni
malessere	lucidità
scontentezza	compostezza
inquietudine	sommare
marasma	ostinazione
esercizio d'esattezza	confrontare

The mediation between the two semantic areas is entrusted to Agilulf's geometric games.

11 The remedy Raimbaut finds for his existential dilemma is really curious, and deserves to be discussed elsewhere (chapter 6).

12 *Il castello dei destini incrociati* originally served as text in a Francesco Maria Ricci art book that elegantly reproduced a Renaissance collection of tarot cards.

13 The text contains archaic lexical forms and constructions: 'Occasionally, I knew other illustrious metropolises ... I elected bride and abode' ('Sparsa-mente conobbi altre inclite metropoli ... elessi sposa e dimora' etc.), as well as bureaucratic and trite formulas: 'using Library Card #2516' ('usufruendo della Carte de lecteur no 2516'). Antithesis obviously guides the text's lexical choices, also.

14 See chapter 3 of this volume.

15 For an interesting reading of Calvino's 'snowfall,' see Tamburri.

16 Much later, in the 'lesson' entitled 'Esattezza' (Exactness), Calvino asserted: 'The crystal, with its exact facets and its capacity to refract light, is the model of perfection that has always been my emblem' ('Il cristallo con la sua esatta

sfaccettatura e la sua capacità di rifrangere la luce, è il modello di perfezione che ho sempre tenuto come emblema'; *Lezioni americane* 69). However, he typically kept wavering between two pulsions, one toward 'the calm and arduous lesson of crystals' ('la calma e ardua lezione dei cristalli'; 70) and the other toward the emblem of the flame.

17   In those years, Calvino was a frequent visitor of artists' studios and exhibitions, and he wrote a number of prefaces and forewords to their programs. It is also useful to remember the importance of the concept of *mobile* in Michel Butor, whom Calvino certainly knew.

18   For this discussion, Ossola's 1987 article has been invaluable. The pattern Ossola draws arranges each chapter as follows:

a1 a2 a3 a4	a5 b5 c5 d5 e5 f5 g5	
b1 b2 b3	b4 c4 d4 e4 f4 g4 h4	h5
c1 c2	c3 d3 e3 f3 g3 h3 i3	i4 i5
d1	d2 c2 e2 f2 g2 h2 i2	l3 l4 l5
	e1 f1 g1 h1 i1 l1 m1	m2 m3 m4 m5

where a= Le città e la memoria; b= Le città e il desiderio; c= Le città e i segni; d: Le città sottili; e= Le città e gli scambi; f= Le città e gli occhi; g= Le città e il nome; h= Le città e i morti; i= Le città e il cielo; l= Le città continue; m= Le città nascoste.

19   Much has been written on *Palomar*. For some keen reflections, see Ossola's article.

20   In this text, a simile with a Montalean flavour and a touch of humour appear, as if dredged up by the return to a past atmosphere: 'It's been years since I have stirred up these memories *holed up like eels in the puddles of my mind*' ('Da anni non ho più smosso questi ricordi, *rintanati come anguille nelle pozze della memoria*'; *Romanzi e racconti* III 50. Emphasis added).

21   For this analysis, see Marietti.

22   For the importance of this technique, see de Lauretis's 1975 articles.

23   See Pirandello's novel *Il fu Mattia Pascal* (The Late Mattia Pascal), where Mattia Pascal, being alive and dead at the same time, attempts to rearrange his own life; and in *Novelle per un anno* (Short Stories for an Entire Year), see 'La vita nuda' (The Naked Life), 'Distrazione' (A Moment of Distraction), 'La rallegrata' (The Prance), 'La cassa riposta' (The Hidden Box), and especially 'Resti mortali' (Mortal Remains).

24   'I prefer to trust in the straight line, hoping that it will continue to infinity and place me beyond reach. I prefer to plan carefully the trajectory of my

escape, as I look for the moment when I can dart away like an arrow and disappear at the horizon' ('preferisco affidarmi alla linea retta, nella speranza che continui all'infinito e mi renda irraggiungibile. Preferisco calcolare lungamente la mia traiettoria di fuga, aspettando di potermi lanciare come una freccia e scomparire all'orizzonte'; *Lezioni americane* 47).

3

Survivors, or The Pastoral Denied[1]

The world had revealed to him its changeable and unstable face ... Things were menacing and elusive. ('il mondo gli si era rivelato mutevole e instabile, ... le cose erano minacciose e sfuggenti.')

Natalia Ginzburg, Opere

Idylls and Not

Nature was never 'just nature' for Calvino (assuming that any human being can differ from him on that point). He saw nature's materiality and conceptual construct filtered through a combination of scientific and literary models. The magnificent autobiographical piece entitled 'La strada di San Giovanni' (The Road to San Giovanni) testifies to the double pattern of organization and contemplation his mind elaborated. On the one hand, there was the severe model of paternal and maternal thought and practice (*pace* Bonura 19, who seems to forget the impact on the young Calvino of his botanist mother's stern world-vision); on the other hand, there was literature's wealth of motifs, which enchanted him. A useful contrast could be established between Calvino's perception of the natural world and that of Pavese, who mythified the country and its inhabitants and chose as his guidebook to the natural world Frazer's *Golden Bough*. Calvino, as was his custom, imaginatively but also consciously explored his idiosyncratic rapport with the natural world, describing his readings, acknowledging his descent from landowners, and humorously retelling the mannerisms of his learned and eccentric parents. His first short stories contain a lively bestiary of orchard and garden dwellers; they are true Calvinian zoological emblems that owe their charm equally to the precision of realistic observation and to the comic bent of the author's whimsy. As for the characters that inhabit the early Calvino stories, they are either country gentry (barons and viscounts) or manual labourers of all sorts, gardeners and the like. Even his female characters waver between an attention to natural phenomena reminiscent of eighteenth-century passions for the natural world and a healthy scepticism about the benignity of those phenomena. We see this, for instance, in *Il barone rampante* and *Il visconte dimezzato*, where the young nun who is Cosimo's sister, Viola, and Pamela follow precisely that model.

When, in 1958, Calvino collected most of his short fiction in the volume entitled *I racconti*, that concern with the natural world informed ten of the stories, which had as their central character a man named Marcovaldo. The table of contents visually emphasized that those stories, written from 1952 to 1956, formed a separate cluster in the volume's 'Libro primo,' within a larger subset entitled 'Gli idilli difficili' (Difficult Idylls). Curiously, that first version of the Marcovaldo stories is seldom, if ever, quoted by scholars. Quotation tends to come from the later collection entitled *Marcovaldo*. And yet the first edition's paratextual elements[2] are essential clues for a reading of both collections. First of all, for an author such as Calvino and for all reasonably well schooled readers, the term *idillio* (idyll) evokes a major literary tradition, that of the pastoral. Calvino's lexical choice is a sign, and holds the promise of familiar themes: Edenic experiences, bittersweet love, and nurturing Nature. Yet the subtitle is an oxymoron, as it juxtaposes two antithetical concepts: the idyll is named, but its conventional connotations are contradicted by the qualification, with the result that the statement made by the first term is almost negated by the second. In addition, the clustering of the ten stories in a separate group within the 'idilli difficili' clearly indicates the importance of the central character, Marcovaldo, who was not just a casual creation.

The First Marcovaldo Cycle

Each story follows a fairly regular outline: the same protagonist, with constant characteristics, in the same emblematic city, lives adventures that are similar in content and development. Out of a latent desire, a need for fulfilment emerges; some clue registers with Marcovaldo, and is given content by some object, which becomes the object of desire.

Then an obstacle materializes, the attempted acquisition of the object of desire ends up in loss, and the story closes with a negative conclusion.[3]

The first three stories were all written in 1952, but the one placed third, 'La pietanziera' (The Lunch-Pail) is probably the oldest, as it is still thematically and stylistically connected to a phase of the Calvinian narrative which has been called Neorealistic. Everyday objects and gestures loom large in it, in their concreteness and functionality. Its first paragraph is a detailed description of a socially connoted object, the 1950s Italian equivalent of the American lunch-box, which becomes the story's iconic centre. Also, Marcovaldo's disappointment when he has almost reached the fulfilment of his desire is caused by sociocultural factors (his being a proletarian in a society that is still stratified, and where privilege is still blatantly codified) rather than by a concrete obstacle or by existential impediments. Still, the short story includes light-hearted fantasies, and the references to social parameters carry a hint of irony, as a manual labourer and his food are contrasted in rather comical ways with the poor little rich kid and the things that make up his lifestyle.[4]

While 'La pietanziera' conveys a sense of confinement and sadness, the other stories begin with a statement, of varying lengths, suggesting openness and a poetic imagination. 'Funghi in città' (Mushrooms in the City), appropriately placed first since it fully introduces the protagonist, establishes this pattern. On a technical level, the agility of its first paragraph is achieved by the use of metric and rhythmic patterns familiar to the school-trained ear of the Italian reader.[5] The beginning is a combination of three and nine syllables with very conventional stresses, and the closing is an *endecasillabo* with accents on the sixth and tenth. The tone is poetic, but touched with humour, thanks to the use of the expression 'anime sensibili' ('sensitive souls'). While suggesting fastidiousness with its connection to a whole lexical family related to eighteenth-century French *sensibilité*, the expression is downgraded to a clinical twentieth-century term for a respiratory ailment, hay fever. So prosaic sneezes ring noisily right in the middle of the protasis, creating a comic interference in this poetic prose. Then, a new paragraph begins with 'Un giorno ...' ('One day ...'), in the classic manner of a tale whose atmosphere has already, and economically, been set.

Marcovaldo is presented as an 'anima sensibile' too, but of a different sort. Rather than being impelled to uncontrollable sneezing by purely physical sensitivity, he is attuned to the vibrations of what escapes everybody else's attention. He is alerted by details that are listed in a progression that goes from the poetic – 'a leaf yellowing on its branch' ('una foglia che ingiallisse sul ramo') – to the whimsical – 'a feather caught on a roof tile' ('una piuma che si impigliasse ad una tegola') – to the humorous evocation of pratfalls – 'a fig peel smashed on the sidewalk' ('una buccia di fico spiaccicata sul marciapiede').[6] In his childlike 'difference,' Marcovaldo looks either above or below the normal line of vision, and is oblivious to the conventional value judgments characteristic of adults. Each story programmatically insists on Marcovaldo's uniqueness, which sets in motion the mechanism of his adventures.

'Il piccione comunale' (The City Pigeon) follows the same outline. Birds flying high above hills and fields, along the alliterative 'invisible flyways of the wind' ('vie invisibili del vento'; 137), open the first paragraph, providing the occasion for daydreaming and adventure. The fourth, fifth, and sixth stories, all written in 1953, form a triptych of variations on the theme of the search for a healing Nature. As in the earlier stories with the exception of 'La pietanziera,' Marcovaldo's dreams are the product of a delusion. Even the supposed folk wisdom is a lie. The bitterness of a medicine is no guarantee of its effectiveness, the woods available to the poor woodcutter and his family in the fairy tales do not exist, and the only air worth breathing is found on the grounds of a clinic for lung patients.

Two 1954 stories introduce representatives of the domestic fauna, but since these are *favole*, not *fiabe*,[7] the animals do not need to undergo metamorphoses. They are not mythified, nor are they representatives of Nature, where they could certainly not survive; they are, rather, legitimate participants in the urban adventure, in their own guises. A rabbit is found to be poisonous because of its having been subjected to laboratory experiments, and a journey to the mountain pastures with a herd of cows turns into a bitter work experience. In both stories, Marcovaldo's disappointment is shared by another creature. In 'Il coniglio velenoso' (The Poisonous Rabbit), the rabbit fathoms the depth of his own estrangement from nature and humanity, and 'Un viaggio con le mucche' (A Journey with a Herd) is a harsh maturing experience for Marcovaldo's young son Michelino. However, Marcovaldo grows no wiser, because his illusions have deep roots. In 1955 and 1956, he is the protagonist of two more adventures, which close the cycle, 'La panchina' (The Park Bench; this is its title in the first collection) and 'Luna e Gnac' (Moon and Gnac).

There is a ghostly presence in the background of all ten stories. It is the image of a nurturing Elsewhere, a fantasy born of desire. The location of each story is unchanged and double. It is always the city, but behind it, as essential to the adventure as the city itself, there is 'nature.' As is the case with all ghosts, Nature is unseen by most people and could not emerge from its absence without a medium or catalyst, who inevitably is Marcovaldo. It is his presence that is the discriminating factor in the author's clustering of this group of ten short stories. Although schematic from the point of view of psychological construction, Marcovaldo is a complex mediating presence. He is a Bakhtinian 'contact,' who makes it possible for writer and readers alike to acknowledge their shared familiarity with several provinces of the literary universe.[8] In the deceptively simple texture of the stories, all connections run through him. Marcovaldo's 'situation' between narrating voice and reading presence is most ambiguous from the point of view of the narrative strategies. The ambivalent positioning of the narrator vis-à-vis the character implies potentially different readers, and multiple outcomes in the realization of the text.

On one level, the extradiegetic narrator introduces each episode with a lyric and descriptive paragraph and occasionally makes comments.[9] He addresses an implicit listener, who is placed at a greater distance from the protagonist than the narrator is, and is supposed to be a naïve audience. For the latter's benefit, the narrating voice maximizes the incantatory quality of the text, by privileging repetitive plot lines, manipulating literary clichés, and choosing certain syntactical patterns dear to storytelling – for instance, the inversion of subject and predicate and the appropriation of the character, as in the following example: 'He had, this Marcovaldo, an eye that was not really made for city life' ('Aveva *questo Marcovaldo* un occhio poco adatto alla vita di città'; 134).

On another level, the narrator seems to address a reader who is familiar with literary conventions, that is, someone aware of the complexities of formal work, ideological content, and intertextuality. The choice of language and the ironic tone indicate a conniving posture and posit a reader who is not naïve but rather is placed at the same distance from Marcovaldo as the narrator is, both pragmatically and culturally. For this reader, who is an equal of the narrating voice, the name 'Marcovaldo' and every word accompanying that name are not purely humorous bits of language.[10]

As for the author (at least, the Italo Calvino who wrote this collection of short stories), his closeness to the narrator is revealed by the sociohistorical concerns of the discourse. It is in this exchange among author, narrator, and expected readers that Marcovaldo is particularly important to the success of the narrative enterprise. He is an invention suited to the specific context of a prospering Western society in the third quarter of the twentieth century.[11] His place at the lowest end of the social spectrum, but politically not defined, his essential characteristic (his sensitivity to the not-obvious), and his fundamental incongruity with his milieu, as proclaimed by his name, are all stated peremptorily in one key sentence: 'No one noticed it except the labourer Marcovaldo' ('Nessuno se ne accorse tranne il manovale Marcovaldo'; 134). Marcovaldo is a marginal human being, unskilled in practical matters and isolated in the social context, but he is neither an intellectual nor a rebel nor a child nor a bum. The expected readers were not likely to be intimidated by him, because, while they were aware of his difference, they were not threatened by it. On the other hand, they shared the narrative's ambiguous empathy with him, since they too felt ambivalent toward their own experiences, baffled as they were by triumphant urbanization, and feeling in turn nostalgic and ironic toward the mythology of a benign Nature.

On the formal plane also, Marcovaldo's presence is essential. If the linguistic medium, with all its characteristics, is the sign of textual strategies, in the Marcovaldo cycle it points unmistakably to a literary matrix. Who speaks here, and how? The distinction between narrator and protagonist seems at first to be clearly marked through a division of tasks, which allows a distancing of reality, and makes irony possible. The narrator speaks the lyrical introductions and uses rhetorical figures, while the character is limited to a prosaic, instinctual dimension, simply registered by the narrator, and to conversational locutions.[12]

Yet the text's double nature soon becomes evident at the formal level also. There is a convergence between the two voices. The observer slyly tends to absorb the observed, as the narrating voice appropriates the character's perspective, naming his sensations and hidden feelings. Not only the lexical and syntactical choices in the descriptive passages but even Marcovaldo's indirect discourse and mental processes become manifestations of the narrator's speech.[13] Marcovaldo becomes the echo of a voice whose vocabulary is often ancient and worn, although refreshed by its context; whose grammatical choices are as close to standard written usage as any purist could desire; whose syntax consistently uses the most harmonious and economical patterns; and who is not in the least tempted by dialectalisms, but makes frequent use of poetic techniques. As a matter of fact, Marcovaldo speaks in the poetic mode in the last two stories, where he is made to use deliberate rhetorical devices (hypallage, isocolon, alliteration, metaphor, and antithesis) as well as rhythmically expert closures.[14]

Necessarily embedded in the cycle's discourse, the thematic continuum also has its centre in Marcovaldo, evoking literary commonplaces, for instance the theme of apparently opposite but actually complementary realms, the urban and the natural. Inevitably, Marcovaldo and his socio-existential status have attracted the attention of critics, eliciting evaluations that Calvino confirmed or reinforced with his own reading of the text (see the cover blurb for the 1963 edition, and the preface to the 1966 edition, both written by him). According to that reading, Marcovaldo is an exile in the city, he arrived there from somewhere else ('L'aria buona' [Clean Air] 152), and he is of peasant origin. But the early Neorealistic colour of Calvino's narrative may lead us into error. Actually, Marcovaldo is an utterly atypical immigrant from the country. He is poor and he is an exile in the city, but his memory of the country, far from being that of a former peasant, is a literary memory. 'Nature' lives *inside* Marcovaldo, as the conventional sign for an ideal construct and a literary signifier, whereby all that contradicts the urban experience carries a positive sign and becomes the motive for an obsessive but inevitably unsuccessful pursuit.

It is clear that Marcovaldo never turned a spadeful of country soil in his life.[15] He could not survive in the 'real' country even for a day, and shows no inclination to attempt the experience. The country is for him a place for contemplation and daydreaming, a land of milk and honey, as it can be only for the quintessential city dweller. The city where Marcovaldo lives may be a prison; nonetheless, it is his only home. In Calvinian terms, it is a labyrinth, an 'inside' which is also an 'outside,' and a dream machine that reveals the ambivalence of all experience. In fact, Marcovaldo, rather than being oblivious to his city environment, is highly sensitive to its potentialities, which he almost miraculously brings out. The urban experience is indispensable to his retrieving a hidden dimension, which constitutes the essential core of the text: the memory of the pastoral.[16]

The Pastoral Universe

What form can the desire of urban dwellers possibly take? The pastoral tradition provides them with an entire range of powerful conventions, and the scene of the 'natural' idyll is one of the dominant metaphors of Western culture. The antithesis in the Calvinian subtitle underlines a contemporary text's close but polemical links with the universe of the pastoral. The whole first book of *I racconti* asserts in its subtitle that the 'idyllic,' contrary to its most trite meaning, is not 'outside,' a realm of serenity and beauty, but rather is the realm of longing and frustration, because it embodies the contradiction within us. Over the centuries, the pastoral vision may have gone from apparently solid staticity to ambiguous self-negation due to a sort of internal collapse, and yet the utterance of the word *idillio* – a coded term in an immense field – still has the power to evoke it.

If a genre is the sedimentation of a literary model of the world in the collective memory, as Mikhail Bakhtin has suggested, it is also true that the shifts and transformations that take place in generic forms, in their formal characteristics, language, tone, and themes, relate to sociocultural change. That is particularly clear for major genres, whose elaboration lasted for centuries, as is the case with the pastoral in European culture. Because of the adaptability of genres, in spite of the recent questioning of all memories and models, writers are still confronted with 'modèles d'écriture,' in Todorov's words (50), and readers with 'formes phantôme,' in the words of Riffaterre (16 n). As readers, we are sensitive to *déjà-lu*. The recurrence of formal elements, themes, and ideological content, however manipulated or disguised, provides points of reference for writing, and clues for reading. The tone of the utterances, for its part, creates the atmosphere that makes the dialogue between authors and interlocutors possible. There was never any doubt in the minds of Calvino's readers that his writing, rather than a mimesis of the factual, was a filtering of multiple givens through a complex apparatus linking the individual and the social, the formal and the ideological, the linguistic and the thematic (de Lauretis 'Italo Calvino' 1975). In the first Marcovaldo cycle, what is left of the utterly transformed pastoral supplies the underpinnings of the narrative.

There are some major constants in that model. In the formal realm, the constant is the lyric configuration of the text, whether or not the writing is in verse, with all the conventions associated with the lyric mode. Chief among the conventions is the literary form that is chosen, usually brief and connected to a constellation of other brief compositions. Each piece reiterates the theme, without demanding a resolution but rather seeking the conventions' confirmation at each moment of a closed pattern. Book of eclogues, wreath of sonnets, sequence of octaves, or collection of short episodes, the pastoral text refuses action and the complexities of mimesis. Several of the pastoral's rhetorical devices are in fact present in the Marcovaldo cycle, and include lyrical imagery; metaphors; similes with terms of comparison drawn from nature; descriptions of privileged locations (a bower), objects (the moon, the constellations), and situations (cool shades, silence, and exquisite natural sounds); and the use of antithesis and repetition at all levels, linguistic, thematic and compositional.[17]

Thematically, the major constant in the pastoral genre is the topos of Nature. Again, the Marcovaldo cycle is the humorous retelling of an obsession. From scattered clues, Marcovaldo extracts, in the artist's fashion, the material for 'ragionamento' (134). This is a methodical reflection about familiar coordinates (passing time, human desire, and the narrowness and repetitiveness of existence) and the re-creation of a myth. The occasion for such reflections is provided by categories of objects long delegated to such a function. Yellowing and falling leaves do not even need to have a phenomenological referent in order to be appropriated, today, for the purpose of philosophical meditation. In the pastoral perspective, the passing of time can be seen only in the guise of seasonal cycles, those 'mutamenti di stagione' (134) that are an integral part of pastoral discourse and faithfully return in each Marcovaldo story.

On the ideological plane, the generic constant is the construction of a country of the mind, placed in varying positions of antinomy to the 'real' social context. Born in the city, written by urbanites for urbanites (Poggioli 1–41), the pastoral cannot indulge in realism. It is constitutionally ambiguous, and in modern times it is allied with the comic and fantastic modes. Through its numerous reincarnations, from bucolic poem to romance to chivalric epics and parodies to fairy tales, myths of new worlds, and Romantic narratives, the pastoral is imprinted in our consciousness as one of the prototypical constructs of our culture. The instantly recognized components of the pastoral include the sense of loss implicit in the evocation of a benign natural habitat; the sense of menace associated with the 'outside' of that idealized place (an outside that is, paradoxically, Western society); the humble social status of the characters, at times voluntarily assumed; the idyllic beauty of the scenery, which is not simply a description but a quotation (in it, flowers are 'roses' and birds are 'nightingales'); and the cathartic sleep in the woods. The connections of the pastoral with its cultural context led, it is true, to the destruction of the perfected construct (witness the fate of the gardens of Alcina and Armida),[18] but led also to its reappearance, from Don Quixote to nineteenth-century idylls, and occasionally to contemporary pulp fiction and popular song.

Marcovaldo, then, is not simply a poetic soul and a hero in whimsical adventures. His images of Arcadia and, especially, the manner of his imagining reveal his family connections. In his proletarian disguise, he is the epigone of the Poet, isolated among other city dwellers for whom poetry is an alien territory, and hopelessly out of touch with the Rimbaldian 'réalité rugueuse' ('rough reality'). His identity as the new embodiment of an archaic character of our culture is subtly suggested, and his name – an allusion to ancient heroic constructs – signifies his status in the world of fantasy. However, neither straightforward nostalgia nor parody suits the spirit of these times, or this author. The text must acknowledge its circumstances, or what has been called 'postmodernity.'

Dealing with the pastoral as a cultural and literary memory, while at the same time unmasking its ambiguities and dysfunctional survival, is made possible by the tone of the utterance, which is ironic, and by a quintessentially Calvinian procedure, which consists of mixing techniques from incongruous modes of discourse, in what I will call *contaminazione.*[19]

Irony permeates the entire text, most often in subtle ways but at times very explicitly. It marks the tension between a code (however diluted), with its formal, thematic, and ideological constants, and the requirements of this text as a self-reflexive twentieth-century construct. Literary conventions, mythological themes, and immediate experience are inexorably dissected and recomposed by the writer's consciousness, which is itself divided between rejection of and unacknowledged nostalgia for an overused model of the world. At the end of 'La panchina,' paradoxically the conventional images of the idyll appear dusty and tired, compared with the energy and freshness of a morning in the city: water runs cool from the hydrants, the streetcars 'scalpitano' ('paw the ground') like impatient horses, the workers run on their motorbikes, the store blinds roll noisily toward the sky, windows open and their glass panes sparkle in the sun's rays, and only Marcovaldo re-emerges from his night visions tired, aching, and out of tune with his environment.

We realize now that the ambiguity of the text is due to the narrator's position, for, in actuality, the narrator and Marcovaldo are two halves of a self-observing character, whose daily attempts and defeats we are called to witness in ambiguous amusement. Detachment and involvement are two faces of the same enterprise. There is no historical flow, here. Each episode follows the same pattern, and each time we circle back to the beginning. Given the seriousness of Marcovaldo's misunderstanding of his situation and the regularity with which his basic condition of disadvantage is challenged by him, a comic outcome is the only one possible; but the connections among author, narrator, protagonist, and reader colour laughter with sadness.[20]

The ironic tone is most often obtained in this text by abrupt antithesis, as unexpected occurrences or petty concerns break the lyrical momentum. For instance, in the previously mentioned sequence of occasions for meditation, poetic allusions to leaves and bird feathers are followed by the mention of an insect and a piece of squashed litter, two caricatures of the nobler manifestations of the 'natural.' In other instances, after an assertion there is a contrary effect, or a hyperbolic (and damaging) confirmation of Marcovaldo's naïve expectations: 'Be patient, the wasps will be here very soon, – when the door opened and the swarm invaded the room' ('Abbiate pazienza, adesso arrivano le vespe, – quando la porta s'aperse e lo sciame invase la stanza'; 147). Irony is emphasized by images of incongruity (mushrooms in the city, rabbits on the roofs of buildings, and cows on city streets) or by straight-faced repartees: 'The best place we can send them to ... is the street' ('Il posto più bello dove possiamo mandarli ... è per la strada'; 151). It is also displayed in certain cinematic effects, particularly at the close of an episode, when Marcovaldo is seen as if in a cinematic long shot, immobilized and surrounded by people he has angered. Throughout the cycle, though, the major source of irony is the quest for a bucolic retreat, as a conspiracy of adverse circumstances, various antagonists, and formal conventions methodically frustrates the character's efforts.

As for the reduction in status of a genre, most often inherent in the chronological shifting and/or transcoding of it, – in other words, as for the genre's 'descent' on the hierarchical ladder – it is explicitly effected here by *contaminazione*. The distance between the two signifying universes, the poetic and the practical, the gap between ideal constructs and givens, between fantasy and actuality, had already found a twentieth-century expression in comic films and strips of a certain vintage, mostly of the thirties. The comic strip provided Calvino with several suggestions for the retelling of a delusion in an ironic key. The crucial suggestion was the narrative model, which echoes the one dear to the earlier poetic tradition: short episodes repeat in a quick succession of frames an identical plot. In addition, the technique of fragmenting and speeding up the narration, characteristic of drawings and films, is a perfect tool for transcoding. The pastoral text is broken up and transcribed, as a sequence in the tenth story beautifully illustrates. Two moments of a character's experience are recorded on two contrasting registers:

> *There was the night's darkness and Isolina, who was all of eighteen years old, felt transported by the moonlight ... Sounds like the refrain of a serenade reached her. There was the GNAC, and that radio seemed to catch a different rhythm, a jazz rhythm, and Isolina stretched in her tight little dress ('C'era la notte e Isolina coi suoi diciott'anni si sentiva trasportata per il chiar di luna ... le arrivava[no] come i rintocchi di una serenata; c'era il GNAC e quella radio pareva pigliare un altro ritmo, un ritmo jazz, e Isolina si stirava nella vestina stretta'; 173. Emphasis added).*

Language (notice that 'si sentiva trasportata' and that 'pigliare,' the one lyric, the other colloquial), images (the moonlit night and the neon sign), and rhythms (a mandolin and jazz music) proceed on parallel and antithetical tracks. The last image, with its realistic mimicry, is in visual contrast to the abandon of the earlier ecstatic mood.

As in the pastoral scene, there is no progression in the comic strip. Space is a clearly defined enclosure, a fixed urban landscape drawn by the cartoonist within the rigid sides of the rectangular frame. Time is immobile. The focus is on the hapless protagonist, who also remains unchanged, a mask, a marionette, Fortunello or Signor Bonaventura,[21] a 'regressive' character, in several ways. On the thematic level, the comic strip tells about the search for fulfilment, which implies desire for escape; but in the claustrophobic existence of the character the only freedom is that of the imagination. However, where the comic strip at times concludes with the triumph of the character, perhaps only for reasons of publishing policy, Marcovaldo's stories regularly end in defeat. The lyricism present in Marcovaldo's universe may be a reminder of the seductive power of the pastoral vision, but the character's defeats pointedly unmask its deceptiveness.

An additional connection, of which Calvino was by no means unaware but which he and other readers simply mentioned in passing, is Marcovaldo's kinship with the cinematic presence of another marginal character, Chaplin's Tramp. It is easy to find points of similarity between the two characters: not least among them is their incongruous (because archaic) refinement of manners, which in the film is iconically manifested through certain details of gesture and clothing, and in Calvino's texts is signified by the choice of a certain level of language and by the character's name. It is more important to our discussion, though, to note a fundamental dissimilarity: the Tramp is a drifter who vainly tries to become an integral part of any society, whereas Marcovaldo is an 'organic' proletarian with a job and a family, someone who belongs to the city of today, where an outcast such as the Tramp would hardly be viewed as poetic.

Important as the characters may be, however, the determinant factors in the *contaminazione* of short story with film are those that foster the ironic tone of the Calvinian discourse. I might mention the incisiveness of the scenes, based on attention to gestures, even minimal;[22] the precision of spatial and cultural definition; the sado-comic insistence on a negative conclusion for each episode; and the choice of the poetic-comic option, which provides the necessary margin for the narrative's fantasy, just as sentimentality once did in Chaplin's films, with delightful self-irony.

A text lives in and through its medium. We must return to considerations of linguistic choices made by Calvino for the Marcovaldo stories. The pastoral tradition in Italy was inextricably linked with the construction of a literary medium, which was significantly removed from dialectalism, in an ideologically motivated incongruence with the pastoral's supposedly 'rural' settings. The comic film was basically mute, although it borrowed the linguistic material for its captions from melodrama. The comic strip, on the other hand, from the late 1920s to the 1940s spoke standard, middle-class Italian and was in its own way ruled by rigid conventions.[23] Its ambition was to address a linguistically 'national' and middle-class young audience, to whom society was determined to impart knowledge of the *lingua*, through schooling and informal example: an audience that the comic strip must powerfully have contributed to shaping and cultivating, in the days before television and in a country where children's literature was extremely scarce.

Calvino, faced with making a fundamental decision about linguistic choices, as Italian writers always have been, unhesitatingly opted for a medium that children's literature had already tested and developed.[24] That medium reflects the tormented history of the Italian language, in which cultural and political motives mesh with literary ones. Calvino was very much a writer concerned with giving his own solution to the 'questione della lingua.' He was also concerned with pedagogy in its widest sense, and aware of reception even before he directly addressed a specific public of children and young people, as he did in the 1963 and 1966 editions of *Marcovaldo*. Clarity, precision, and accessibility were characteristics he viewed as basic to all writing, and consistenly pursued.[25] Thus, the poetic tradition and the comic strip revealed some intrinsic connections, as they concurred in affecting the linguistic and ideological aspect of Calvino's writing practice.

In the first Marcovaldo cycle, Calvino's writing is as respectful of grammatical standards as any school would recommend. The lexicon is rich and precise, with preference given to the medium-high level of the Italian word population. Tuscanisms and dialectalisms are very rare. Even uncertainties about graphic doubles are minimal.[26] The syntactical choices clearly show Calvino's concern with sober complexity. At times rapid because of paratactic patterns, the phrasing is most often made up of elegantly structured subordinates. Yet the discourse remains transparent, thanks to the writer's control of his tools, and his self-critical restraint.

Two Exemplary Texts, and a First Conclusion

The first Marcovaldo cycle finds its culmination and closure in the last two stories, which develop to the fullest the motifs of the entire cycle. The familiar narrative pattern (search for idyllic experience, obstacle, disappointment) returns, but with a progression that is evident at all levels, cyclical in 'La panchina' and catastrophic in 'Luna e Gnac.' In both stories, a greater insistence on the pleasure of repetition, the lyric quality of the text, and the intensity of the protagonist's desire emphasize the sense of loss, as the pastoral dream is annulled in the very act of being formulated.

Marcovaldo's torments have nothing to do with heroic passions. His troubles, urban overcrowding, noise, and technological barrenness, all made more oppressive for him by poverty, are typical of twentieth-century life. Yet, as all the pastorally inclined characters before him did, he yearns for rest and contemplative ease in the bosom of Nature. While a park bench, the urban equivalent of a mossy bank and no less mythical for Marcovaldo, is the focus of 'La panchina,' a night sky with its marvels is the backdrop for 'Luna e Gnac.' In the former story, Marcovaldo's antagonists define with Calvinian precision the coordinates of the urbanites' world (two lovers, two city policemen, two black market vendors, a team of city repairmen, and a street-cleaning crew). In the latter story, the antagonists become more elusive but no less distracting, and ultimately more powerful in their impersonality: a neon sign and two big commercial firms. In both stories, a miraculous equilibrium is attained between protagonist and narrator, desire and actuality, promise and outcome, as each term of the pair opposes the other yet depends on it for definition. Only a literal cold shower, in the first short story, can scare away the dreamy half of the story's divided consciousness. With felicitous progression, in the second short story, a blinding intermittent light erases all the protagonist's sensorial and imaginative powers, in a subtly ironic transcoding of the blinding light of revelation that shines at the zeniths of canonical poetic journeys.

Formal factors again reveal the text's strategy. 'La panchina' is the most revised of the Marcovaldo stories. As a matter of fact, Calvino, well aware of the lyric and comic potentialities of this text, used it as a basis for the libretto of a chamber opera, that most conventional of artefacts issued from the pastoral matrix.[27] Its opening paragraph is a contrappunto of pastoral allusions and realistic touches, which achieve a comic-ironical effect. Curt comments by the narrator sharpen the contrast between delusion and actuality, as the overall poeticity of the text is increased: the lexicon is more selective than usual, the syntactical patterns follow poetic modules, particularly in the placement of adjectives, and the rhetorical devices, from repetition to hypallage, and synaesthetic notations are very frequent.[28] The lovers' quarrel, entirely made up of conventional phrases and abstractions, is an exquisite transposition of a fixed topos from the literary love tradition. As a counterpoint to it, the theme of 'L'avventura di due sposi' (The Adventure of Two Spouses) is discreetly announced. The quotation of the stereotype of the moonlit night, obbligato of Italian poetry, expands into a delicate analysis of the tonalities of the colour yellow, a subtle sensorial discrimination between two warring orders of phenomena. The two tones of luminosity, one elusive and nuanced, the other abstract and mechanical, each attuned to a different rhythm, signify the rending of the consciousness by opposite mechanisms, that of conventional poetic connotations and that of present-day mechanicity. Technological reality is harsher for Marcovaldo, because it is not something filtered through the poetic memory. Only those for whom poetic memories do not exist, such as Marcovaldo's wife, a new Xanthippe, and Marcovaldo's children, with their trite little names, can cope with urban reality.

Marcovaldo's path in the night is a circling motion – 'He went ... he went ... he returned ... he went ... he returned' ('andò ... andò ... tornò ... andò ... tornò'; 167) – down into the oneiric retrieval of conventional items that bear the unmistakable imprint of 'high' culture: sounds of nightingales, fresh lymphs, the mysterious pallor of a Leopardian moon 'large above trees and roofs' ('grande sugli alberi e i tetti'; 167), healing silence, murmuring brooks, and the fragrance of roses. Marcovaldo's senses, programmed by literary experiences, are charmed by ghostly echoes and reflections. A new Don Quixote, he pursues what never was, except in poems.[29]

In the later short stories, the observation post has appropriately been moved from lowly basement to sublime mansard, with obvious spatial implications and operatic allusions. Suspended close to the firmament, Marcovaldo and the little human tribe that is his family must witness the extinction of their illusions, in 'Luna e Gnac.' Not only does the natural light of the moon disappear, but with it must go the consoling accretions of adventure, learning, daydreaming, and romance, the fragile superstructures built by each character. A deeper melancholy pervades this text, as the poetic flights become more extensive and intense, and the identification between narrator and character becomes closer. Antithesis and chiasmus rule, right from the first paragraph: 'Darkness lasted twenty seconds, and for twenty seconds there was the GNAC' ('La notte durava venti secondi e venti secondi il GNAC'; 173). As a matter of fact, the title has already placed in antinomic position two groups of four letters, *Luna/Gnac*. They are separated by a disjunctive 'and' ('e'), which is the equivalent of a *vs.*, but not quite, since it marks also, as an equals sign (=) would, the transition from poetic myth (Marcovaldo's) to technological myth-in-the-making (for Marcovaldo's children).[30] Emblematic presences out of a pastoral universe irretrievably archaic are also the two lovers unable to communicate, Fiordaligi and the 'moon girl' ('ragazza lunare'). They are not quite made of the same flesh as young Isolina, so alive in her skimpy dress, whose romantic fantasies are metamorphosed into rhythmic energy by neon lights and jazz music. As for Marcovaldo, the mediating presence, he is right in the eye of a 'storm of passions' ('tempesta di passioni'). Alas, he is overcome by an unexpected disaster. The spectacle of the starry night disappears, and the love duets of cats and human beings are forever silenced, as Arcadia and *Bohème* are blasted off the stage by commercial advertising.

Calvino's transcoding of the pastoral was not simply a game of formal skill. This cycle of short stories is a last goodbye to an ideological construct in which an entire culture had found consolation and alibis for centuries, a beautiful construct, but deceptive ('menzognero'). The Marcovaldo cycle is a pivotal text at the intersection of a writer's maturing and societal history in the making. In the ten stories produced between 1952 and 1956, Marcovaldo was designated to carry the burden of the internal contradictions of an ideology, as the bourgeois myths of rural life and individualism were undone by the new order of postwar society, and as questions about the definition and roles of a 'working class' emerged. Calvino, the quintessential bourgeois, had gently deconstructed some bourgeois myths right from the beginning of his career. His beloved Robinson Crusoe myth, too, which he more explicitly critiqued in those same years with *Il barone rampante*, was undermined by the creation of Marcovaldo, inept *bricoleur* and survivor without an island. He, Marcovaldo, the distancing but also the connecting factor, is poised between the old, a poetic universe of fragmented symbologies and conventional myths, and the new, the two-dimensional but energetic world of his own children, whose budding myths imply a disenchanted aggressiveness toward the unknown. Lyric melodies *in sordina* accompany his appearance; but since lyric abandon is unthinkable in our times, he must be content with being a comic character and the target of irony. So he is *déclassé* in societal terms, and he behaves like a child, a misfit, an 'empty head' ('testavuota'; 137).[31] Yet he performs his blundering forays into a vacant pastoral universe with amazing obstinacy, confirming without tragic posturing both the inevitability and the incredibility of the failure of illusions. Marcovaldo the lonely dreamer cannot be a competent interpreter of biological, organic nature, then, and the actual countryside is too tainted with memories of toil and poverty to be evoked as it really was. Nature is symbolic here, a cultural ideogram. Mushrooms, in this version of nature, need to be as luridly speckled as those in Walt Disney's films in order to be recognized as poisonous. Otherwise, a brown cap and a stem can only denote 'mushroom,' something said to be edible and miraculously free of cost.

In this universe, birds also are emblematic animals, not sparrows but nightingales ('La panchina'), not pigeons but fowl to be roasted ('Il piccione comunale'). The sound of rain in the night evokes a storehouse of poetic memories, through the intermediary of Marcovaldo's well-tuned senses ('Funghi in città'), while the other characters remain deaf, blind, and noseless to all messages but the most abstract: road signs, advertisements, and the two-dimensional drawings of the comics. The clearest expression of this perceptual dichotomy can be found in 'Un viaggio con le mucche.' For a deluded Marcovaldo, the mountain meadows are still a theatre for Vergilian activities, faithfully cited from the first eclogue: rest in the shade of ancient trees, *'whistling with a blade of grass in your mouth, looking down* as the cows *move slowly across the meadow,* and listening to the rustling of water *in the darkening valley'* ('zufolando con una foglia d'erba in bocca, *guardando giù* le mucche *muoversi lente* per il prato, e ascoltando *nell'ombra della valle* un fruscio d'acque'; 164. Emphasis added). For Michelino, Marcovaldo's small son, his journey with the herds is a maturing rite, and he sums it up with a pragmatic, narrow definition of his situation: back-breaking work for miserable pay. Michelino's words and gestures, so grown-up in comparison with those of his father, challenge Marcovaldo's residual fantasies, and ours, about 'the deceiving, languid fragrance of hay, and sound of cowbells' ('i menzogneri e languidi / odori di fieno e suoni di campani'; 165). The *settenario* plus almost *endecasillabo* of the closure clearly evokes the poetic aura of those smells and sounds, which are breathed and heard (perhaps only) in the older generations' shared literary experience.

Neither are we faced, in this Marcovaldo collection, with the modules of oral fairy tales, statically ready to receive new fillings according to a Proppian recipe, atlthough Calvino knew Propp, too. The mechanics of the structure, with their repetitiveness, point in other intertextual directions, as the collection is fully integrated in the fabric of written tradition. The Marcovaldo stories say that dreaming the idyll means surrendering to the deceptive myth of Eden. Formally, the myth is evoked in effective ways, thanks to Calvino's profound familiarity with the literary storehouse. Thematically, the texts pre-empt the ongoing debate over the relationship between the artificial and the natural (city vs. country, culture vs. nature, artefact vs. natural object). Calvino once asserted, 'I know that nature is neither good nor bad, but rather something impassive and ambiguous like Melville's white whale' ('So che la natura non è né buona né cattiva, ma qualcosa d'impassibile e di ambiguo come la balena bianca di Melville'; Falaschi 1976, 113). But, at a more mature stage of his life, he went beyond that youthfully Leopardian image of Nature's impassivity. The antithesis between city and country has collapsed, as the latter can live only *in* and *through* the former. The Marcovaldo stories expose the conventional universe of the pastoral for what it was, a lie that promised oneness and harmony in spite of the pastoral's own ambiguities, and offered the mirage of consolation in spite of its obvious inadequacy to deal with the anguish of human experience. The search for the idyllic, it turns out, is not only 'difficult,' but pathetic and humorous in its delusional quality.

At the end of each short story, the observing eye pulls away from the protagonist, becoming as distant as the voice that speaks at each beginning – except in 'Luna e Gnac,' where the narration reaches a cosmic range, thanks to a rapid inversion of perspective. First the movement is centrifugal, in one of the most lyrical passages of Calvinian prose, which ought to be quoted in full; it begins with 'Aaah! – they all exclaimed, and the canopy of the sky rose infinitely starry above their heads' ('Aaaaah! – gridarono tutti e la cappa del cielo s'alzò infinitamente stellata su di loro'; 175–6). Then the movement becomes centripetal, even claustrophobic in its frantic repetitiveness: 'And there was neither moon nor firmament nor darkness of night any more, but only Cognac Tomawak, Cognac Tomawak' ('e non c'erano più luna né firmamento né notte, soltanto Cognac Tomawak, Cognac Tomawak'; (177). The horizon has definitely closed,[32] escape into a dream Arcadia has become impossible, and the death of illusions evokes not Leopardian despair but a melancholy astonishment.

The Second Marcovaldo

Copying a text, even letter by letter, is writing anew, as Borges taught us. Words, phrases, and sentences do not mean what they once did, when they are drawn again on the page, reproposed in a new format, and reread in a new context. The second collection of Marcovaldo stories, which Calvino published in 1963 as a paperback entitled *Marcovaldo ovvero Le stagioni in città* (*Marcovaldo, or The Seasons in the City*), is that intriguing product, the rewriting of a previous text. The first collection remained embedded in the volume of *I racconti* and almost disappeared from the consciousness of Calvino's readers, in part because it had become less accessible, hidden as it was in a large and relatively expensive volume.

What is the significance of Calvino's re-elaboration of the Marcovaldo pieces? Given the transformations of the collection and the changed historical and literary context, how does the 1963 reformulation build on the elements of the first version and relate to the works that followed? I submit that the second *Marcovaldo* is the major work that announced and prepared all the future phases of Calvino's activity.

It is by now commonplace to say that the late fifties marked the end of an era in Italian post–Second World War history, particularly in the lives of those intellectuals who were in any way connected with the Italian Communist party.[33] Bitterness about the practices of Soviet Communism compounded disappointment with the way Italian politics had evolved after the Resistance. Many felt increasing perplexity as to the direction they were to take in their personal and political activities. In 1956, Calvino wrote the last short story of the first Marcovaldo series, 'Luna e Gnac.' In 1957, he published *Il barone rampante*, in which playfulness and energy disguised a sombre coming to awareness appropriated by the novel's narrator: 'The ideals of our youth, all is ashes' ('gli ideali della giovinezza, tutto è cenere'; *Il barone rampante*

283). In that same year, Calvino also withdrew from specifically political commitments. In 1958, he published *I racconti*,[34] after selecting and carefully rearranging the greatest part of his short fiction (but not all of it). Clearly, he was rethinking his personal positions and literary practice. The reflective statements he made shortly thereafter insist on two or three concepts: the primacy of a lucidity that does not indulge in pessimism, the importance of filtering every memory through irony and fantasy, and the need for what Calvino repeatedly called 'obstinacy without illusions.'[35]

By 1963, a mere six years later, something clearly had shifted in Italian cultural life. At forty years of age, Calvino already appeared as representative of an earlier generation. His major essays centred on the crisis experienced by writers over their inability to reconcile words and deeds – that is, writing and being in the world – but they also called for a challenging of the sense of entrapment felt by many, and for an exorcising of the fascination exerted by the 'labyrinth,' that world of objectification proposed by consumerism as the new human environment.[36] The essays' posture, as well as the spirit of *La giornata d'uno scrutatore*, published that same year, 1963, met with cutting criticism from some young critics. In retrospect, it is clear why those works seemed out of tune with the early sixties: they brought to the emerging new Italy echoes of the literary and cultural discourses elaborated over the previous thirty years. Meanwhile, the 'nouveau roman' was triumphant in France, flaunting its disdain for obvious political commitment and for the common pleasures of a fiction wedded to characters and plots. Today, Calvino's 1963 publications (the essays, *La giornata d'uno scrutatore*, and especially *Marcovaldo*) appear more complex and in tune with their times than his critics believed. Calvino's move, also in 1963, from the Turin of the so-called Italian economic miracle to the Paris of structuralism and semiology further suggests a symbolic shift in perspective. But the significant gesture of a writer is writing, and the second *Marcovaldo* is that gesture.

Speaking of the two Marcovaldos in 1975, Maria Corti asserted that, as compared with the first collection, the second one did not have a cohesive model or generative structure; it had moved very far from the spirit and the nature of the first collection, and, although artistically very valid, was not a unitary textual body, or macrotext. Calvino, self-reflective writer that he was, mulled over some of her conclusions, as we learn from a note to the 1978 reprint of Corti's essay, where she quotes from a letter Calvino wrote her. Calvino insisted:

What remains open is the possibility of studying the transformational model from macrotext 1 to a new (perhaps only potential) macrotext 2. In the latter, the calendar structure becomes crucial, starting with the title *The Seasons in the City*, and a historical dimension is suggested ('resta aperta la possibilità di studiare il modello di trasformazione dal macrotesto I a un nuovo [possibile, forse non realizzato] macrotesto II, in cui la struttura di calendario diventa decisiva [a cominciare dal titolo *Le stagioni in città*] e viene sottintesa una dimensione di sviluppo storico'; Corti: 'Testi o macrotesto?' 1978, 200n).

These remarks cannot be attributed simply to the writer's sensitivity to criticism, or to his necessarily idiosyncratic perspective on his own work. Calvino's keen critical awareness provides us with some valuable clues: structure is a crucial addition in the new collection, a historical perspective is an integral element of it, and the text's cohesiveness may be of a different kind from that of the earlier cycle.

The original cluster of ten stories, linearly constructed and located within the volume *I racconti*, was extracted from its context and dismembered. Each story became a movable component in a new order, and part of a free-standing text. Gaps were created and filled by new stories. A visible scaffolding was erected to support and define the whole, which had previously been held inconspicuously together by implicit connections. Paratextual clues draw attention to the changed identity of the collection: the volume has its own title (*Marcovaldo*), a subtitle (*Le stagioni in città*), a blurb on the jacket, and illustrations.

The most obvious elements of a book are often also the most significant clues for an analysis of the text, as the writer suggested in the letter cited earlier. The title and subtitle of the new volume effect a break with the past. The title is a message emphasizing the centrality of the protagonist's presence. Marcovaldo is the first Calvino character to give his name to a book. Only Palomar, twenty years later, would perform the same function. The subtitle translates, in less abstract but more peremptory terms, the oxymoron present in the subtitle of the earlier cycle, 'Gli idilli difficili.' The paradoxes of the protagonist's universe are now made explicit. The term 'the seasons,' with its pastoral overtones, is linked to the 'city,' which traditionally indicates a stressful, exciting reality in oppposition to the 'natural.' The preposition 'in' inserts the first term of an antinomy, which is conventional but by no means proven, into the second term. The simplicity of the subtitle (what could be plainer than 'the seasons in the city'?) is further contradicted by the controlled patterning of the collection. For the first time in his career, Calvino plays consciously with grids, headings, cycles, and repetition, which control through the camouflage of seeming transparency the proliferation of unmanageable elements in the protagonist's universe. As for the 'ovvero' linking title to subtitle, it is a playful and not translatable archaism. The fables are inserted in a tradition of storytelling.

On the volume's front jacket flap, an anonymous voice speaks of authorial intent, underlining the communicative dimension of writing while distancing and objectifying author and text.[37] The blurb says that the author has remained faithful to 'his stylistic ideal of a supple, agile, and limpid prose' ('[il] suo ideale stilistico d'una prosa articolata, agile e limpida'). The new collection is part of a series called 'Libri per l'infanzia e la gioventù,' and the audience is now specifically mentioned. It is composed of children of various ages ('bambini e ragazzi'), although it does not exclude an earlier public: 'Even readers who are no longer children will find in it the caustic fun they are accustomed to expect from a book by Calvino' ('Anche il lettore non più ragazzo vi troverà il divertimento pungente che è abituato a cercare nei libri di Calvino'). Do Marcovaldo's adventures – as the blurb says – remain 'faithful to a classic narrative structure, that of children's comic strips' ('fedeli a una classica struttura narrativa: quella delle storielle a vignette dei giornali dell'infanzia')? The assertion needs to be qualified, as I will seek to do in the analysis of the text. For now, I will only point out that indeed the text's visual apparatus was provided by a major author of Italian comic strips for children, Sergio Tofano, a significant choice.[38]

Formal changes in the original ten stories fall, by and large, into two categories. All the characters acquire names, and some acquire new ones. The maid in 'Il piccione comunale,' Teresa, becomes Guendalina, the night watchman in 'La panchina' becomes Tornaquinci, and the foreman becomes Signor Viligelmo. The author confirms the dichotomy he had already established between two groups of characters. Adult characters of humble station are burdened with archaic, noble names, which signify their estrangement from their sociohistorical context.[39] The children, on the other hand, being at ease in a world that is not a disappointment to them, acquire more realistic names modified by diminutive endings: Paolino joins the earlier Michelino, Filippetto, and Teresina, while an earlier Daniele becomes Pietruccio.

Some changes are related to reader reception. In order to bring up to date the allusions to popular culture, the Superman of the early fifties (*I racconti* 173) is replaced by the Nembo Kid of the early sixties (*Marco-*

valdo 84).[40] Also, what Calvino saw as appropriate only for a text that was not consciously directed at young people is eliminated and transformed. For instance, the episode of the women selling cigarettes on the black market (*I racconti* 169) disappears from 'La villeggiatura in panchina' (*Marcovaldo* 17); talk about 'money' ('quattrini'; *Marcovaldo* 55) replaces talk about 'girls' ('ragazze'; *I racconti* 163); 'the four-nippled udders and filthy tails' of the cows ('le quadruplici mammelle e sozze code'; *I racconti* 163) disappear; allusions to breasts (*I racconti* 156) and to the mechanics of rabbits' reproduction (*I racconti* 157) also disappear (see *Marcovaldo* 63 and 64).

Two crucial stories experience major changes, which attune them with the sixties but also stress the stories' lyric quality. 'La villeggiatura in panchina' (Vacation on a Park Bench) is an extensive reworking of the story that was called simply 'La panchina.' The mention of 'la villeggiatura' adds an ironic sociocultural connotation, as extensive summer vacations used to be the privilege of the upper-middle class (as Goldoni had already testified in his comedies) and still remain out of reach for the perpetually – and inevitably – city-bound Marcovaldo. In the second version, the poetic/comic aura is accentuated, while many realistic touches are erased. For instance, a pillow reminiscent of Linus's blanket replaces the old rolled-up shirt that originally served as a pillow (*I racconti* 166, 167, and 168; *Marcovaldo* 14 and 15). An episode with Neorealist tones, concerning two black market vendors and their arrest, is eliminated (*I racconti* 169). A factual remark disappears: 'In the summer they turned it off, given the reduced water supply available in the city system' ('d'estate, data la minor disponibilità dell'acquedotto, la chiudevano'; *I racconti* 170). The timid announcement (*I racconti* 169) of the theme that will be movingly developed in 'L'avventura di due sposi' (*I racconti* 345–8) is sacrificed, so that it will not distract from the Marcovaldian themes. A sentence on page 171 of *I racconti* – 'He found it with his eyes half-closed, as happens to someone with a sharp eye' ('Come succede a chi ha occhio, lo trovò a occhi semichiusi') – through a shift from past tense to present becomes an aphorism, in keeping with the playfully didactic character of the new collection: 'He who is on the lookout finds what he is looking for, even with eyes closed' ('Chi ha occhio trova quel che cerca, anche a occhi chiusi'; *Marcovaldo* 19). The colloquialism 'to drag up' ('tirar su'; *I racconti* 171) becomes 'to empty' ('vuotare'; *Marcovaldo* 19); another, 'Darn it!' ('Orcalorca'; *I racconti* 145), is eliminated. On the other hand, some rhetorical devices are insisted upon: the exclamation 'O, if I could ...' ('Oh, potessi ...') is added in the first paragraph of the story, and 'one could hear it down there' ('da sentirlo laggiù'; *I racconti* 170) becomes 'almost indistinguishable in the distance' ('che appena s'indovina laggiù'; *Marcovaldo* 18), with its added poetic indeterminacy.

In 'Luna e Gnac,' in addition to the changes in the children's names indicated earlier, there is a major transformation of Isolina and Fiordaligi, from proletarian adolescents to romantic dreamers. Isolina 'coi suoi diciott'anni' (*I racconti* 173) has become less specifically 'by now ... a young woman' ('ormai ... una ragazza grande'; (*Marcovaldo* 83), and has lost the vividness that a graceful gesture of physical yearning gave her (*I racconti* 173). Fiordaligi, in love with the unattainable 'moonlight girl' ('ragazza color di luna'), from a 'precociously developed fifteen-year-old boy' ('ragazzo quindicenne precocemente sviluppato'; *I racconti* 174) has become a 'melancholy youth' ('giovinotto melanconico'; *Marcovaldo* 84).

Language contains a text's fundamental clues. Since it bears the traces of all previous users and acts like a societal record, it does not disguise connections but rather acknowledges them. The discourse of the first Marcovaldo was already exquisitely literary, which is to say written in a medium rich in allusions and supremely controlled. The cartoon-like quality of the early stories is accentuated now, and reveals clearer traces of other reminiscences. For instance, and most significantly, Collodi's voice is now more audible. Certainly *Le avventure di Pinocchio* (The Adventures of Pinocchio) was a much more important influence in Calvino's formation and in shaping his linguistic medium than many texts he read later in life. The voice of the Author, open to dialogue but as elusive as that of the older Tuscan writer, speaks here about a more naïve and stubborn *burattino* than Pinocchio, that is, Marcovaldo, who never learns his lesson and is never subjected to the indignity of becoming a nice little boy ('un ragazzino per bene'; Collodi 280), but rather disappears for good.

The two major voices speaking in *Marcovaldo* are interconnected in even more ambiguous ways than was the case in the earlier cycle. The narrating voice, with its interferences that take the form of asides and poetic flights, boldly appropriates Marcovaldo's voice, his point of view, and his feelings. Very early in the collection, the narrating voice suggests the total control it exerts on the character, by evoking the ghost of the page where Marcovaldo exists in 'La città smarrita nella neve' (The City Hidden in the Snow), and by making the physical ink trace that gives Marcovaldo life the focus of the story entitled 'I figli di Babbo

Natale' (Santa's Children). As Calvino was to assert later, the ink drawing on the page 'presupposes a pen that traces it, and every pen presupposes a hand that holds it' ('presuppone una penna che la traccia, e ogni
penna presuppone una mano che la impugna'; *Una pietra sopra* 295). The
story, for Calvino, is clearly the storyteller's domain.

The major change in the new text is the grid formed by two coordinates, time and space. This grid distances the narrative episodes and
further stresses the intersection of 'nature' and 'history.' The natural
cycle of the seasons, determinant and yet curiously distant in its
mechanical repetitiveness, structures life in the city, while the city
expands its function as an indispensable prison and a dream machine.
Each coordinate bears the weight of the text's contradictions. Time runs
on two tracks: on one side there are memory and desire, those condi-
tions determined by historical forces; on the other side, there is the rigid
pattern of a calendar, whose ahistorical phases mark the parallel boundaries of Marcovaldo's existence and the narrator's storytelling, as each
season affects the protagonist's life and controls each short story. Space
also is two-faced. Although the episodes take place in a narrowly
defined urban environment, glimpses of another world emerge from a
cityscape that is familiar and rich in allusions. What was suggested in
the original ten stories is now made more explicit. In the first Marcovaldo, the world's duplicity was an intrinsic necessity; in the second, the
measuring of time and space emphasizes the impact of external constraints on internal motives, magnifies the labyrinthine quality of existence, and exasperates the need for a way out. The nature–history
dichotomy is more emphatically negated, as its two terms reveal their
inescapable connection. Marcovaldo's adventures acquire intensity, in a
multilayered urban context which, more clearly than in the earlier collection, is both the impregnable fortress of the 'real' and the necessary
ground on which to plot an escape.

The historical background in which poetic production takes place
informs the text's structural and thematic shifts in subtler ways even
than those suggested by Calvino in his letter. The first Marcovaldo was
the humorous undermining of an aristocratic literary tradition, where
the city lay within a fantasy landscape of bountiful serenity, called
Nature. The second version heightens the urgency of the search for
escape, as dysfunction becomes a widening phenomenon in economic,
social, and cultural terms. Ultimately, this text provides also a thread
out of the labyrinth, as literary metaphors of pastoral daydreaming give
way to surreal happenings, then to the magic of writing. Where the orig-

inal ten stories had reiterated a statement about the powerlessness of desire in the 'miseria' of existence, and had regularly closed with the defeat of the protagonist, the theme now is a potentially successful escape. Two paradigmatic tales in this regard are 'Il giardino dei gatti ostinati' (The Garden of Stubborn Cats) and 'I figli di Babbo Natale,' which illustrate the shift in perspective from 1954 to 1963. Now the city is riddled with hideouts, and the text intentionally revalues poetic discourse, in its flexibility, playfulness, and transformative power, as a tool for the enactment of that escape.

If we look more closely at the twenty stories, we see a new pattern emerging (see the appendix to this chapter). The first three stories remain faithful to the early narrative triad of desire/obstacle/defeat; but the added fourth tale, 'La città smarrita nella neve,' where the city is not lost but *hidden* by a snowfall, evokes for the first time a realm of fleeting and menaced freedom that only the quintessential city dweller can imagine. Silence and snow also introduce for the first time the metaphor of the white/blank sheet of paper ('un foglio bianco,' with its untranslatable ambiguity).

The sixth tale, 'Un sabato di sole, sabbia e sonno' (A Saturday with Sun, Sand, and Sleep), develops two earlier and more discreet Marcovaldian themes, of a sleep visited by visions, and of the protagonist's literal 'flying' away from everyday reality. Then, 'La fermata sbagliata' (The Wrong Stop), number twelve of the new series, reiterates and intensifies the need for escape felt by the protagonist, an escape that he actively pursues by viewing films about exotic locales. The oneiric quality of his flying away is conveyed by the darkness of the movie theatre, which contrasts on the one hand with the colourless fog that has washed over the city and erased the sharpness of lines and sensations, and on the other hand with the colourful 'splendour' of the films. The theme of escape in flight becomes more concrete, as Marcovaldo actually boards a plane bound for faraway places.[41]

The tales numbered thirteen, fourteen, and fifteen play with a surrealistic motif, orchestrating it in various ways: 'Dov'è più azzurro il fiume' (Where the River Is More Blue) leans toward the fairy tale; 'Luna e Gnac' revisits with nostalgia its earlier farewell to the illusions and marvellous lies of the idyll; and 'La pioggia e le foglie' (The Rain and the Leaves) allows the protagonist to experience a near-metamorphosis (into a plant) and then a vicarious flight, a secular Assumption confirmed by the appearance of a rainbow.

After two attempts to escape through consumerism fail, in 'Marcovaldo al supermarket' (Marcovaldo at the Supermarket) and 'Fumo, vento e bolle di sapone' (Smoke, Wind, and Soap Bubbles), the eighteenth and nineteenth stories – 'La città tutta per lui' (The City All to Himself) and 'Il giardino dei gatti ostinati' – return to the theme of the discovery of a hidden city, the city that is present in its invisibility, a 'negative' of the visible city, a mosaic of empty spaces. The city of summer, that other city 'glimpsed for barely one instant, or perhaps only dreamed' ('intravista solo per un momento, o forse solamente sognata'; *Marcovaldo* 115), like the city erased by snow, allows Marcovaldo a playful freedom: 'He wandered along the streets with the zigzags of a butterfly' ('percorreva le vie con zig-zag da farfalla'; *Marcovaldo* 115). In 'Il giardino dei gatti ostinati,' the 'counter-city' has become as real as the city, its upside-down double, where the protagonist comes close to another metamorphosis, this time into a cat, that icon of obstinacy and freedom. As the seasons pass swiftly, the cats slyly enforce a stalemate on a demolition and construction site at the heart of the technological wonder-city. 'The ancient cat people' ('L'antico popolo dei gatti'; 118) embodies the obstinacy without illusions that lies at the heart of Marcovaldo's tenacious resistance and of Calvino's writing. It is the function of the twentieth story to bring Marcovaldo's odyssey to a close.

Escaping the Labyrinth

An odyssey is a song of return. The destruction of the 'city of men' is literally effected by the 'children of Father Christmas' ('figli di Babbo Natale'; something is lost in the English 'Santa's children,' namely, the very traditional, Tuscan, and Collodian term *babbo*). As their happy destructiveness is swiftly co-opted by a consumption-crazed socioeconomic system, Marcovaldo goes back into the streets. He loses himself among the crowds. The narrative thread that is his essence unravels and feeds a frenzy of detailed drawing, which always announces a closure, however ambiguous, in Calvino's writing.[42] In the chaos of the urban scene, with its artificial lights and artificial night, an exquisitely familiar yet portentous detail emerges: the open fire of the roasted chestnut vendor, a 'round black opening all aflame' ('tondo fornello nero ardente'), which turns into the magic fire of a sorceress. A lyrical mode, subdued but unmistakable, has materialized.[43] The round, dark, but red-hot crucible evokes the 'dark mysterious mountains' ('buie misteriose montagne') glimpsed at the beginning of the story. Thus the world in its multiplicity is reduced to a symbiotic double image, as the encompassing gaze recedes with vertiginous speed. Whose perspective is it, the one for which 'the city seemed *smaller, curled in a luminous globe*, buried *in the dark heart of the woods,* among the ancient trunks of chestnut trees and an infinite mantle of snow' ('la città sembrava *più piccola, raccolta in un'ampolla luminosa*, sepolta *nel cuore buio d'un bosco,* tra i tronchi centenari dei castagni e un infinito manto di neve'; *Marcovaldo* 130. Emphasis added)? The city is the matter in the alembic of the alchemist, who contemplates in it the desired metamorphoses. Marcovaldo's eye has ultimately been absorbed by the eye of the narrator.

A spider's stratagem has been engineered under our very noses. The thread of narration busily follows the narrator's fantasy and fills the page with dark print. Onomatopoeia and alliteration are used to evoke characters out of ancient fables, like the wolf and the hare. The narration becomes pure pleasure, a light symphony of three vivid colours: black, white, red, then white on white and black on black, separated by an impassable line. That line and the miracle of suspended flight prevent both chaos and total closure.

The thread now quickly sketches the animated cartoon of a chase sequence, deadly and playful in its exact grace of movement and gesture. The disappearance of the pursued, announced by the hare's invisibility and by the acceleration of monosyllables and question marks, accomplishes the sleight-of-hand performed by the text: 'Is it here? Is it there? No, it's a little bit farther' ('È qua? è là? no, è un po' più in là'; *Marcovaldo* 139). The metamorphosis of the character allows character and narrator to fuse and then escape. The stress placed on the chromatic factor disguises the trick enacted, as the expanse of snow and the empty page alone remain, testifying in their whiteness/blankness to the ambiguous success of writing.

The old model has indeed been erased. The term macrotext could be used, but has become irrelevant to a definition of the new text. This text incorporates the splintered elements of its own past in a different game, as it places them in new configurations and constricts them within deterministic grids. It tests more stringently the options for an escape, while remaining a mobile structure, a Calder-like artefact. Building on the model of the first collection, where a search for the idyll inevitably led to comical disappointment, 'leaving no margin for escape or consolation' ('senza lasciare margini di fuga e di consolazione'; Ferretti 43), this set of episodes progressively introduces new themes. One theme is that of the formalized game, in which cards, tassels, chips, or pieces are movable and subject to different interpretations, depending on their placement in a context. The other theme is that of the enactment of escape, as vicarious 'flights' less and less frequently conclude with a 'fall' back into 'reality.' Now, the escape attempts are dynamic. In 'Un sabato di sole, sabbia e sonno,' Marcovaldo is poised in the air, and surveys the teeming beach scene beneath him. In 'La fermata sbagliata,' he is off on an actual journey, only partly unintended. Through trial and error, the 'invisible' face of the city fully emerges. Though surreality and consumerism are unmasked as erroneous paths to escape, just as the pastoral dream had been, the text has opened a gap in the wall of necessity. A way out is revealed in the protagonist's quest, even though success remains uncertain. The new metaphor is the chase fraught with danger, while writing and fantasy are offered as a possible salvation in this narrative 'challenge to the labyrinth.' While the suspense of the chase points to the impossibility of a final closure, writing is proposed as the thread leading out of the maze toward an ever menaced freedom. A new 'ameno inganno' for a besieged humanity may have been found.

Appendix: The Sequence of Stories in the Two Marcovaldo Cycles

The number in parentheses in the second column indicates the position of the story in the earlier collection. The asterisk indicates that the story is an addition to the earlier collection.

I racconti (1958)	*Marcovaldo ovvero Le stagioni in città* (1963)
1. Funghi in città (1952)	1. Funghi in città (1)
2. Il piccione comunale (1952)	2. La villeggiatura in panchina (9)
3. La pietanziera (1952)	3. Il piccione comunale (2)
4. La cura delle vespe (1953)	4. La città smarrita nella neve*
5. Il bosco sull'autostrada (1953)	5. La cura delle vespe (4)
6. L'aria buona (1953)	6. Un sabato di sole, sabbia e sonno*
7. Il coniglio velenoso (1954)	7. La pietanziera (3)
8. Un viaggio con le mucche (1954)	8. Il bosco sull'autostrada (5)
9. La panchina (1955)	9. L'aria buona (6)
10. Luna e Gnac (1956)	10. Un viaggio con le mucche (8)
	11. Il coniglio velenoso (7)
	12. La fermata sbagliata*
	13. Dov'è più azzurro il fiume*
	14. Luna e Gnac (10)

15. La pioggia e le foglie*
16. Marcovaldo al supermarket*
17. Fumo, vento e bolle di sapone*
18. La città tutta per lui*
19. Il giardino dei gatti ostinati*
20. I figli di Babbo Natale*

1 Portions of this chapter were published in 'Requiem for the Idyll: Italo Calvino's First Marcovaldo Stories,' *Stanford Italian Review* 10:2 (1991): 177–98, and in 'Escape from the Labyrinth: Italo Calvino's *Marcovaldo*,' *Annali d'Italianistica* 9 (1991): 212–29. The quotations are from the 1983 edition of *I racconti*.

2 For this term, which indicates all the elements that define the 'pragmatic dimension' of any work by offering among other clues 'generic indices,' see Genette 9–10.

3 For a discussion of the structure and repetitive patterns of the Marcovaldo stories, see Corti's 'Testi o macrotesto? I racconti di Marcovaldo di I Calvino' (1975 and 1978). Corti saw in the repetitive model a generative structure or macrostructure, which, combined with the progressive pattern of the discourse, gave cohesion to the first cycle of short stories. Thus, the ten short stories, Corti concluded, are components in a macrotext, or unitary textual body.

4 It is interesting to note how cultural conventions vary with ethnic and chronological contexts. Sausage and turnips widely connote a coarse diet, but I very much doubt that fried brains conveys to the North American reader (or to an Italian reader, today) the connotation it carried in the original Italian of the 1950s, that of a refined and wholesome delicacy.

5 'The wind, *reaching the city from afar*, brings it unusual gifts that only *rare sensitive spirits* notice, such as hay fever sufferers, who sneeze *because of pollens from exotic flowers*' ('Il vento, *venendo in città da lontano*, le porta doni inconsueti, di cui s'accorgono solo poche *anime sensibili*, come i raffreddati del fieno, che starnutano *per pollini di fiori d'altre terre*'; *I racconti* 134. Emphasis added).

6 The last item is a culturally marked equivalent of the Anglo-Saxon 'banana peel.'

7 The term *favola* is closely related to speech itself (*favella* derives from a diminutive of the Latin *fabula*); it indicates a 'life story,' the Petrarchan 'la mia favola breve è già compita' ('The brief story of my life is already concluded'). Or it may refer to the telling of historically rooted legends, such as Dante's

'favoleggiar di Fiesole e di Roma' ('telling tales of Fiesole and Rome'), and usually has an instructive dimension. *Fiaba* is a parallel term, which enjoyed particular favour from the seventeenth century on. It always includes magic and supernatural beings (see Battaglia; Cortelazzo).

8 The works of the Bakhtin circle are all essential to this discussion of the Marcovaldo stories, particularly on the connections between author, character, and reader. More specifically, see Bakhtin and Medvedev 21–30 and 129–141. See also Vološinov and Bakhtin 46–58, 'La parola nella vita e nella poesia.'

9 The narrator's comments may be brief – 'Marcovaldo, always with his nose in the air' ('Marcovaldo sempre a naso in aria'; *I racconti* 137); 'Easier said ...' ('Una parola'; 148) – but often pertain to psychological motivation: 'doubting thoughts,' 'full of apprehension,' 'with relief,' 'even he didn't know why' ('ragionamento sospettoso,' 'pieno d'apprensione,' 'con sollievo,' 'non sapeva neanche lui perché'; 135); 'anger, rage ... the bursting of those passions' ('ira, rabbia ... tracollo di quelle passioni'; 136); 'very worried' ('molto preoccupato'; 138); etc.

10 The narrator's interventions may be descriptive – 'shoulder-blades as frail as the wings of a featherless baby bird' ('scapole fragili come le ali d'un uccelletto implume'; 151); 'Marcovaldo, tall and thin, and his wife, short and stocky' ('Marcovaldo, lungo e affilato, e sua moglie, bassa e tozza'; 151) – but more frequently in later stories they are couched in aphoristic terms, as if they referred to a shared knowledge or wisdom: 'Children, you know how they are' ('I bambini, si sa come sono'; 145); 'Where does a kid run when he is chased? He runs home' ('Dove scappa un bambino inseguito? Scappa a casa!'; 147); 'The possibility that it was a female rabbit, that Marcovaldo had not imagined' ('alla possibilità che fosse una coniglia, Marcovaldo non ci aveva pensato'; 157); 'Dogs, for whom nothing that is human is alien' ('I cani, cui nulla di quel che è umano è alieno'; 163); 'All you have to do is to start questioning your present situation, and who knows how far you can go' ('Basta cominciare a non accettare il proprio stato presente e chissamai dove si arriva'; 170); etc.

11 More specifically, that society was the Italian society emerging from postwar times, with all the implications of that fact in terms of linguistic choices and cultural allusions. Interestingly, the Marcovaldo stories were among Calvino's last works to be translated into English and remain the least known outside Italy.

12 'He bent down' ('Si chinò'; 134); 'This is what I am saying' ('Ecco quel che vi dico'; 135); 'It's getting late ... It's cold. Let's go home' ('È tardi ... Fa freddo. Andiamo a casa'; 154); 'Lucky him' ('Beato lui'; 164); etc.

13 Describing the appearance of mushrooms, Marcovaldo 'explained *with trans-*

port the beauty of their many species, and *the delicacy of their flavour'* ('spiegò con trasporto la bellezza delle loro molte specie, la delicatezza del loro sapore'; 135). Observing the supposedly barren city environment, Marcovaldo discovers items which become 'the object of his reflections, as he discovered *the changes in the seasons, the desires of his heart, and the misery of his existence*' ('oggetto di ragionamento, scoprendo *i mutamenti della stagione, i desideri del suo animo, e la miseria della sua esistenza*'; 134). The city seen from afar 'looked to him like *a leaden moor, stagnant, covered by the scales of a myriad of roofs*' ('gli parve *una landa plumbea, stagnante, ricoperta dalle fitte scaglie dei tetti*'; 152). Emphasis added.

14 One example will suffice: 'O, if I could awaken at least once with the chirping of birds instead of the alarm clock ...! O! if I could sleep here, in the cool greenery, and not in my room, low and hot; here, in this silence, and not in the snoring of the whole family and the rumble of streetcars ...; here, in the natural darkness of night, and not in the artificial darkness streaked by the glare of streetlights; and see tree leaves and sky when I open my eyes!' ('Oh, potessi destarmi una volta al cinguettare degli uccelli e non al suono della sveglia ...! Oh, potessi dormire qui, solo in mezzo a questo fresco verde e non nella mia stanza bassa e calda; qui nel silenzio, non nel russare ... di tutta la famiglia e correre di tram ...; qui nel buio naturale della notte, non nel buio artificiale ... zebrato dal riverbero dei fanali e vedere foglie e cielo aprendo gli occhi!'; 166).

15 See, for a curious preview of this theme, the early 'apologue,' entitled 'L'importanza di ognuno' (The Importance of Each Person), *Romanzi e racconti* III 786.

16 A brief list of recent works on the pastoral is included in the bibliography.

17 These observations are supported by Calvino's own later reflections in *Lezioni americane* 48.

18 Again, this is a convention in many writings about the pastoral. Bàrberi-Squarotti explored with particular keenness the conflict between *otium* and *negotium*, or pleasure and duty, in the late Renaissance and early Baroque periods.

19 *Contaminazione* is a term coined by classicists to indicate the technique, originally attributed to Roman playwrights, of combining in one text procedures and elements drawn from supposedly incompatible sources. The Battaglia dictionary cites the use of this term in Carducci, Pascoli, and Pavese.

20 For the matter of melancholy in the pastoral, see Garber.

21 For a brief discussion of these comics, see chapter 4. For Calvino's own reflections on the matter, see *Lezioni americane* 6.

22 'He bent over to tie his shoelaces' ('Si chinò a legarsi le scarpe'; *I racconti* 134);

'He was bent over' ('Era così chinato'; 135); 'He sat up in bed' ('si levò a sedere sul letto'; 136); 'he pedalled faster' ('pedalò più forte'; 137); etc.

23 For instance, no dialectalisms were included, except some Tuscanisms ('babbo' and 'figliolo'). Melodramatic language and quotations from operatic librettos were often used for parodic effect: 'sorrowful laments,' 'noble steed,' 'Cowardly I am not,' etc. ('mesti lagni,' 'nobile destriero,' 'sí vil non sono,' etc.)

24 In addition to the comic strips from children's periodicals, Collodi's *Avventure di Pinocchio* performed a crucial function in Calvino's artistic formation. For this topic, see Jeannet 1994.

25 Calvino refers to those three characteristics in several articles that are now gathered in *Una pietra sopra*, for instance in 'La sfida al labirinto' (The Labyrinth Defied), and then more pointedly in 'L'italiano, una lingua fra le altre' (Italian, a Language among Other Languages) and 'L'antilingua' (The Antilanguage).

26 An example of graphic uncertainty is in 'La pietanziera,' which uses the two forms 'salsiccia' and 'salciccia' to indicate a type of sausage.

27 'La panchina' has a complex history, which Maria Corti has documented ('Un modello' 1978, and 1990). It was first a short story, then a libretto for an opera produced in 1955, with music composed by Sergio Liberovici, then the short story in *I racconti*, and finally the revised version in *Marcovaldo*. In the libretto, the protagonist has no name, he is 'l'uomo insonne' ('the insomniac').

28 Numerous examples of contrasting registers are found on page 166: Marcovaldo's trudging to work is juxtaposed with strolling in the woods. His immediate launching into idyllic visions – 'He raised his eyes to the branches ... where they were thickest ... in the shade transparent with lymph' ('Alzava gli occhi tra le fonde ... dov'erano più folte ... nell'ombra transparente di linfa') – is juxtaposed with the meagreness of the pretext: 'the square of a public garden carved out from the middle of four streets' ('un quadrato di giardino pubblico ritagliato in mezzo a quattro vie'). Also, 'the noise of tone-deaf sparrows' ('Il chiasso dei passeri stonati'), which 'to him sounded like nightingales' ('a lui parevano usignoli'), mocks the literary memory of the Petrarchean bird's pure notes.

As for the bench, it is a mirage – 'There was coolness and quiet ... a wood – he was sure of it – soft and hospitable' ('Là era il fresco e la pace ... un legno – ne era certo – morbido e accogliente') – and the transition to its negation is effected through a laconic sentence – 'The coolness and the quiet were there, but not a free bench' ('Il fresco e la pace c'erano, ma non la panca libera') – with an ellipsis that underscores the finality of the denial.

Here is a list of poetic lexical choices, which it would be pointless to translate: 'le fronde, l'inveire, prescelte' (166); 'si ritrasse, il mondo terrestre, pallore misterioso' (167); 'acqua che rampolla' (170); 'anfratti' (171); 'si premeva, colmarsi l'olfatto' (172).

And here is a list of the syntactical patterns and rhetorical devices mentioned, which again may yield rather different English constructions and lexical choices: 'lasciavano dardeggiare gialli raggi nell'ombra trasparente di linfe' (166); 'sottili reti di nubi' (167); 'assoluta serenità naturale; falsa luna intermittente; un occhio giallo che ammicca, solitario; come dormirei bene ...! come dormirei bene! quello sciocco giallo; un gran nastro sbiadito' (168); 'bocche storte e dipinte' (169); 'cupo soffio aspirante; raggrinzito guanciale; alto castello; scorrere querulo e sommesso; illustre opera di scultura; ninfe, fauni, dei fluviali; zampilli, cascate e giochi d'acqua' (170); 'alti getti; liquido fuoco d'artificio; ecco ... ecco ... voci cupe e rotte; opachi gong; alone soffice d'attutimento; la fantasia delle narici' (171); and, at the climax, 'il convulso mazzo di ranuncoli' (172).

See also note 14, for an important example of the same stylistic strategies.

29 Don Quixote is a character whose connections with the pastoral universe are too complex to be analysed here.

30 There was an interesting exchange of views between Calvino and Anna Maria Ortese on the subject of the moon, for which see 'Il rapporto con la luna' (The Connection with the Moon) in *Una pietra sopra* (182–3). There, Calvino refused the 'consolatory' myth of astronomical contemplation, but also the myth of technological progress, and proposed Galileo's writings as exemplary texts. Marcovaldo 'was going to look at the stars for a moment, and then was going to close his eyes in a restoring sleep' ('avrebbe guardato per un momento le stelle e avrebbe chiuso gli occhi in un sonno riparatore'; 166). The past conditional underlines the wishful charge of the vision.

31 'Testavuota,' written as one word, is like a nickname for Marcovaldo, who is utterly 'different.' As a matter of fact, in a sharp departure from pastoral conventions, Marcovaldo is not even given a love object. The love motif is absent from his experience, in what is really a 'pastoral of solitude,' to borrow Poggioli's words.

32 For the concept of the 'orizzonte negato' ('deleted horizon'), see the interesting article by Milanini.

33 For an extensive treatment of this historical moment and its impact on cultural life, see Asor Rosa 1982. On page 614, a heading reads 'Il 1956: fine di un ciclo' (1956: End of a Cycle). Among those who have addressed Calvino's sociocultural context, see Falaschi 1976, who drew one of the first major portraits of Calvino and asserted, speaking of the late fifties' crisis, 'The period

1956–7 is so important for at least two generations of Communists that ... the context ... carries more weight than the positions of the individuals' ('il 1956–'57 è cosí significativo per almeno due generazioni di comunisti che ... lo sfondo ... conta più delle posizioni del singolo'; 544). De Federicis, in an excellent school edition of *La giornata d'uno scrutatore*, devotes an entire section to 'Il cambiamento culturale dal 1953 al 1963' (Cultural Changes from 1953 to 1963). That is the decade that elapsed between the planning and the actual publication of that work, as well as between the two Marcovaldos. Ferretti reiterates, 'Calvino's reflection ... and his search for the integration of man and world continues ... even after the 1956 crisis, but something certainly changes' ('Il discorso di Calvino ... e la sua ricerca di un'integrazione uomo-mondo continua ... anche dopo la crisi del '56, ma qualcosa certamente muta'; 46). Then he adds an interesting correction: 'However, substantially, the year 1956, more than representing a *leap*, or a *turning point* in Calvino's itinerary, fully illuminates what Calvino carried inside right from the beginning' ('Ma nella sostanza il '56, più che rappresentare un *salto*, una *svolta* nell'itinerario di Calvino, fa piena luce su quanto Calvino stesso recava fin dall'inizio dentro di sé'; 46–7; Ferretti's emphasis).

34 For an analysis of the entire volume of *I racconti*, see Ricci, especially 1–17, where the short stories are defined as steps in a 'labyrinthine journey' (10).

35 The major essays in which those concepts appear are 'Natura e storia del romanzo' (The 'Nature and History of the Novel, 1958), now in *Una pietra sopra* 19–38, where the expression 'ostinazione *nonostante tutto*' first appears (38; 'obstinacy *in spite of everything*'; Calvino's emphasis), and 'Tre correnti del romanzo italiano d'oggi' (Three Currents in the Contemporary Italian Novel, 1959), now in *Una pietra sopra* 39–45, where 'ostinazione senza illusioni' ('obstinacy without illusions') is used as a closing expression.

36 The concepts I paraphrase are presented in 'Pavese: essere e fare' (1960; *Una pietra sopra* 58–63), 'Dialogo di due scrittori in crisi' (Dialogue between Two Writers, 1961; *Una pietra sopra* 64–9), 'La sfida al labirinto' (1962; *Una pietra sopra* 82–97), and 'Un'amara serenità' (A Bitter Serenity, 1963; *Una pietra sopra* 98–9).

37 Actually, Calvino himself would write the material used in the publisher's blurbs. His analysis of *Marcovaldo* is like a preview of the critical readings that were to follow. He mentions the book's comic-poetic whimsy, the Neo-realistic concern with day-to-day struggles, the satire of the 'economic miracle,' etc., in one of his many playful forecasts of the reception awaiting his own books.

38 Sergio Tofano (1886–1973) was a writer of whimsical books, and the creator of several comic strip characters. One of them, Signor Bonaventura,

appeared in children's periodicals such as *Il corriere dei piccoli*, an insert of *Il corriere della sera*. Tofano was much admired and cited by Calvino.

39 This technique is reminiscent of the convention established in the comic strips of the thirties and forties, where, for instance, Jiggs and Maggie, whose names carried a connotation of blue-collar roots in the American original, became the formal and archaic Arcibaldo and Petronilla in the Italian translation.

40 Interestingly, he became the Lone Ranger in William Weaver's translation (72).

41 Arthur Rimbaud's 'bateau ivre' metaphor looms in the background, among many echoes that haunt Marcovaldo's blind search. As is often the case with Calvino, one could list a number of intertextual allusions in this tale about the hero's journey toward the place of his desire. Calvino's literary knowledge was truly encyclopaedic.

42 As examples of this Calvinian technique, one might see the endings of 'La formica argentina' and 'L'avventura di un poeta' in *I racconti*, and of *Il barone rampante* and *Il cavaliere inesistente*.

43 The use and placement of adjectives are important signs of the text's shifting toward a poetic tone and level of writing, as one can see in 'La villeggiatura in panchina' and 'Luna e Gnac,' two of the most poetic of Calvino's short stories. Calvino insisted on his preoccupation with stylistic factors (Corti 1985): 'I believe that prose writing requires an investment of all the verbal resources one has available, exactly like poetry' ('Credo che la prosa richieda un investimento di tutte le proprie risorse verbali, tal quale come la poesia'; 49).

4

Telling Stories

Telling stories protects souls, according to Balinese belief.

Robert Darnton, *The Great Cat Massacre*

The Castle of Literature

Calvino's coming of age took place under the contradictory signs of private comfort and dramatic public events. Then, from the leaden years of dictatorial regimes, a period emerged when Europe seemed to have become as young as the protagonists of a victorious struggle. Through it all, even in spite of the drawing power of action during a time of armed struggle, another domain had beckoned to the young man: 'The faraway castle of literature drew near and opened up as a welcoming haven' ('il lontano castello della letteratura s'apriva come un porto vicino ed amico'; *Il sentiero dei nidi di ragno* 20). The image of that mythical place, at the same time remote and magically approachable, was not accidental, with its suggestions of medieval architecture, Renaissance fantasies, and travel adventures. And even though the words that evoke it were meant to refer to Calvino's own entry into writing, they apply equally to his experience as a reader. He often spoke of his profound affinity with the written word, and his 'basic distaste for the spoken word' ('un disgusto fondamentale per la parola parlata'; Camon 1973, 183). The abuse of rhetoric over the preceeding one hundred years, and not only during the period of Fascist hegemony, probably had something to do with the posture he adopted. But his distaste and mistrust had to do mostly with a certain notion of human communication, and of the discipline needed to practise it at its best. Writing was a guarantee of commitment to work and of seriousness in using language, and proof of the skill one had acquired in that trade – concepts that 'dated' Calvino and placed him within a specific cultural perspective. But his premises were going to be less limiting than some of his early critics had believed, as far as his writing career was concerned.

Well before writing his first works of fiction, Calvino had frequented the castle of literature, where he had discovered that a whole universe of order, fantasy, and playfulness existed, beyond the disorder and chaos that were only one part of human experience. That awareness led him to ever deeper probings of the connections between the mechanics of history, the complexities of individual journeys, and the questions posed by the act of writing. Naturally, all sorts of voices make their echoes heard in the Calvinian texts, flowing together to quicken a quintessentially 'Italian,' as well as cosmopolitan and idiosyncratic, unitary whole. The exploration of the links between his fictions and a multitude of other writings has only just begun, in part, I believe, because Calvino perfected literary self-analysis, seeming elegantly to pre-empt that favourite scholarly exercise. What I wish to discuss first is the place held by so-called children's literature in the Calvinian universe, and the significance of that place. It will then be easy to move on to consideration of Calvino's legacies.

For the great majority of Italians, Carlo Collodi's classic of children's literature, *Le avventure di Pinocchio. Storia di un burattino* (The Adventures of Pinocchio: Story of a Marionette), is the first real book, often not read, but heard read by a beloved adult. Calvino stated more than once, in articles and interviews, its importance in his own formation: 'Any [reading] list, I think, must begin with *Pinocchio*, which I have always considered a model of narration' ('Ogni elenco [di letture] credo deva cominciare con *Pinocchio* che ho sempre considerato un modello di narrazione'; Corti 1990, 48). Not only did Collodi provide the first experience of fiction for the child Calvino, but his example was fundamental for the future writer from the linguistic, structural, and thematic points of view.[1] Above all, Collodi demonstrated something that was to become a fundamental tenet for Calvino, that literature is first and foremost storytelling. Collodi also provided the equally essential proof that a reconciliation of opposites is possible, since his novel confirmed that the storytelling activity is at the same time playful and serious, gratuitous and instructive, the sign of private imagination and collective imaginary, in short, a complex and necessary manifestation of human existence.

The key to intertextual factors is often a word, a name, or a gesture. 'Kim' comes from Kipling as a prototype for Pin in *Il sentiero dei nidi di ragno*. Both Kim and Pin are orphaned urchins; they are shrewd and street-wise, and they walk through a world of mysterious symbols. Both are caught in a world they do not understand, and pretend to know more than they do when they talk with grown-ups about war and secret messages. Both live and barter in the midst of confusing events and heterogeneous crowds. Also, some of Kipling's narrative techniques serve Calvino well, for instance the use of an impersonal narrrating voice that affords glimpses into the boy's character – 'Kim will remember till he dies that long, lazy journey' (Kipling 353) – and the vivid description of an array of jewels, such as we might find in *Le cosmicomiche*: 'It [the table of the jeweller] blazed in the morning light – all red and blue and green flashes, picked out with the vicious blue-white spurt of a diamond here and there' (Kipling 362). Pin is Kim's new avatar; yet it is a grown-up, the other half of Calvino's persona in the context of the Resistance, who bears the name 'Kim' in *Sentiero*. It is almost as if the impact of Kipling's memory had to be acknowledged indirectly, or diffused by being shared by more than one character. At the same time, the name (which, we must remember, is an assumed name for the young Resistance fighter) confirms the importance of Calvino's encounter with the British writer. Similarly, the loan of a name, Trelawney, from *Treasure Island* and the return of the same type of character in both *Il visconte dimezzato* and *Il barone rampante* are not just obvious clues to a superficial Stevensonian reminiscence. They are an indication of theoretical and structural affinities with the old adventure story. Calvino must have approved his beloved model's stress on the mediating function of writing ('I take up my pen ...'; Stevenson 3). And he, like Stevenson, opted for a first-person narrative that is 'distanced' and therefore devoid of sentimentalism. Like his predecessor, the Italian author usually chose to look at the world through the observing eyes of a young boy, a marginal and naïve watcher and witness to events, but both authors had their characters tell the story of events only after reaching adulthood. A time gap is placed between happening and retelling, between the excitement of action and the writing about it, so that the story enjoys simultaneously the privileges of memory and of immediacy. Just as Calvino had Cosimo's brother say, 'I remember as if it were today' ('Ricordo come fosse oggi'; *Il barone rampante* 11), and made Qfwfq repeat often, with felicitous effect, that 'he was there,' Stevenson had his storyteller use that same truth-affirming device: 'I remember him as if it were yesterday'

(Stevenson 3). Not least in importance is the fact that Calvino admired in Kipling and Stevenson the elaboration of a transparent medium, a prose that used a precise and rich lexicon in order to speak of adventure.

When Calvino named the readings that were influential in his formation well beyond childhood and adolescence, he consistently placed first on the list works that are classified as children's literature: Collodi, Kipling, Stevenson, Defoe, and, yes, the comic strips. At least two reasons motivated him. First, as we have observed, Calvino had absorbed from them messages about style that he deemed fundamental. In addition, those authors, like Calvino, were highly conscious of the presence of an audience, and had a sense of the importance of their connection with a collectivity; which connection, in turn, with all due regard for changed contexts and personalities, agreed with the young writer's political stance in the forties and fifties, and later fit well with the tenets of the new theories he explored on the subject of writing, literature, and reception. The writer Calvino did possess some of the essential characteristics of one of his creatures, Cosimo di Rondò: he had a keen sense of the presence of an audience, in spite of his posture of reserve and almost aloofness, and was immensely concerned with the reception of his works. It must also be pointed out that most of the authors who presided over Calvino's entry into literature belong to the second half of the nineteenth century, the great storehouse of Western fiction's traditions, when the ruling middle classes' concern with fostering a specific linguistic and cultural competence among the young was exceptionally high.[2] The intended audiences, however imaginary and hypothetical, were audiences of 'bambini e ragazzi' (*Marcovaldo* 1966, 11), as Calvino put it. It is true that the concern with reception was ambiguous, in spite of its being so explicit; it could not influence the 'quality' of the works, or even the direction of their impact, since ultimately those fictions found their place on a variety of shelves, those of young people, of adults, and even of scholars. Yet there is no doubt that the young people of various generations were very much on the writers' minds, as projections of their own selves as young readers, and as virtual audiences well into the future. These were also matters of definite concern to publishers, as the young at all levels of the middle classes seemed a very promising and expanding new market.

All these remarks are even more apt, if, with Calvinian eclecticism, we look at the comic strips that appeared in Italian publications in the period between the two wars, for their impact extended well beyond the young readers' immediate enjoyment of them, as Calvino himself often ackowledged. A rapid glance at the strips that appeared in the prime periodical for children, the *Corriere dei piccoli* is revealing. The 1930s issues are particularly interesting: they contain translations of American comics (most notably Maggie and Jiggs, and the Katzenjammer Kids) as well as the work of young Italian artists. Most successful among the latter was Sergio Tofano, the creator of 'il signor Bonaventura,' with his 'nero ombrello' (a 'black umbrella' we find blowing in the wind in the first story of *Le cosmicomiche*) and books under his arm; the character's name, Mr Goodluck, was not entirely ironic, since his adventures always ended with a fabulous win of one million liras (at 1930s value!). Tofano, who signed himself 'STO,' would become a writer of books, too, and was much admired by Calvino. The comics based on American material, in which new captions were written by Italians in place of the original ones, and, even more, the Italian strips used a curious mixture of language levels that hinted at their continuity with several types of Italian popular storytelling. Not excluding the ever influential *Pinocchio*, their models, used with parodistic tones, were the works of the epic and chivalric tradition of the *cantastorie* or balladeers (which were going to be combined with Ariosto's voice by Calvino), the *commedia dell'arte*, the puppet show, and the melodrama. Again, it is the style of storytelling that is the ground for Calvino's attention: the strips, within the ironclad limits imposed by the space available and the audience addressed, are visual, spare, humorous, and very much creatures of their time, in spite of their farcical archaisms and apparent disengagement. They too are the product of adult imagination, which finds in this genre a miraculous freshness thanks to the distancing effect that is the privilege of maturity. Their concision is functional to their effectiveness. They are perfect narrative machines, and that characteristic has guaranteed their inexhaustible success down to our day, when many Italians of all ages continue to read only comic strips. The wide public foreseen by the comic strip writer was made up of reading parents and grandparents, of older siblings and former aficionados too old to indulge overtly in such 'literature,' and, finally, of the children to whom the strips were supposedly directed. Writer and audience favoured a mixture of language levels, wacky pastiches, and a light-hearted reliance on pervasive irony.

The characters and adventures that fill the three volumes of *I nostri antenati* (Our Ancestors) and the Marcovaldo short stories are certainly indebted to the adventures and crowds of pseudo-aristocrats, capricious women, pesky children, and inept men that filled the comic strips. The language and rhetorical devices of Calvino's stories, after his brief fling with Neorealist modes, are – among other things – a revisitation, at a more refined technical level, of the melodramatic, conventional-poetic verse that the comic strip authors lifted from lesser chivalric poems and opera librettos. Most Italian comic strips, we must remember, used poetic forms such as rhyme, verse, and the quatrain. Rhetorical question marks often punctuated the narration, to create suspense and establish a direct connection with readers, a technique well known to storytellers, particularly when addressing an audience of children. As we said earlier, the names of the characters in any fiction are often markers of intertextuality, and in the comics published in the *Corriere dei piccoli* we find the prototypes of Calvinian characters: Ugone, who emulates Charlemagne's paladins (24:1–4 [January 1932]), a Petronilla (22:10 [9 March 1930]: 3); a Guendalina, some terrible children, frequent policemen (called 'gendarmi' in the *Corrierino*, in a Collodian vein), and a 'fonda buca scura' (22:14 [6 April 1930]: 1, for which see the end of 'I figli di Babbo Natale' [Santa's Children]); a 'Barbanegra pessimista, l'ottimista Zeffirino' (22:17 [27 April 1930]: 9; see *I racconti* 9–15); and a 'figlioletto – un po' debole di petto' (24:27 [3 July 1932]: 1, as in 'L'aria buona' [Clean Air]). By 1941, the comic strips in the *Corrierino* had become fewer, the loans from American authors were slowly disappearing because of censorship, and the new comic strips had become war propaganda. From then on, only three or four moments suggest Calvinian names and situations. There is the story of a comic character who eats a pigeon (34:2 [11 January 1942]: 1), for which see 'Il piccione comunale' (The City Pigeon). A Pin Focoso (Fiery Pin) goes skiing and is upstaged by the blond Lia (34:4 [25 January 1942]: 1): the name Lia appears in *La giornata d'uno scrutatore*, and the situation appears in 'L'avventura di uno sciatore' (The Adventure of a Skier). For an Abelardo, 'uomo di neve' (41:2 [9 January 1949]: 8), see ' La città smarrita nella neve' (The City Hidden in the Snow).

A vagabond and watcher in an all-inclusive realm of literature, Calvino metamorphosed into elements of a scenario of his own the suggestions that came from centuries of fiction. It is no wonder that he became more a storyteller than a novelist.

Myths and Folk-Tales

As he entered the fifties and the adventure of the Resistance receded into a past that was more and more problematical to retrieve, the still young Calvino began reflecting on what he was as a writer, and on the direction the world around him was taking. If the situation of literature had changed, as Jean-Paul Sartre, Elio Vittorini, and Nathalie Sarraute were asserting, Calvino -- being of a younger generation – found in that realization, which we have reason to believe he shared, a challenge and a sense of freedom. He always favoured new beginnings, hoping for the best even when expecting to be disappointed by events – as he repeated often in his fiction and essays. Being deeply involved in Italian cultural life as a journalist and editorial reader, he started writing essays that attracted attention. However, much as 'Il midollo del leone' (The Lion's Marrow), written in 1955, has been cited, praised, and attacked since then, not least because of its poetic qualities, no explicit mention has been made of the roots of its metaphor. The myth of Chiron the Centaur, the idealized teacher of an idealized pupil, Achilles, whom he fed with lion's marrow, has reappeared frequently in the poetic tradition since its Classical beginning and Rabelaisian rebirth. Most notably for Italian readers of Calvino's generation, Chiron is the protagonist in an ode by the eighteenth-century Italian poet and moralist Giuseppe Parini.[3] The genealogy of the image was not designed to endear Calvino to a new crop of intellectuals, who for a variety of conflicting ideological reasons were determined to bury the concept that literature in any way is inclined to connect with history or society. But the essay marked an important phase in Calvino's activity. In the resistance offered by the world to the dream of a new society synonymous with a new literature, the speaker found the incentive to make explicit his combative vision of life and writing. The image of the lion's marrow celebrated the concept of the sustenance to be found in literature, a concept that was at the core of the Western tradition but was rejected by those who saw and cheered the demise of humanism. In Calvino, the generous conception of litera-ture as a means of acting upon history by understanding 'the man of the future,' of providing him with a voice, an ethical impetus, and a way of looking at the world, paralleled the essayist's insistence on literature as dialogue. Calvino's imagined audience was the same one the Resistance had mythified, the young, the workers, and the peasants. Curiosity, hope, and wonderment formed the triad of emotions the author pro-jected onto those who turned to literature by opening a new book. The function of the writer, then, was the maternal-paternal function of the Centaur: to stimulate the imagination, nurture a rigorous morality, and strengthen the reader to master life's circumstances. As the author pro-claimed his refusal of an 'intellectual shrewdness [that is] withdrawn and allusive' ('furbizia intellettuale avara e allusiva'; *Una pietra sopra* 15), he placed his own voice in a line that went back to the origins of Italian literature, where the tension of ethical voluntarism nourished a profound, if implicit, pedagogical interest. The inheritors of that tradition closer in time to Calvino were an Alfieri, a Foscolo, and a Parini, who operated at a historical moment Calvino privileged, at the meeting point of the eighteenth and nineteenth centuries. Clearly, several factors contributed to defining the affinities that shaped the Calvinian voice. In serendipitous confluence, they were his family background, as he stated many times in spite of his protested dislike for personal reminiscing; historical junctures; and his readings. His posture vis-à-vis life and literature, serious yet livened by humour and ironic playfulness, not uncommitted yet careful to protect the essential quality of distance, would survive the historical-political context of the fifties and inform his literary and political views into the seventies and eighties. The coordinates of his universe remained basically the ones he traced early on, except for a more probabilistic view of the future: 'The literature we would like to see emerge, while keenly aware of the negatives that surround us, ought to express the same clear and active energy that prods the knights in the ancient ballads, or the explorers in the eighteenth-century travel journals' ('la letteratura che vorremmo veder nascere dovrebbe esprimere nella acuta intelligenza del negativo che ci circonda la volontà limpida e attiva che muove i cavalieri negli antichi cantari o gli esploratori nelle memorie di viaggio settecentesche'; *Una pietra sopra* 15).

The writing of the 1955 essay paralleled a work in which Calvino was engaged at that time, the rewriting of a selection of folk-tales drawn from the Italian dialectal tradition. In his preface to *Fiabe italiane* (*Italian Folktales*), he returned with muted accents to the substance of 'Il midollo del leone.' The treasure trove of stories he 'translated' firmed up, first of all, his criteria for style. When speaking of Perrault's work, he underlined his function as a writer: 'At last [he re-creates] on the page a precious equivalent [of the] folk-tale simplicity of tone' ('finalmente [ricrea] sulla carta un prezioso equivalente [della] semplicità di tono popolare'; *Fiabe italiane* vii). The French folk-tale seduced him with its 'play of imagination, elegant and tempered by the symmetries of a Cartesian rationality'('gioco di fantasia elegante e temperato di simmetrica razionalità cartesiana'; vii). The Italian folk-tale combined opposites, 'exact rhythm [and] light-hearted logic' ('esatto ritmo [e] allegra logica'; xxxii). In addition, his concern for a special audience he thought empathetic and immensely receptive was strengthened: 'I had to keep in mind the children who were going to read them, or who were going to be read to' ('ho dovuto tener conto dei bambini che le leggeranno o a cui saranno lette'; xxiv). Addressing a public, just as the oral storytellers had done, gave concreteness to his work, even though that contact was such as *he* wanted it, mediated by writing. Also essential was the folk-tale's confirmation that in literature a form of truth was available, a truth partial and never final, but truth nonetheless: 'Folk-tales are true' ('Le fiabe sono vere'; xii). They were sustenance for human beings, imagination as antidote to resignation, and a potential tool for that access to freedom that would become one of the recurrent motifs in Calvino's work. In that, a moral could be found: 'The true moral [of the folk-tale is that] the storyteller escapes [lack of freedom] and is able to speak of what is close to his heart' ('La sua [della fiaba] morale vera [è che] ... il narratore sfugge [alla mancanza di libertà] per parlarci di quel che gli sta a cuore'; xxxv). And Calvino concluded that, far from retreating into escapist dreams, the folk-tale demonstrated 'an awareness of one's situation that does not exclude imagining other destinies ... the power of a reality that is transformed totally into fantasy. Folk-tales could not give us a better lesson, both poetic and ethical' ('un'autocoscienza che non rifiuta l'invenzione d'un destino ... forza di realtà che interamente esplode in fantasia. Migliore lezione, poetica e morale, le fiabe non potrebbero darci'; xxxvi).

There is no doubt that Calvino liked to surprise his reader with paradoxes and contradictory assertions, which were sincere statements nonetheless. A good example is a later reconstruction he made of his encounter with the folk-tale, which seems to have come about as the result of a fortunate editorial initiative. Calvino's own scenario satisfied his perception of a search based on conscious choices: 'It was my need to stress the rational and contrived elements of storytelling, order and geometry, that pushed me in the direction of folk-tales' ('è stato il bisogno d'accentuare l'elemento razionale e volontario del racconto, l'ordine, la geometria a spingermi verso la fiaba'; 'I racconti che non ho scritto' [Stories I Have Not Written] 12). The folk-tales caused Calvino, the editing subject, to be absorbed into the story and become a presence in the flow of fantasy: 'I plunged into that submarine world without the weapon of professional harpoons, not provided with doctrinaire lenses, and not even supplied with that oxygen tank that is the enthusiasm ... for anything spontaneous and *naïf*' ('io m'immergevo in questo mondo sottomarino disarmato d'ogni fiocina specialistica, sprovvisto d'occhiali dottrinari, neanche munito di quella bombola d'ossigeno che è l'entusiasmo ... per ogni cosa spontanea e primitiva'; *Fiabe italiane* x). It is not unimportant that the metaphors, sustained for an entire paragraph, are the same we find, in explicit and implicit forms, in 'Pesci grossi, pesci piccoli' (Big Fish, Little Fish), 'L'avventura di un poeta' (The Adventure of a Poet), and *Palomar*. In all four texts, the plunging of the Calvinian characters into a hidden sea-world of disorder and murkiness aims at bringing back an ambivalent 'prey': the confirmation of the human desire to create order, bound to a continuously menaced but necessary pleasure.

Frequenting the records of oral storytelling, even though they were already translations into writing by earlier collectors, also showed Calvino the usefulness of the lively devices of 'spoken' narration, designed to create suspense and therefore curiosity – for instance, the well-known expression 'which I will tell you later' ('che dirò più in là'; x). And the effectiveness of choosing the perspective of a naïve narrator, a child or a speechless youth or a marginal adult, even in first-person narratives, is confirmed as the prime distancing device, essential to Calvino's approach to fiction: '*I* was that child' ('quel bambino ero io'; *Il visconte dimezzato* 26).

What of the pedagogic intent of children's literature? The Italian tradition, poor in works meant for young readers until well after the First World War, could rely only on the dialectal oral storytelling and on two nineteenth-century works, the already mentioned *Le avventure di Pinocchio,* and *Cuore* (1886) by Edmondo De Amicis. The latter has been the target of ferocious parodying over the years, because of a sentimental moralism that seemed to be the expression of a self-righteous bourgeoisie (the 'benpensanti'). *Cuore* was not a text made to please Calvino, who subscribed until the end to a fundamental statement he made in the mid-fifties on the relationship between moral and storytelling:

> The moral of the folk-tale is always implicit ... It is almost never insisted on in a sententious or pedagogic manner. And perhaps the moral function of telling stories ... is to be found not by looking to the content but in the very institution of the folk-tale, in the act of telling the tales or hearing them told ('la morale della fiaba è sempre implicita ... quasi mai vi s'insiste in forma sentenziosa o pedagogica. E forse la funzione morale che il raccontar fiabe ha ... va cercata non nella direzione dei contenuti ma nell'istituzione stessa della fiaba, nel fatto di raccontarle o d'udirle'; *Fiabe italiane* xxxv).

In the years after Fascism and the Resistance, a new (perhaps too brief) season began for Italian children's literature. The stories told by the new practitioners of the genre were whimsically realistic, rich in fantasy and nourishment, and, above all, well removed from 'the narrow world of convention' ('il mini-mondo di convenzione'; Rodari vi).

An Editor Named Tonio Cavilla

The sixties saw Calvino perfecting his disguises, from Amerigo Ormea the Watcher to a 'meticulous teacher and pedagogue' ('meticoloso docente e pedagogista'; preface to a 1965 school edition of *Il barone rampante* 4). Once, he chose a name that is a witty anagram, self-mockingly combining rusticity (Tonio) with slyness and even sophistry (Cavilla is linked to the word *cavillo*, which corresponds to 'quibble' and 'chicanery'). His alter egos were critical readers of every book written by Italo Calvino: they wrote prefaces for them, prepared blurbs for jacket flaps, drafted biographical notes, and penned various commentaries. At first, there was a naïve quality to these rereadings, as in the comments Calvino made about the changes in *Il sentiero dei nidi di ragno*: 'I thought that ... the readership would be a few hundred ... When I saw instead that so many people read it, the book changed aspect for me too' ('pensavo che ... avrebbe avuto un pubblico di poche centinaia di persone ... vedendo invece che lo leggeva tanta gente, il libro è anche cambiato di fronte ai miei occhi'; *Romanzi e racconti* I 1247). As if intrigued by his own artefacts, the writer/self-reader placed further distance between himself and the finished work, with analytical creative detachment. The themes and rhetorical figures of those early reflective texts convey the writer's malaise due to changing historical and cultural circumstances, as well as the pleasure he found in invention and dialogue. In 1980, in a less playful mood, he performed a similar review of his past production, when he edited the collection of essays entitled *Una pietra sopra*. In addition to the paratextual materials for his own books, and at times within them, Calvino wrote autobiographical texts – for instance, his responses to questions in an interview for *La generazione degli anni difficili* (The Difficult Years Generation), in 1962; 'La strada di San Giovanni' (The Road to San Giovanni), in 1964 (which was also the year of the by now famous preface to the school edition of *Il sentiero*); a manuscript note at the end of *Tarocchi*, in 1969; and the preface to *Gli amori difficili*, in 1970.

The backward look toward the first part of a life that already seemed quite remote was accompanied by the urge to gather all his writings in 'collections.' The writer-reader became his own dissatisfied editor, as he manipulated, cut, shuffled, and regathered existing and projected materials, in a restless pursuit of order. The publishing history of *Ultimo viene il corvo* (The Crow Comes Last) is an example of that phenomenon. Also, several themes returned again and again in the numerous interventions Calvino made in the first person (at times by interposed person), which defined the writer's consistent perception of his rapport with storytelling. First, he insisted on the impact of the changed circumstances on the direction taken by his imagination: 'It was the music in the air that had changed' ('Era la musica delle cose che era cambiata'; 1960 postfazione, *I nostri antenati* vi; see also the 1964 preface to *Il sentiero*, and numerous other conversations, letters, etc., now available in the five-volume 'I Meridiani' edition of Calvino's works). Then, he foregrounded the ethical dimension implicit in the texts, naming it the primary narrative theme in his vision – 'A person decides to choose difficult rules for himself, and follows them to their last consequences, because without them he would not be himself, neither for himself nor for others' ('una persona si pone volontariamente una difficile regola e la segue fino alle ultime conseguenze, perché senza di queste non sarebbe se stesso né per sé né per gli altri'; *Romanzi e racconti* I 1213) – where 'discipline' ('regola') has to do with an ethics of writing, and is increasingly embodied in stylistic constraints, as well as life choices. The ambiguity of the position of writer and text vis-à-vis existence was also a frequent theme: 'To be truly *with* other people, the only way is to be separated from them ... as is the vocation of poets, explorers, and revolutionaries' ('per essere *con* gli altri veramente, la sola via era d'essere separato dagli altri ... cosí come è vocazione del poeta, dell'esploratore, del rivoluzionario'; *Romanzi e racconti* I 1214. Calvino's emphasis). And finally there was the repeated assertion that the text finds its fruition in the reader's response; the ethical concerns ultimately dissolved in the storyteller's integrity and in the give-and-take of unforeseeable questions and answers from readers (*Romanzi e racconti* I 1219).

The intended interlocutors for many of these reflections were primarily young readers, who were closest to Calvino's heart, even though behind them, as always, were the adults who bought and perhaps read the books. The Bakhtinian concept of ideological horizon (for which see *The Formal Method*) finds here one of its most striking exemplifications, belying the supposed simplicity and disengagement of a literature that is designed to entertain. Calvino explicitly declared his desire to entertain – 'The one who must have fun is the reader' ('chi deve divertirsi è il lettore'; *I nostri antenati* xiv) – adding cheerfully that the game involved the writer, too. He laboured at fitting what he had written to the changes in the expected audience, carefully explaining how and why he did it, when he edited his own works for use in the classroom. He played with paradoxes, on the one hand stressing the control exerted by the author, and on the other hand 'opening' the text by throwing in offhand remarks that are familiar to conversation – 'You can go ahead and believe it, if you want' ('siete ... padroni di crederlo': *I nostri antenati* xv). However, fiction '*is not* gratuitous fantasy; it is anchored in time, space, and personal experience' ('*non* fantasia gratuita; ancorata nel tempo, nello spazio, nell'esperienza personale': 'I racconti che non ho scritto' 12. Calvino's emphasis). The triangular relationship writer/writer-reader/ reader never moved outside the realm of the 'written' ('scrittura'), but the dialogue was supposed to pursue the elaboration, initiated by the text, of a multitude of elements: sociohistorical factors, linguistic matters, free play of the imagination, communication through the literary forms that existed before the user in any given culture, and the (only apparently) paradoxical goal of a simple and clear organization of multiplicity. In his preface to a book written by schoolchildren, *I quaderni di San Gersolè* (The Notebooks of San Gersolè), Calvino expressed his admiration for those qualities of the book he found congenial: precision of expression, cool objectivity in the description of a world in the process of being discovered, and an absolute absence of sentimentality. He saw in *I quaderni* the genuine, choral chronicle of a Tuscan village. However much his situation and perspectives may have changed in later years, his dialogue with the young pursued through the written page never ceased, because he found in that portion of the reading public what he prized, seriousness in play, lack of sentimentalism in sorrow, and directness in the use of language. To those same things he felt that most adults and their whole consumerist society had become insensitive.

In a question-and-answer interview about the characteristics and place of textbooks, Calvino stressed the complexity of his position and his enduring concern with young people, by placing his own voice in the company of the best comics: 'My pedagogic ideal, when I published this series of short stories [*Marcovaldo*] as a children's book ... was an education to pessimism, which is the true message one can draw from the great humourists' ('Il mio ideale pedagogico, quando pubblicai come libro per l'infanzia questa serie di storielle ... era quell'educazione al pessimismo che è il vero senso che si può ricavare dai grandi umoristi'; *Romanzi e racconti* I 1367). In the same breath, his self-as-commentator reiterated that 'the moral postures also, such as the individualism based on will-power that animates Alfieri's life, return in this work almost as caricatures made by a distorting mirror' ('Anche gli atteggiamenti morali (l'individualismo fondato sulla volontà, che anima la vita dell'Alfieri) qui ci ritornano come caricaturati da uno specchio deformante'; *Il barone rampante* 7). In fact, the only essential element of storytelling, he said, was and remained the image that originated it (*Il barone rampante* 1965, 10).

'These are times that are not favourable to totalizing interpretations of the world, or to great novels' ('Questi sono tempi poco propizi alle grandi spiegazioni del mondo come ai grandi romanzi'; 'I racconti che non ho scritto' 11) – so asserted Calvino in 1959, well before the Lyotard pamphlet described the root sources of the postmodern condition. He added that what fiction needed was to focus on objects close at hand, and on limited biological and archaeological details, the eye of an ant or a fossil vertebra, things on which something could eventually be built. And in fact, nothing can be more useful in tracing the transformations undergone by the various components of the Calvinian universe, including the writer, than the evolution of its animal inhabitants. Well before Calvino engaged in the rewriting of Italian folk-tales, his pages were filled with the presence of small creatures from the domestic realm, those that are not particularly appealing to grown-ups but are the favourites of children because of their size, liveliness, and whimsical shapes: ants, crickets, spiders, bees, snails, toads, and fish. In the short stories written in the forties, the animals inhabit a natural world where human beings are interlopers, often destructive and usually alien, as in 'Il bosco degli animali' (The Animals' Woods). Then, increasingly, the animal world becomes more sparse and is enclosed in an urban environment, as in a short story written in 1948 ('Il gatto e il poliziotto' [The Cat and the Policeman]); with the Marcovaldo stories, the animal world becomes a pretext for human daydreams about lost natural paradises, even though the animals are as estranged from a hypothetical wilderness and as actually bound to an artificial environment as any other city dweller. By the sixties, the Animal, having traversed all the eras of cosmic events, has become an integral part of the human consciousness, to be acknowledged and tamed, in true Calvinian fashion. As he looked at a Carpaccio painting of St Jerome and the lion, Calvino mused:

> The theme at the heart of these scenes is the relationship with a wild animal ... perhaps the animal we carry within ourselves that changes shapes with every change in our lives ... A major step will be to accept that presence ...

what haunts us as a biological inheritance descended from our species and the species before ours, the dark side of our collective and individual history. We must change it into our living and suffering shadow, come to a pact with nature inside and outside our selves, and transform the destructive impulses into strength, as the lion that accompanies the wise old man ('il motivo di fondo di queste scene è il rapporto con un animale feroce ... forse l'animale che portiamo in noi stessi e che cambia forma nelle epoche della nostra vita ... Il grande passo sarà accettare questa presenza, ... ciò che incombe su di noi come eredità biologica della specie e delle specie che ci hanno preceduti, come parte oscura della nostra storia collettiva e individuale, farne una nostra ombra vivente e dolorosa, stabilire un patto con la natura dentro e fuori di noi, trasformarne le pulsioni distruttive in una forza, come il leone del savio vegliardo'; unpublished, 1973; *Album Calvino* [A Calvino Album] 283).

The Games of the Magician and the Temptations of the Writer

The seventies opened with Calvino's rewriting of Ariosto's *Orlando furioso*, and continued with an intense series of contacts with the reading public through participation in radio programs, prefaces to volumes of the most diverse authors (for instance, an inspired and personal introduction to a bilingual edition of Xenophon's *Anabasis*), letters to his critics, and introductions to catalogues for art exhibitions. There also continued to be collections of fables for children, such as *L'uccel belverde* (The Bird Named Handsome Green, 1972), and *Il principe granchio* (The Crab Prince, 1974). Among the many prefaces, the most enlightening for us is the one written for Ovid's *Metamorphoses* (1979), which describes well Calvino's vision of the function of storytelling in the world's multiplicity:

> The *Metamorphoses* aim at representing all that it is possible to narrate ... *without making choices among possible keys for interpretation* – as is appropriate given the ambiguous quality of myths ... *accepting within the poem all the possible stories*. The author of the *Metamorphoses* can be sure in this way that *he is not serving a partial goal but rather the multiplicity of life* ('Le Metamorfosi vogliono rappresentare l'insieme del raccontabile ... *senza decidere* – secondo l'ambiguità propriamente mitica – *tra le chiavi di lettura possibili* ... *accogliendo nel poema tutti i racconti*. L'autore delle *Metamorfosi* sarà *sicuro di non servire un disegno parziale ma la molteplicità vivente*'; *Perché leggere i classici* 40–1. Emphasis added).

Calvino was a well-established writer, and he increasingly involved himself in the literary and cultural life of his times, as if wanting to draw on all its resources in all their variety. For instance, in 1978 he participated with educators, psychiatrists, and psychoanalysts in a conference whose title contained three key words, 'Creativity, Instruction, and Culture.' His intervention focused on the function and characteristics of the Author, and gave a shorthand preview of what he was writing at that moment, the novel that was to become *Se una notte d'inverno un viaggiatore*. The central theme of the talk, entitled 'Il romanzo e il suo suggeritore' (The Novel and Its Prompter), is the lack of 'originality' of the individual writer (Calvino says 'poet'). Each act of poiesis, or individual poetic creation, originates in a pre-existing mass of elements for which the individual is a new conduit, synthesizer, and interpreter. Calvino was very fond of these concepts and returned to them in a more coherent and peremptory way in a 1980 dialogue with Tullio Pericoli. He asserted that reading is an appropriation, and writing its logical follow-up. Or, as he put it more vividly, 'There is theft with breaking and entering in every true reading' ('c'è un furto con scasso in ogni vera lettura'; *Saggi* II 1808).

Those were fertile years for him, informed by current theoretical thinking and also rich in successful fiction publishing. There is no doubt that the structuralists (first among them Claude Lévi-Strauss, and, even more, as subtle a theoretician/artist as Roland Barthes), as well as the reader-oriented or reception theorists, greatly fascinated Calvino. However, we must keep in proper perspective the connections between his involvement in the ferment of ideas and theories surrounding him and his continuing elaboration of personal concepts of authorship, reception, and the characteristics and function of storytelling. What is often forgotten is that actual artistic realizations contain the seeds of reflection, and are the basis for the elaboration of theoretical systems. The family air shared by ideas, or theory, and fiction, or praxis, is the evidence that a writer's elaboration of a point of view has been given wider currency. Calvino, like writers and artists of all times, often anticipated what was about to be theorized. His writing is 'a game of today that is aware of structuralism's discoveries and combinatorics, but blends with them imagination and poetic invention' ('un gioco d'oggi, che conosce le scoperte strutturaliste e le possibilità combinatorie, ma che a queste unisce fantasia e invenzione poetica'; *Tarocchi* 14). In the seventies, his image of an audience is shaped by anthropological metaphors, where tribes are entranced by storytellers who are the conduits and elaborators

of tribal mythologies; his vision of creativity is informed by the termi-
nology and suggestions of cybernetics (he had already given a talk in
1967 entitled 'Cibernetica e fantasmi' [Cybernetics and Ghosts], which
is now an essay in *Una pietra sopra*). Calvino loved hypotheses, games
played with seriousness, and multiple possibilities. Whether he spun
images around the theoretical constructs of structuralism, semiotics, or
the postmodern, he was fundamentally an explorer, an experimentor
who tested independently all the materials he had available, while
maintaining a distance from whatever he observed. His name may have
been added to the membership lists of several movements, but there is
no evidence of his subscribing to an implicit or explicit faith in the uni-
versality of the human spirit, or to a belief in the total dissolution of the
individual consciousness.

Here is an intriguing example of the independence of fictional artefacts from theoretical principles, and also of their parallelisms. Recalling
a letter Calvino had sent her, Maria Corti once observed, 'Calvino is
keen on looking in depth at issues pertaining to the construction of each
of his texts' ('a Calvino preme approfondire ogni questione strutturale
riguardante la costruzione di ogni suo testo'; Corti 1990, 140). Corti's is
an accurate statement, although coloured by her own interests as a theo-
retician accustomed to strict codifications. A further passage in the same
letter leads us to an understanding of a Calvinian technique. Calvino,
referring to Corti's allusion to the surrealistic quality of the endings in
his later series of Marcovaldo short stories, stated in his letter, that he
was using a technique that belonged to 'a *wider formal category, a final
sweeping vision crowded with objects,* an opening up of the visual field into
a minutely detailed panoramic view that may be surrealistic or not'
('*una categoria formale più estesa* di *quadro finale visionario gremito di figure,*
di allargarsi del campo visivo a una panoramica minuziosa, che può
essere surreale o non esserlo'; 140. Calvino's emphasis). The comment
fits precisely the long shot at the end of 'I figli di Babbo Natale,' but
could apply as well to the endings of 'L'avventura di una bagnante'
(The Adventure of a Swimmer), 'L'avventura di un poeta,' 'La formica
argentina' (The Argentine Ant), and *Il barone rampante.* That technique,
which is often combined with another stylistic device typical of Calvino,
chaotic enumeration, is also the implicit foundation for the descriptions
in *Le città invisibili* and *Se una notte d'inverno un viaggiatore.* On the other
hand, in *La pensée sauvage* we find a passage that suggests a possible
direction for the analysis and interpretation of such a technique. Lévi-
Strauss speaks of a pictorial technique that he defines as 'an illusion that

gratifies intelligence and sensibility' ('illusion qui gratifie l'intelligence et la sensibilité'; Lévi-Strauss 35). He is speaking of the miniaturization of reality that is common in the works of painters and artisans (33–6), a technique that – in the anthropologist's mind – has the specific effect of producing

> a sort of reversal of the process of knowledge. *In order to apprehend the object in its totality,* we always tend to address each part separately. The resistance offered by the object is overcome by its division. The reduction in scale overturns the situation: the totality of the object appears less redoutable, as it is reduced in size, and *the fact of its quantitative reduction makes it seem qualitatively simpler. More precisely, this quantitative transposal augments and diversifies our power over the homologue of the real object.* Through its homologue, *the object can be appropriated ... apprehended with a single glance* ('une sorte de renversement du procès de la connaissance: *pour connaître l'objet réel dans sa totalité,* nous avons toujours tendance à opérer depuis ses parties, la résistance qu'il nous oppose est surmontée en la divisant. *La réduction d'échelle renverse cette situation: plus petite, la totalité de l'objet apparaît moins redoutable; du fait d'être quantitativement diminuée, elle nous semble qualitativement simplifiée. Plus exactement, cette transposition quantitative accroît et diversifie notre pouvoir sur un homologue de la chose;* à travers lui, *celle-ci peut être saisie, ... appréhendée d'un seul coup d'oeil';* Lévi-Strauss 34–5. Emphasis added).

Calvino's pursuit of simplicity and control in the midst of chaotic complexity may have found one of its forms of realization in a device akin to the one observed by Lévi-Strauss: thus he created the minutely detailed images that bring closure to a number of his fictional texts.

Calvino's activity, then, proceeded on three fronts: he paid close attention to the work of other art practioners, he wrote fictions in which he demonstrated technical virtuosity, and he further elaborated some of his favourite images, following what he called a 'discipline of greater rigour and austerity, however hidden behind the screens of irony and paradox' ('una lezione di rigore più essenziale e severa, sia pur dietro lo schermo ironico del paradosso'; *La memoria del mondo* 8).

Actually, one must not 'read' Calvino's books, but play along with his fantasy: that was the lesson of his fiction. The trilogy *I nostri antenati* had been not so much a reappropriation of a tradition as a challenge to a certain way of 'seeing' literary eras and stylistic conventions, time and space, narration as invention and narration as manipulation. When

Calvino took his readers on a more distant journey, along the light-years of the universe's evolution, cosmic consciousness had to be an intensely individual anthropomorphic presence, even before acquiring any form. The first spark of consciousness had to be an urge to look for, and see, what is 'other,' hidden, invisible but necessarily there; it had to be a leap of the imagination. The themes of estrangement and obstinate search were projected against the background of a vastly expanded grid of time/space coordinates. The only stance the writer found conceivable for a reflection on the immense questions raised by a universe of which the boundaries stretch further and further away as we learn more about it, was the comic stance. While Pascal's monologue reached out from an abyss of anguish, the voice of *Le cosmicomiche*, sensuous and mellow, involves the reader in a dialogue, in discursive and humorous storytelling sessions. The cosmic consciousness in its changing habitat speaks through storytelling, for it is the storyteller who is the rightful inhabitant of the cosmos and its eras. No god interferes; and the history of a dark and chaotic universe becomes a collection of stories, a myriad of probabilistic interpretations of the universe's experience.

As he gained in virtuosity, Calvino enjoyed nonchalantly flaunting his tricks, as he did in *Il castello dei destini incrociati*, for the greater joy of critics and literary theorists. He had considered the tarots ideal illustrations for his collection of folk-tales (*Fiabe italiane* xxxv), but he had had to abandon the idea at the time of that project. A favourable set of circumstances allowed him to go back to it and play with a set of tarots, in one of his most elaborate handiworks equally divided between structuring and inventing. That tells us something about the stubborn persistence of his plans, and confirms Northrop Frye's assertion that 'every poet has his own distinctive structure of imagery, which usually emerges even in his earliest work, and which does not and cannot essentially change' (*Critical Path* 1971, 22).

What attracted Calvino to the tarots was not their connection with magic, but the patina of history and the mystery of mythologies that had settled on those decks of cards, as well as their receptiveness to being shuffled and interpreted a seemingly infinite (and yet necessarily finite) number of times. Through the centuries, as in a solitary theatrical performance, each card reproduced with ever more static and laconic impassivity the faces of humanity's obsessions, ideas, dreams, fears, and ideals. The players, looking at the hand they had been dealt, could reread each time ancient stories with unchanged characters, and interpret them to fit their own stories. From India or China, and from Italy's fifteenth-century courts to clubs and taverns in later times, and on to our own time, fond of evasion and thirsty for prophecy, the tarots perpetuated the Game. The cards were there, ready to be picked up, and Calvino's new game took shape using old ingredients: the woods, the castle, a heterogeneous crowd around a table, and the silence of private obsessions. The protagonist had reached the hub of the forest, the heart of the labyrinth, only apparently by chance. It was the telling of stories that had called to him and had drawn him there. He found himself – perhaps by discovering, thanks to the writer's memory and inventiveness, forgotten meanings, lost correspondences, and all sorts of narrative options for his task, from the fable to the quest, and from the *conte philosophique* to the comic and epic poems.

Creation is nothing casual, as Calvino reminded one of his readers with some of the most amusing expressions of irritation and temper he ever displayed in writing. Angelo Guglielmi had had the unfortunate idea of suggesting (*Romanzi e racconti* II 1390–1) that Calvino may have made certain choices inadvertently in *Se una notte d'inverno un viaggiatore*. The documentation available is proof, on the contrary, of the long gestation and even longer reflection that preceded each one of Calvino's texts. The writer was concerned not only with expression, but also with the elaboration of more and more controlled forms to meet the expectations of the reader who was awaiting the book. The appropriate metaphor for writing was the thread, a filament wound in ever more elaborate knots, to challenge the eye that sees it and unwinds it by reading. The collaboration between writer and reader was a new Ariadne's stratagem, and fiction was defined as a writing of stories elicited by the reader who desired to read them.

However, we must not fall for the Author's programmatic assurances and metanarrative constructs. His declared availability and openness are to a large extent the tricks of a sorcerer. After all, Calvino did not admire poets like Ariosto just because of their skill and imagination. 'Atlas, or Ariosto? The role of the sorcerer ... and the role of the poet ... overlap until they become indistinguishable. The fair of illusions is the palace, the poem, the entire world' ('Atlante o Ariosto? La parte dell'incantatore ... e la parte del poeta ... si sovrappongono fino a identificarsi. La giostra delle illusioni è il palazzo, è il poema, è tutto il mondo'; *Italo Calvino racconta l'Orlando Furioso* [Italo Calvino Retells *Orlando Furioso*] 80–1). Concern with the audience and awareness of one's own gift for storytelling, the pleasure of awakening and, yes, manipulating the readers' emotions, are powerful persuaders for the writer to metamorphose into a magician. We can sense the shifting mood, from pedagogical to incantatory and vice versa, in a passage from one of Calvino's best interviews:

I ... am dreaming of a periodical that would be completely different, not theoretical or technical, and not for the usual three or four specialists, but above all for a different public, a magazine with serial fictions, like those that Dickens and Balzac published. True writers also would write for it, they would write on command (I am a firm believer in writing on command). Through that magazine we would reclaim the true function of a rapport with the public: to weep, to laugh, to be frightened, to discover adventure and enigmas ... And many sections would exemplify diverse narrative strategies, character types, reading modes, stylistic traditions, and anthropological-poetic functions, all through stories that are fun to read. In short, it would be a type of research done with the tools of popularization. Celati says that you must not give lessons to anyone, that we cannot act as pedagogues. But I believe that, through showing these things to other people, perhaps we would get to understand them, too' ('Io ... sogno una rivista tutta diversa non speculativa o tecnica, non per quattro gatti), diversa come pubblico innanzitutto: una rivista di romanzi a puntate come quelle che facevano Dickens, Balzac. Anche qui dovrebbero scrivere scrittori veri, scrivere su commissione (io credo molto allo scrivere su commissione), attraverso questa rivista ritrovare le funzioni vere d'un rapporto col pubblico: il piangere, il ridere, la paura, l'avventura, l'enigma ... E molte rubriche che esemplificano strategie narrative, tipi di personaggi, modi di lettura, istituzioni stilistiche, funzioni poetico-antropologiche, ma tutto attraverso cose divertenti da legggere. Insomma un tipo di ricerca fatto con gli strumenti della divulgazione. Ma Celati dice che non bisogna fare la lezione a nessuno, non si può tenere un atteggiamento pedagogico. Invece io credo che spiegando queste cose agli altri forse riusciremmo a capirle anche noi'; Camon 1973, 191).

What Calvino said to Camon places in context, and helps us to analyse, the fictional text that decreed Calvino's success beyond the Italian readership, *Se una notte d'inverno un viaggiatore*. It is not surprising that the Italian writer attained fame in the English-speaking world with that novel, since the discourse on the postmodern was becoming a dominant feature of North American creative and critical life. The novel 'obstreperously proclaims its participation in the postmodern aesthetics of simulation, textual spectacle, masquerade and self-reflexive excess' (de Lauretis 1989, 131). Actually, Calvino had long been operating in the postmodern mode, consciously although less overtly. He delighted in using his talent for masterful *bricolage*, game playing, and grid constructing, moving back and forth from creative pleasure to tongue-in-cheek insistence on quotation; he emphasized the self-referentiality of the text, and created multimedia narratives, playing with a variety of structuring strategies. In 1975, commenting on the artefacts shown at an exhibition, he objectified his own project: 'The writer, looking at them, can already read the beginnings of innumerable volumes, that library of apocryphal texts he would like to write' ('Lo scrittore guardandole già riesce a leggere gli incipit d'innumerevoli volumi, la biblioteca d'apocrifi che vorrebbe scrivere'; 'La squadratura' [The Squaring], *Saggi* II 1990). His complex background and commitment to planning and 'discipline' found a congenial echo in some of postmodernism's statements. These are contradictory at times, but no matter which definition of postmodernism one selects,[4] certain recurring themes are part of it. First of all, there is the ambiguity of the postmodern historical positioning. Andreas Huyssen writes, 'As the word "postmodernism" already indicates, what is at stake is a constant, even obsessive, negotiation with the terms of the modern itself' (Huyssen x). While self-reflexivity is variously defined either as modern or as postmodern, the past – for the postmodern – is not certainty of origins but an occasion for reminiscence, a spectacle of ruins, a storehouse yielding the fragments that are endlessly reordered in repetitive narratives. On the other hand, the future holds no promise of resolution. The ground of conventions has shifted, becoming an unsafe basis for any durable structure that in Horace's words was 'monumentum aere perennius' (*Opera* 100). Character representation has gone from a subjective to a functional mode, having been compromised by the crisis of the self and the problematical legitimation of knowledge. It follows that the postmodern can only revisit the past without innocence, disbelieving all social constructs, of which literature is one, and using them in ways necessarily playful and ironic. Finally, the postmodern operation is dependent on the presence of an audience, preferably endowed with a shared cultural and textual competence, but naïve nonetheless. All this could not be foreign to the writer whose work we have been examining up to now.

However, something dry and sterile, like preciosity, threatened Calvino's texts, as he engaged in a frenzy of experimentation. If one accepts E. Ann Kaplan's distinction between a 'utopian' and a 'commercial' or 'co-opted' postmodernism, where the latter is a fashionable trend and the former revalues the body and rejects a binary world-view, then the 1969–79 Calvinian season, with its extraordinary outcomes, wavered between the two. It hesitated between virtuosity, 'relishing ... the eternal recurrence of dejà-vu' (Huyssen 182), and the search for a way to prove the intelligibility of chaos. Calvino's *bricolage* was in some ways counter-productive, and Calvino himself later complained about the reductionist readings he had helped to foster, as the formal components of his texts were dissected by critics. In the Calvinian universe, the body, physical immanence, and the literary text always mattered. Writing, for him, was not a simulation model developed by a computer, detached from actualization in history. Calvino's pen had intercepted early, as if it were the sensitive point of a seismograph, the changes in its sociocultural environment; but his awareness of a 'crisis of tools' and of the wider crisis of his culture did not induce a postmodern indifference in him. The text's pleasure and its worth, for Calvino, had to do with the interpenetration of style and ethics. Language and the senses continued to interact, in a stubborn and spare dialogue, in spite of the apparent collapse of the old order. Calvino's characters continued to be entrusted with the task of chronicling the ongoing search for a new contact with the 'real,' however uncertain.

What does Calvino do in *Se una notte d'inverno un viaggiatore*, that over-analysed fictional tour de force? One of the many titles planned for it was: 'Here the Adventure Begins' – 'Qui comincia l'avventura' – which was the consecrated first sentence of Tofano's Signor Bonaventura comic strips, still echoing like a refrain, and almost a mantra, in all his readers' heads. The ironic dimension of what he was writing and his masterful caricaturing of all theories and practices of fiction, narrative, and the novel have not been given sufficient importance. His was no ponderous demonstration of theoretical perspectives; the 'obstreperous' quality of it tells us as much. Perhaps the most humorous sleight-of-hand of *Se una notte d'inverno un viaggiatore* is the resurrection of the Author, with a capital *A* and an aggressive 'masculine' profile. The Author is definitely not dead; as a matter of fact, since the ideal reader, the one who reads in a disinterested way, for pure pleasure, is female, the male readership is reduced to a pale figure, admonished, pushed and pulled and bullied by the authorial voice that turns from instruction to manipulation and sarcasm. So much for dialogue! Is it a wonder that the story would veer toward eroticism, and an arranged marriage? The (male) reader is a tool in the seduction of the (female) reader; he is a convenient 'obstacle' in a triangular love affair, which, in good literary form, unfolds through a written text. The female presence used to be called 'Muse' by Classic and Romantic alike, but here she is desire, the embodiment of a capricious and insatiable passion for reading that stimulates the writer's prolificacy, by helping him overcome his moments of impotence. And to think that this author is a brother, or perhaps the double, of the author who said, 'How beautifully I would write if I were not there! ('Come scriverei bene se non ci fossi!'; 'Al di là dell'autore' [Beyond the Author] 128), leading the more credulous among his readers to list him as a member in the band of those who were mourning the Death of the Author.

Let us return to style, and pedagogy. The writer is in a perverse mood: the freedom he offers his readers is illusory, he knows it and gloats, as he displays virtuoso variations on his basic motifs, as in a magician's show. His is the world of monologue disguised as dialogue, of make-believe, tricks, and cheerful authoritarianism, where the pleasure of the text is ambiguously shared. This is the clearest evidence of the profound impact a historical period often linked with Calvino's name, the Enlightenment, exerted on the writer's formation.[5] A conflicted 'faith in reason' is inseparable from a disenchanted view of human ventures and adventures, and of the vagaries of a probabilistic universe. No metaphysical perspective forms a backdrop for the Calvinian text; ever since the young writer drafted his first apologues, he showed Christian principles in fundamental conflict with the institution of religion. The stern requirements of a 'religious ethics without religion' ('un'etica religiosa senza religione'; Romanzi e racconti I 1212) seemed to be his only foundation.[6] The literary game is a rigorous game, played for the passion of the suspense, and to teach the pessimism of the intellect, the same lesson that Candide and Pinocchio once learned (Bàrberi-Squarotti 1976, 105). The ideas and world-vision of the Enlightenment were accompanied by all-important lessons about the elaboration of a style. Denis Diderot ('our brother,' Calvino called him in an article published in La Repubblica in 1984)[7] was a supreme practitioner and teacher of cat-and-mouse games, particularly in Jacques le fataliste et son maître, 'his antinovel-metanovel-hypernovel' ('il suo antiromanzo-metaromanzo-iperromanzo'; 'Il gatto e il topo' [The Cat and the Mouse]). The central importance of storytelling, the distancing devices, the abrupt interruptions of the textual flow, the comical buffeting of a mesmerized reader, the changes in textual direction, the false open-endedness, the peremptory orders given a hapless listener, and the utter disregard for, or rather the flaunting of, the obviousness of it all, these are examples that Calvino found in this exhilarating reading and took to heart. Deception is indeed the basis of literature; the writer/narrator/editor is a puppeteer who must elicit the public's curiosity, keep its attention, and manage to share with it his or her own pleasure, while manipulating the direction the whole enterprise will take. The surreal show is the assertion, in a world of constraints, that only artistic expression can break the bonds of determinism, and teach at the same time how dark the human condition is and where the possibility of freedom can be found. Perhaps speaking for himself, Calvino wrote: 'Diderot had intuitively seen that it is from the most rigidly deterministic worldviews that one can draw the impetus toward individual freedom. As if free will and choice could be operative only when they break through the hard rock of necessity' ('Diderot aveva intuito che è proprio dalle concezioni del mondo più rigidamente deterministe che si può trarre una carica propulsiva per la libertà individuale, come se volontà e libera scelta possano essere efficaci solo se aprono i loro varchi nella dura pietra della necessità'; 'Il gatto e il topo'). Style of life and style of writing find their description in this prose that relies on the orchestration of familiar concepts and words: determinism, freedom, leap forward, will, free choice, passages, rock, and necessity. Yet neither aesthetic autonomy nor a confusion between literature and life found favour with Calvino. The boundaries remained intact between the two equally essential and contiguous dimensions of the human experience: 'Only the white margin between life and book marks the book's limit, and the boundary of life' ('Solo il margine bianco tra vita e libro segna un confine al libro, e alla vita'; *Romanzi e racconti* II 1400).

Preparing the Future

For those who saw in Calvino's later writings, particularly *Palomar*, the expression of a dark vision of life, the very last words he wrote are a clear denial. Not only did he turn his eyes toward the future, but the next millennium opened up before his imagination as a realm full of potential for the flourishing of literature. Explicit concern for the future was not something he expressed on isolated occasions. In 1977, distressed by the political and social turmoil racking Italy, he had written an editorial in the *Corriere della sera* entitled 'Our Next 500 Years' ('I nostri prossimi 500 anni'). That was his political statement, firmly rooted in a conception of life as 'discipline ... firmness ... and rigour, more profoundly liberating than any libertarian wishfulness' ('disciplina ... fermezza ... severità, più sostanzialmente liberatrici di qualsiasi velleità libertaria'; *Saggi* II 2299). The 'memos' he drafted in 1985 for his favourite audience, the young, elaborated the same themes, which were now transferred to the domain of that 'written world' he could claim as his own. He had always seen writing as a discipline, even to the point of accepting a sort of playful invitation by Umberto Eco, who had praised the classical exercises practised and hated by all Italian schoolchildren, to write summaries ('Elogio del riassunto'). Twelve writers took up Eco's challenge, and wrote fifteen-line summaries of famous novels. The twelve included Calvino, who chose *Robinson Crusoe*, and then wrote comments on the initiative in a brief article entitled 'Come to the Point!' ('Poche chiacchiere!' 1982). No task was too elementary for him, when it came to studying the techniques of that technology he saw as fundamental in human experience. As he had said, there was 'something to be saved, and only writing in a certain mode (a style) could do it' ('qualcosa da salvare, e solo lo scrivere in un certo modo (uno stile) può farlo'; *I nostri antenati*; now in *Romanzi e racconti* I 1221).

The effort to acquire technical mastery could turn into an empty exercise, and Calvino was well aware of it. In one of his prefaces, reflecting on the commitment to technical precision demonstrated by Xenophon in his tale about a routed army returning home (certainly a familiar and painful reminder for all those who had lived through the Second World War), he reminisced about the dilemmas of his youth, divided between a 'moral all involved in "technique" and "pragmatics" and the awareness of the void gaping under them. But even now that it seems so far removed from the spirit of the times, I find that it had its positive side' ('morale tutta "tecnica" e "pragmatica" e la coscienza del vuoto che si apriva sotto. Ma ancora adesso, che sembra tanto lontana dallo spirito dei tempi trovo che aveva la sua parte di buono'; *Anabasis* 8–9). We may be justified in saying that Montale's and Hemingway's models had found their uneasy truce in Calvino's oeuvre.

Shortly before his death, Calvino returned to the (apparently) simplest exercise, of observing and describing the world's multiplicity through its objects ('The Written and the Unwritten World' 39). A new image of the writer now paralleled the new focus of his writing. Whether being interviewed by schoolchildren (13 May 1983) or writing for the Italian dailies the short pieces that would be collected in the *Palomar* volume, the Calvinian persona increasingly chose understatement and a sly humility. 'The Writer? He Is an Idiot Like Flaubert' reads the title of the 1983 interview. 'Why do you write?' asked the children. And he, after answering that he was not good at anything else, continued in a more serious vein: 'It's a way to be oneself and to communicate ... to become an instrument for something that is certainly greater than I am, which is the way men see, reflect, judge, and express the world; to filter it, and put it back in circulation' ('è un modo per realizzarsi e comunicare ... farmi strumento di qualcosa che è certamente più grande di me e che è il modo con cui gli uomini guardano, commentano, giudicano, esprimono il mondo: farlo passare attraverso di me e rimetterlo in circolazione': 'Lo scrittore? È un idiota come Flaubert' 1). That dialogue with young interviewers yielded a sort of testament, touching on literature's function as entertainment as a matter of social responsibility; on fun as serious business; on Calvino's own constitutional lack of talent for introspection and explorations of the irrational; and on life, which 'is not rosy, but precisely because of that is our element' ('non è rosa ma proprio per quello è il nostro elemento'; 20).[8]

The publication of *Palomar* had been long in the making. Ten years earlier, in 1973, Calvino had expressed a need or desire that he had finally satisfied: to work at 'the intersection of a certain abstract, deductive way of building a story ... and a mode of accretion of experiential details, a painstaking description of objects, and places, and gestures' ('il punto d'incontro tra un certo modo astratto, deduttivo, di costruire il racconto ... e un modo d'accumulazione di particolari dell'esperienza, di descrizione minuziosa di oggetti e luoghi e atti'; Camon 1973, 186). During the late seventies, he began writing isolated pieces that had the same protagonist, a Mr Palomar. The eye of an older and socially more 'respectable' avatar of Marcovaldo turned all his energies, drained as they were, toward intercepting signals outside all codices, as he focused his attention 'only on those things that [fell] under his gaze in his everyday life' ('solo sulle cose che gli capitano sotto gli occhi nella vita quotidiana'; *Palomar*, blurb).

Ultimately, it is again through writing that the writer plots the capture of each instant, in another 'hare and wolf' game[9] with space and time. The telling of the story of Mr Palomar's experiences is again delegated to an extradiegetic narrator, as was the telling in *Marcovaldo*. The writer is in the wings, invisible yet in total control, and the exploration of the apparently simple (one wave of the sea, one blade of grass in the lawn) is constructed by him as a form of ascetic exercise, an *askesis* available to the secular human being thirsty for understanding. Silence is one of the tools in that progression, and a simulation of death is Mr Palomar's ruse 'to see how the world goes on without him' ('per vedere come va il mondo senza di lui'; *Palomar* 121). As for the narrator, he has the last word; it can be assumed that he is going to continue his lonely search, since he is the one who closes the series of episodes with a brief announcement of the character's disappearance.

Much has been said about the watcher who is Mr Palomar, and the possible interpretations of his functions in the text and in Calvino's oeuvre. Little has been said, on the contrary, about the environment in which he operates (or fails to operate). Calvino, without explicitly calling attention to it, insists on placing Mr Palomar in a very clearly connoted social milieu, the universe surrounding a well-to-do bourgeoisie.[10] The deceptive placidity of that lifestyle, with its afternoon pauses on a city deck filled with plants, its strolls along the beach in the evenings, its visits to well-stocked butcher and cheese shops, and its trips abroad, again suggests this work's closeness to the paradoxical atmosphere of the Pirandellian universe. The dull comfort of an existence devoid of surprises is as far as one can be from postmodern hyper-reality. Its dailiness, just as in Pirandello's 'bourgeois dramas,' suggests the depth of the abyss that threatens to open up under its surface. Unlike the plots of the fiction and dramas of the first half century, the Calvinian 'plot' does not require sudden crises (unexpected pregnancies, earthquakes, and duels) to allow for the protagonists' coming to awareness. There is no plot in *Palomar*. The historical flow seems to have been almost stilled. As in other writers of the century, the issue here is what the salvation of humanity might consist in. It turns out that the character's disappearance has been the writer's ruse, ultimately a leap toward what lies beyond the supreme escape. For Calvino, as the 'six memos' of the *Lezioni americane* say, what endured was – again – the realm of literature.

Mr Palomar and the observer hiding in the pieces of *Collezione di sabbia* insist on calling on the senses in order to get a grasp on the world. Actually, contrary to what was accentuated in many readings of Calvino's works, his characters question reason's hold on reality, while sensual experience provides the few clues they can rely on. The senses gained increasing ground in Calvino's work, until the celebration of their triumph in the pieces posthumously collected in *Sotto il sole giaguaro*. There is a curious pattern to this accelerating enterprise. We must keep in mind, first of all, that in Calvino the senses are consistently part of a totality that includes reason and will, as they once powerfully were in Dante's world-vision. What is also important to note, in both authors, is that these are 'written' senses, the analogues of a sensory world filtered and given form by a 'poet of exactness, who knows how to seize the most subtle sensation with an eye, an ear, and a hand that are quick and self-assured' ('poeta della precisione, che sa cogliere la sensazione più sottile con occhio, orecchio, mano pronti e sicuri'; *Lezioni americane* 61). In fact, we must lend an attentive ear to the hints left here and there about the process that translated those senses into writing. Textual expression becomes leaner as it acquires intensity; it communicates a world-view and a view of the practice of writing that have become one and the same. Once, Calvino said in a serious vein, 'Any operation toward stylistic "impoverishment," of reduction to the essential, is an act of literary ethics' ('ogni operazione di "rinuncia" stilistica, di riduzione all'essenziale, è un atto di moralità letteraria'; *Fiabe italiane* xvii). Later, he declared that talk about 'expressing oneself' was something akin to talk about excretions, and made him think of squeezed lemons: 'If the writer wished to choose a fruit to be compared with, he would choose a species that cannot be pressed, a walnut, an almond, or – in his most generous moments – a dried fig' ('Se lo scrittore dovesse identificarsi con un frutto, preferirebbe una specie non spremibile, una noce, una mandorla, o magari – nei suoi momenti più generosi – un fico secco' 'La squadratura,' *Saggi* II 1982).

It is no surprise, then, that in 1984 and 1985 Calvino would mull with renewed appreciation over reminiscences about an icon of literary rigour, Emilio Cecchi, 'a demanding and sarcastic man' ('uomo esigente e sarcastico'). Calvino, who was by then approaching his own old age, lingered on the quality of Cecchi's pedagogic vocation, which was expressed in few words and often was condensed in exclamations and allusions' ('una vocazione pedagogica, sia pur laconica e concentrata in esclamazioni allusive'; 'Cecchi e i pesci-drago' ['Cecchi and the Dragon-fish']). The homage he paid his old mentor is clear:

> Among the great old men who opened our century's history of Italian literature (and I am speaking of those who were moving toward their seventies when I was beginning to take my first steps and look around) Cecchi was the one I frequented most, even more than those who had greater influence on me with their imagination and their style ('Dei grandi vecchi che avevano aperto la storia della letteratura italiana del nostro secolo (parlo di quelli che già andavano verso la settantina quando io cominciavo a muovermi e a guardarmi in giro) Cecchi è quello che ho frequentato di più, anche più di coloro che avevano avuto maggiore influenza su di me come immaginazione e come stile').

In his maturity, Calvino reflected on the significance of shared reading preferences, and the subtle bond they establish across generations. For Cecchi and for him, the favourite texts were those in which 'ethical dimension and adventure became one and the same thing, and that thing metamorphosed into style' ('esperienza morale e avventura diventavano una cosa sola e questa cosa si trasformava in stile'; 'Cecchi e i pesci-drago').

Calvino's first 'lezione americana' was his 1983 lecture delivered at New York University. The first glimpse he provided then into his reflections on 'the written and the unwritten world,' and the place from which he was surveying them as a mature practitioner of the trade of writing, was to be followed by a series of lectures for Harvard University students. One can imagine Calvino labouring at reviewing and organizing for delivery the mass of concepts that went into his *summa* on literature. Its title in Calvino's handwriting, as it appears reproduced at the beginning of the printed text of the 'memos' (*Lezioni americane*, 1988), is simply 'Six Memos for the Next Millennium,' followed by the six words that would head the chapters of the series of lectures. Calvino did not need to say that his memos for the future had to do solely with literature, because – as he reiterated – he saw literature as 'an existential function ... a resistance to the heaviness of living ... [and] a search for understanding' ('come funzione esistenziale ... come reazione al peso di vivere ... come ricerca di conoscenza'; *Lezioni americane* 28).[11] *Mestiere* (know-how), entertainment, and existential integrity, for him, were one.

For a long time, the voice speaking in Calvino's texts asserted that he was 'prepared for the Worst and ever more demanding of the Best.'[12] Similar statements punctuated like a refrain Calvino's essays and fiction from 1960 on, taking the form of aphorisms or functioning as a leitmotif[13] until, in 1983, in the very last chapter of *Palomar*, the narrating voice declared, 'Now, he no longer remembers what there was to expect, whether good or bad' ('adesso non ricorda più cosa ci fosse da aspettarsi, in male o in bene'; 123). No matter what may have been Calvino's personal temperament, that refrain is symptomatic of the writer's concern with what he viewed as the problematic connection between the world of literature and the existential dimension in which literature operates. This is what he found in Cecchi's example: 'I glimpsed ... the answer to my never satisfied expectations in my rapport with literature, and in its coming face to face with the world of action' ('Intravedevo ... la risposta alle mie mai risolte esigenze nel rapporto con la letteratura e nel suo confronto col mondo della pratica'; 'Cecchi e i pesci-drago'). But the naïvely earnest postures of the Calvinian personae, in keeping with Calvino's convictions about literature's value as entertainment, are often the source of humour. The various narrators keep referring to perplexity and disillusionment; in contrast, the characters, in all seriousness, are committed to finding some inclusive unity and meaning in their disjointed universe.[14]

Born of doubt and contradiction yet humorous and functioning with elegant ease, all of Calvino's texts imply a vision of art and history as the heterogeneous but necessarily connected components of human experience. His awareness of the difficulties, but also the potential, of that connection is at the basis of the pedagogic motif that is woven through all his writings. Used here in its most encompassing sense, the term 'pedagogy' has to do with the interlocutory quality of Calvino's work, his concern with reception, his attention to scholastic needs, and his statements on the 'uses of literature.' Calvino searched for coherence in the incoherent universe of experience, but ultimately trusted in the value of language and literature, and devoted to it an entire life. In a way, his death came at the most opportune moment, when he had made the statement that summed up his entire career as a writer and 'pedagogue.' He confirmed that he was a writer 'on the edge,' to paraphrase the title of Rebecca West's fine study of Montale, but his edge was a point of departure, the beginning of a journey into the future that the Montalean persona had not wished to undertake. That is where one can appreciate the generational and constitutional differences between the two voices: one could hardly imagine Montale writing for today's young, especially for children and adolescents. Calvino did, and his 'memos,' a message of secular faith without illusions, were his bequest to them.

1 For a more exhaustive treatment of this topic, see Jeannet 1994.
2 Collodi, Kipling, and Stevenson have been the object of admiration, and more recently of criticism also, because of their impact (real and supposed) on the formation of new political, cultural, and linguistic entities. As far as Italy was concerned, the issue was the emergence of a new nation with a new language in the second half of the 1800s. For the English-speaking world, the issue was the creation of an empire, which was destined to provide the basis for the diffusion of a new lingua franca in the twentieth century, all objections to imperialistic ideology notwithstanding.
3 Giuseppe Parini (1729–99) is best known for his satirical poem Il giorno.

4 The material available on the subject of postmodernism is overwhelming in its abundance and diversity of focus. I have relied, for the concepts that relate more directly to my topic, on Ihab Hassan's view of postmodern literature as a response to apocalypse, on Lyotard's discussion of the crisis of knowledge and the functions of narrative, and on Huyssen's overview of the evolution of postmodernism in the sixties and seventies, for which see part 3, 'Toward the Postmodern,' of his *After the Great Divide.* The volume edited by E. Ann Kaplan includes Frederic Jameson's 'Postmodernism and the Consumer Society' (Kaplan 13–29), which explores postmodernism in the context of mass culture and political thought.

5 On this topic, see Bàrberi-Squarotti, Jonard, and Bryce, among many others, and Calvino's intriguing comment in *I libri degli altri.* In a 1964 letter to Leonardo Sciascia, he wrote: 'The rationalism of the Enlightenment has received the worst beatings and disavowals for almost two centuries, yet continues to coexist with all its challenges. *And I, perhaps, express that coexistence*' ('il razionalismo illuminista per quasi due secoli non ha fatto che ricevere bastonate in testa e smentite, eppure continua a convivere con tutte le sue contestazioni: *e io forse esprimo questa coesistenza*'; 491. Emphasis added) .

6 The choice was not without drawbacks: 'I knew only the secular form of repression, which is more internalized and more difficult to overcome' ('ho conosciuto solo la repressione laica, più interiorizzata e da cui è meno facile liberarsi'; *Romanzi e racconti* III 48)

7 The version published in the *Saggi* unfortunately eliminated some paratextual elements, such as the subtitle 'Diderot fratello nostro' (Diderot, Our Brother), and the title 'Il gatto e il topo' (The Cat and the Mouse), which highlighted those of Diderot's characteristics that Calvino prized.

8 For Calvino's dialogues with his young readers, see also *I libri degli altri,* especially a 1974 letter to a group of middle-school students, about his *Marcovaldo* (605).

9 'Any theory of modern writing must ... be, at the same time, a theory of play' (Suleiman 2).

10 This reading differs from Michele Balice's. In his article he emphasizes the 'hermitic isolation' of the protagonist, and asserts that he avoids any 'celebration of city images' (86).

11 Calvino complained, in his later years, about the excessive attention paid by his readers to the technical aspect of his texts, as he reiterated in a polemical article: 'Issues of content, these days, are never even touched, as if it were unseemly to mention them in conversation' ('i temi di contenuto ... adesso non vengono mai sfiorati, come fosse sconveniente nominarli nella conversazione'; 'La coda di Minosse' [Minos's Tail]). For this topic, see Cases 1973,

'Calvino al bando' (Calvino's Banishment). As for Asor Rosa and his views on the enduring ethical dimension present in Calvino's texts, see Asor Rosa 1985, 'Il cuore duro di Calvino' (Calvino's Hard Core).

12 Appendix to *Tarocchi*.

13 Many examples could be cited from *Una pietra sopra*, and from almost every fictional text.

14 This contrast is wittily exploited by the author even in a collection of essays such as *Una pietra sopra*; see Jeannet 1989.

5

Between Garbage and Cosmos

I prefer to draw ... a confirmation for the opposite conviction: ... familiarity with the vision of the world's end as a firm guarantee of the world's continuation. ('Io preferisco trarre ... conferma al convincimento opposto: ... la consuetudine con la visione della fine del mondo come stabile condizione perché il mondo continui.')

Italo Calvino, 'Con Macchia senza paura'

A Motif

Calvino, as we have seen, was a particularly consistent writer throughout his various 'periods,' a writer faithful to certain thematic and meta-narrative concerns. Right from the start, in the collection of short stories entitled *Ultimo viene il corvo*, which included the short fiction he had written from 1945 to 1949, he privileged a basic motif, that of the world's dual presence, as his protagonists had the sudden revelation of a disturbing reverse side of reality ('il rovescio delle cose'; *Ultimo viene il corvo* 121) that was hidden under the surface of things. The author's interest in human experience and its contradictions was expressed in two distinctively Calvinian ways: he focused on images of 'dimidiamento' (clovenness, for which see chapter 2), and played with two opposing and connected aspects of his characters' environment, the world of garbage and waste, everything we discard, and the cosmos, that which (perhaps) endures. Tracing the transformations of this early motif through the years shows the intensity of Calvino's participation in the dilemmas of our time, and his connections with a tradition of Italian writing that saw the human condition as intimately bound to its envi-

ronment, both artificial and 'natural.' The formative reading of any edu-
cated Italian, which went from Dante, Petrarch, and Boccaccio through
Ariosto and Tasso down to such different writers as Leopardi, Pavese,
and Morante, confirms the Italian culture's predilection for an image of
the human community as a construct immersed in a well-tended habitat
that is also constructed and is named 'nature.'

To the characters of the young Calvino, the world appeared as a sensorial paradise, where plants and animals celebrated a never exhausted
multiplicity. The attention paid by the various narrators to detail and to
the unusual forms the universe could take contributed to giving the Calvinian text that quality of 'magic realism' so often invoked by readers.
Its early fictional settings, however, idyllic as they may have been,
invariably harboured an observer with analytical inclinations, or an
interloper bent on destruction. In either case, the texts suggested
obscure urgings of chaos under the enchanting surface of the real. In the
war stories, for instance in 'Andato al comando' (Sent to Headquarters,
1945), 'Ultimo viene il corvo' (The Crow Comes Last, 1946), 'Campo di
mine' (Minefield, 1946), 'Uno dei tre è ancora vivo' (One of the Three Is
Still Alive, 1947), 'Il bosco degli animali' (The Animals' Woods, 1948),
and, more obviously, 'Chi ha messo la mina nel mare' (Who Put a Mine
in the Sea?, 1948), violence and death were the horrors wrought by men
at war, in a world that had appeared to be the tranquil realm of animals
and plants.[1] On the other hand, stories such as 'Uomo nei gerbidi' (A
Man in the Fallows, 1946), 'Un pomeriggio, Adamo' (An Afternoon,
Adam, 1947), and 'Il giardino incantato' (The Enchanted Garden, 1948)
acknowledged that the incongruity between the images of a mythical,
benign nature and a problematical human experience predated war.
Surprised by an inconsistency, perhaps a secret flaw, in the universe, the
Calvinian characters felt discomfort with their discovery, despite the
fact that they inhabited what was supposed to be their own space, a
realm that certainly beguiled their senses. Their coming to awareness
was prompted by something that previously had been hidden and now
was unwittingly brought into the field of vision. It was the whimsical
zoo of 'Un pomeriggio, Adamo,' the crabs and sea urchins covering the
inside of an abandoned ship in 'Un bastimento carico di granchi' (A
Ship Full of Crabs, 1947),[2] and the unsettling aura permeating an
'enchanted garden' that suggested 'an immense mistake ... a wrong ... an
ancient injustice' ('un enorme sbaglio, ... una ... colpa, ... un'antica
ingiustizia'; 26). It is interesting to note that, right from the beginning,
the uneasy relationship of character to milieu was ascribed to the per-

ception of a social as well as an existential flaw. The awareness of
Calvino's protagonists was thus awakened to the connection between
environment and human constructs, or, more precisely, to the realization that the very concept of 'natural' is evidence of a human perspective. The historical and social universe is not contained by, but rather
contains, what we call Nature (see chapter 3).

The image of garbage appears early, in a 1945 short story entitled
'Angoscia in caserma' (Anguish in the Barracks). The protagonist, who
speaks in the first person, has been rounded up by Fascist militiamen
and forced to serve in the military, in a subservient position, as garbage
collector. While he sweeps and takes away the garbage, 'the mania of
symbols, a road to madness' ('il male dei simboli, la via della pazzia';
Ultimo viene il corvo 99) torments him, but then he muses, 'The trash cart
had a rickety and friendly air, and invited laughter at those chores, even
if they were difficult to do, because everything would ultimately end up
all right' ('e poi il carretto per trasportare la spazzatura aveva un'aria
sgangherata ed amica, insegnava a prendere le cose in ridere, anche se
era penoso farle, chè poi tutto si sarebbe risolto'; 99). The waste produced by humans, and the humble implements used to take care of it,
are consoling, with their homelike connotations, for the adolescent
caught in the fury of incomprehensible events. There is a sense of stabil-
ity, and even a hint of secular purification through good works, in the
supposedly basest but indispensable activities of the human community, and those suggestions redeem them and turn them into symbols.

As for the second image, that of the cosmos, again it is almost moving
to find it already present in a 1945 short story entitled 'La stessa cosa del
sangue' (Like Your Own Blood), which was rejected in the revised edition of *Ultimo viene il corvo* and then recuperated in the third printing of
that same collection. During a brief pause, while waiting to enter a civil
war without mercy, 'the Communist guy kept wondering how the
rocks, and the ravines, and the mountains had been formed, and how
old the Earth was. And together they all debated about the rocks' layers,
and the ages of the Earth, and when the war would be over' ('il comuni-
sta s'andava domandando di come s'erano formate le rocce, e i burroni,
e le montagne, e di quanti anni aveva la terra. E tutti insieme discute-
vano degli strati delle rocce, delle ere della terra e di quando la guerra
sarebbe finita'; 88). That dialogue and those wonderings would be
resumed by other Calvinian voices, from Qfwfq to Mr Palomar.

It is not that cosmic harmony could be remembered as an actual
occurrence by the protagonists of the Calvinian texts, and contemplated

with nostalgia. It is more a case of a vague sense of awe and bewilderment that needs to be acknowledged, and, at other times, of innocence contradicted and disabused by events. In 'Pesci grossi, pesci piccoli' (Big Fish, Little Fish, *I racconti* 195), for instance, the salt water dripping from the young body of the ecstatic underwater fisher Zeffirino – whose very name has idyllic overtones – is juxtaposed, with subtly ironic compassion, with the tears dripping from the eyes of a grieving adult, who has the uncanny ability to discover the hidden wound in each fish the boy catches. A malady has taken hold of the world. Disconsolate or puzzled, the Calvinian characters struggle with that realization. Sweeping, cleaning and washing return with exorcistic regularity in Calvino's fiction, as character after character tries to hold its own by mere stubbornness in the face of a duplicitous reality. Two novellas in 'La vita difficile' (Living Is Hard, *I racconti* 355–495), for instance, speak with escalating grimness of environmental pollution and an infestation of insects; yet they close on visions of cathartic, though very homely, cleansing. One, 'La nuvola di smog' (The Cloud of Smog), ends with a scene of vaguely surrealistic flavour, a procession of carts freeing the city of its dirty laundry, which is being taken to a stream to be washed, and with the fluttering of bright white wash drying in the sun. The other, 'La formica argentina' (The Argentine Ant), closes with the vision of a resplendent sea bottom where all impurities ultimately dissolve into the innumerable grains of sand. Imaginative ways of curing the disharmony that plagues human experience are devised, and the early texts close with fable-like happy endings; but the ever renewed question posed by subsequent texts confirms that all reality is 'cloven,' and the wound of disunity keeps aching inside all the characters. The duality of all experience turns out to be merely the outward manifestation of an internal rift, a puzzlement, a disappointment, which will be explored in ever greater depth in later works. Writing about it is not without delight. In fact, Calvino's fiction never loses its lightness and playfulness, because the search for understanding is cast as an adventure that excites inventiveness, requires energy, and relies on rapidity and surprise.

The solution to the dilemma of incompleteness turns out to be different for different characters, but in each case it is fraught with anguish and danger. That solution may be sought in the dissection and reconstruction of experience, by those aspiring to the rigour of geometric rationality (see chapter 2), or it may lie in the character's immersion in the organic matter that is the stuff of the sensorial universe. In its most humorous instance, a non-existent knight, Agilulf, pursues with icy passion his claim to existence by playing games of order and precision, while his squire, Gurduloo, submerges his overflowing physique in vats of soup and female flesh. Also, throughout the works of the fifties Calvino showed a persistent fascination with the refuse humans produce and the way they deal with it. Agilulf fastidiously disposes of the remains of a meal (*Il cavaliere inesistente* 89), and the enlightened baron Cosimo di Rondò turns his considerable inventiveness to devising an acceptable way of removing bodily excretions (*Il barone rampante* 99–100). Management of the waste produced by humans is entrusted by the text to a human drive whose ideals are rationality, order, and a sense of civic responsibility. The issue of waste disposal has not yet become an emergency, although it is constantly raised; the amount of garbage produced is not overwhelming, and good planning or a mildly compulsive behaviour seems sufficient to keep the matter under control.

The Realm of Contradictions

A contradictory universe, the urban community,[3] hovered in the background of Calvino's fiction right from the start. Even when his characters found themselves in the woods or the countryside, they acted most often as people who were attuned to the symbiotic relationship between the urban and the 'natural' environments. As the narrator of 'La taverna dei destini incrociati' (The Tavern of Crossed Destinies) had to say in 1973, even in hermits' lives 'the city is there, a few steps away. Paintings depicting hermits have almost always a city in the background' ('La città è lì a due passi. I quadri degli eremiti, quasi sempre, hanno una città sullo sfondo'; *Il castello dei destini incrociati* 106). In *Il sentiero dei nidi di ragno*, the urban centre, to which the Resistance fighters and Pin return often, is already an ambiguous place, with its familiar maze of alleys and streets, its poverty, the (precarious) safety of homes, and the (treacherous) warmth to be found in the havens of small-time vice, the bar and a young prostitute's hovel. It is also the village that appears in the distance as an unreachable haven to a hunted man, in wartime, in 'Uno dei tre è ancora vivo', or the *paese* that becomes an emblematic construct in the short story entitled 'Paese infido' (Treacherous Village, 1953). A wounded Resistance fighter straggles into an idyllic *paese* on a hill above a little valley, surrounded by the woods out of which he has emerged. The village seems uninhabited, and looks like a trap. In fact, the few people the man meets are hostile, and plan to capture him to hand him over to the Nazis. Unexpectedly, though, that mixture of country charm and mob ferocity is transformed into a rich and mysterious double universe. The wall of a stable, which had looked like a dead end, reveals an opening, and the locked and shuttered houses harbour compassionate people: 'Every town ... even the one that looks most hostile and inhuman ... has two faces. There comes a time when you discover its good face, which was there all along; only you couldn't see it; and you didn't know how to keep hoping' ('Ogni paese ... anche quello che pare più ostile e disumano, ha due volti; a un certo punto finisci per scoprire quello buono, che c'era sempre stato, solo che tu non lo vedevi, e non sapevi sperare'; *I racconti* 98–9). The urban community turns out to be the ideal metonymy and potential metaphor for the total human experience. In 'La formica argentina' and 'La nuvola di smog,' it is the rational, modern community that also hides destructive forces and decay.

Pollution, proliferation of insects, and garbage, as well as the efforts made by human beings for their elimination, accompany less tangible forms of waste and deterioration. Between 1953 and 1963, two fictional works elaborated that motif. *La giornata d'uno scrutatore* follows a man during a one-day stint at the local polling place, which marks a turning-point in his life, a journey that reveals to him the ambiguities of all that exists, of history and love, and the stubborn efforts human beings make to construct something together. The last paragraph of the novella is a famous Calvinian closure, the view of a city that had until then remained invisible, as a group of residents of a home for incurables in Turin together attend to humble daily tasks, in the declining light of the evening:

> Female midgets went by in the courtyard, *pushing a cart loaded* with bundles of sticks. The load was heavy. Another woman came along, tall like a giantess, and pushed it, almost at a run. *She laughed, and they all laughed.* Another one, also big, came in *sweeping with a broom* made of millet stalks. A big fat woman was pushing by its high handles a huge stockpot on bicycle wheels, perhaps *transporting soup.* Even the ultimate city of imperfection has its perfect hour, thought the watcher, the hour, the moment, when in every city there is the City ('Donne nane passavano in cortile *spingendo una carriola* di fascine. Il carico pesava. Venne un'altra, grande come una gigantessa, e *lo spinse, quasi di corsa, e rise, e tutte risero.* Un'altra, pure grande, *venne spazzando, con una scopa* di saggina. Una grassa grassa spingeva per le stanghe alte un recipiente-carretto, su ruote di bicicletta, forse *per trasportare la minestra.* Anche l'ultima città dell'imperfezione ha la sua ora perfetta, pensò lo

scrutatore, l'ora, l'attimo, in cui in ogni città c'è la Città'; *La giornata d'uno scrutatore* 95–6. Emphasis added).

Some details that return insistently, such as the sweeping and the ever present 'soup,' are the signifiers of what is a form of secular cleansing and of cooperation, and the harbingers of inchoate potentialities.

The Marcovaldo stories, which were written in that same decade, go further in defining the city as the place where the contradictions of human experience are more clearly visible, and in fact are the very evidence of humankind's inescapable identification with what it has constructed. Marcovaldo 'feels' his world. His observations, his *ragionamenti*, and his imaginings, all expressed in limpid prose, are anchored in his actual perception of each detail of a hostile and familiar environment. Ambiguity, even more than dualism, is at the core of his every sensation and reflection, because everything carries a double connotation, even urban litter. In the first short story of the Marcovaldo cycle, 'Funghi in città' (Mushrooms in the City), garbage in the city streets acquires a double function, as a clue to the organic world, an emblem of physicality and oneness, but also as a rotting reminder of corruption and dysfunction. To Marcovaldo's chagrin, the broom wielded by Amadigi the street cleaner is a weapon by which all natural waste must be erased until, ideally, the city is left fully aseptic. On the other hand, the malodorous loads of garbage being ferried nightly through that same city are an intrusion into Marcovaldo's dream world in 'La villeggiatura in panchina' (Vacation on a Park Bench). Caught between such ambivalences, Calvino's character ends up yearning for the reappearance of a 'saviour' validated by the poetic tradition: high above the world of accumulating dross and ambiguity, there is the presence of the moon.

A consolatory literature is very far from Calvino's intentions; his stoic ethos excluded all such temptations. The poetic quality of Marcovaldo's perception of the moonlight in 'La villeggiatura in panchina' underscores the distance between what is man-made and what is not, but also serves to put to rest whatever illusions one might still entertain as to the reliability of archaic metaphors and symbols. It is true that in this short story humankind's ingenuity in providing the darkened urban landscape with its own artificial light is undermined by the realization that its effort is imperfect and even negative. The contrast between the elusive magic of the light of the moon and the blinking of the amber traffic light (*Marcovaldo* 15) is one of the most striking passages in Calvino's writing, since it privileges the 'natural' phenomenon over the industrial creation. But the beauty of moonlight is exactly what is sacrificed at the end of the first cycle of Marcovaldo short stories. Symbolically perched between city chaos and the dome of the night sky, Marcovaldo's family vainly attempts to negotiate a precarious existential balance between pragmatic and poetic needs. The story makes clear that a full moon with its magic belongs to another universe, not of nature but of literature, and is bound to be obliterated in our culture, at least in the form it has taken over the centuries. Although the moon will miraculously reappear in later Calvinian works, as all magic objects do, its presence will have become infinitely more problematical and menaced.

The sixties, in Italy, brought to a head the ambiguities of a society in which *benessere* and *spreco* (prosperity and waste) were the twin faces of technological advancement. The so-called economic miracle was accompanied by the rebellion of those who had made it possible: people, particularly the young, became increasingly aware of the social, economic, and cultural price exacted by precipitous and politically manipulated change. On the literary scene, two voices among many others exemplified the perplexity elicited by the problems inherent in the rapid transformation of a culture. Elio Vittorini reiterated his enthusiasm for a technological future,[4] even though his fictional texts continued to live in a non-urban universe filled with archetypal literary constructs – Mediterranean landscapes, the gestures and rituals of an agrarian culture, and the icon of an all-knowing Mother. On the other hand, the voice of Anna Maria Ortese lamented the loss of a consoling point of reference, which until then had been provided for her by the images of a familiar cosmos. Precisely in answer to a letter written by Ortese,[5] Calvino reflected on his own position vis-à-vis the changed sociohistorical reality that surrounded him, and on his relationship to the literary tradition. He firmly distanced himself from Vittorini's heritage as well as Ortese's lament. He saw 'the literary text as a map of the world and the knowable, and writing as an impulse to learn' ('l'opera letteraria come mappa del mondo e dello scibile, lo scrivere mosso da una spinta conoscitiva'; *Una pietra sopra* 187).

Those years saw Calvino engaged in a writerly project, putting the growing body of his short fiction in order. The publication of *Marcovaldo* was an opportunity to reflect on the increasing deterioration of the environment, an environment that in the Calvinian universe was human, a symbiosis of natural and man-made. In 'Dov'è più azzurro il fiume' (Where the River Is More Blue) and in 'Fumo, vento e bolle di sapone'

(Smoke, Wind, and Soap Bubbles), Marcovaldo's habitat is poisoned by industrial waste and technology's greedy expansion, in which Marcovaldo's children cheerfully partake. In 'La città smarrita nella neve' (The City Hidden in the Snow) and 'La pioggia e le foglie' (The Rain and the Leaves), Marcovaldo vainly attempts to reconstruct the seasons of his daydreams. The rage to consume is the thematic core of 'Marcovaldo al supermarket' (Marcovaldo at the Supermarket) and 'I figli di Babbo Natale' (Santa's Children). The city can become a naturalized urban paradise for Marcovaldo only in the heat of the dog days in 'La città tutta per lui' (The City All to Himself); and only in a single episode is resistance to the prevailing environmental disaster successful, as hordes of felines prevent the paving over of a funky city garden in 'Il giardino dei gatti ostinati' (The Garden of Stubborn Cats).

Cosmic Perspectives

In the late sixties, the poet Marcovaldo, whose city was the entire cosmos, was replaced by the ubiquitous and talkative Qfwfq, for whom the entire cosmos was home. Garbage also acquired greater prominence, as its presence indicated not only the negative impact of humans on the environment, but also the chaotic mass from which the universe sprang up, the matrix and the nurturer of future life forms, as in 'Sul far del giorno' (At Daybreak). The character Qfwfq, with his 'human grimaces and human mutterings' ('smorfie umane, borbottii umani'; *Una pietra sopra* 188), introduced the grotesque and the humorous in the exploration of the knowable, and proposed a new evaluation of the processes by which all that we know came into being. Significantly, the topic of the lead short story in *Le cosmicomiche* was the Moon's increasing distance from the narrator's planet. That widening gulf between a traditionally idealized celestial body and the Earth was accompanied by a disturbing discovery: cosmos and chaos, pure light and garbage, are not antithetical elements of reality, but rather shifting and overlapping aspects of the same universal predicament. So whether it was imagined as a 'butter-coloured light' or a 'black umbrella blown by the wind' ('luce color burro,' 'nero ombrello portato dal vento'; *Le cosmicomiche* 9), the Moon was an organic body. It was a *bestione* (a big beast) whose belly is covered with a crust of sharp scales emitting a fishy odour, and it was strewn with the lost objects of earthly visitors, a sort of cosmic garbage dump. The narrator's yearning for the Moon, consequently, was due not to nostalgia for perfection, but to the conflicting emotions caused by something that attracts and repels at the same time. That yearning was the other face of frustration with the intractable quality of reality. The Moon, alternatively shown in frightening close-ups and in *angst*-producing withdrawal, became a Calvinian metaphor for life.

It was in those years that Calvino also increased the number of his 'cosmicomic' stories and organized them in the new volume entitled *La memoria del mondo*. Like a new Agilulf immersed in painstaking modifications of the arrangement of objects, Calvino seemed to pursue the goal of an ideal order, as he retrieved his own bits of fluid reality – the writer's materials – and rearranged them in numerically defined clusters. The title of the new collection speaks of a 'memory of the world' that may be an ordering principle embedded in the world's very structure or a gaze focusing on the world from the outside. Either way, for Calvino memory makes visible or, better, writable the long experience of consciousness, by organizing it. Pointedly, in each of the first four stories, different and even contradictory scientific hypotheses as to the Moon's origins provide the pretext for a tale.[6] The dual metaphors of garbage and cosmos collapse, earthly and celestial phenomena reverse and then coincide, and the world of celestial bodies and the world of filth, of 'sudiciume,' trade sides. The four short stories have in common a vision of the universe as an organism in which matter and living species are not discrete components of a static order, but rather entities sharing a fluid symbiotic relationship. The Moon now is described in minute and often humorous detail as a repulsive globe, soft, full of oozing growths; it is 'pale ... slow, sickly' ('pallida ... lenta, malata'; *La memoria del mondo* 65), whereas the City in its modernity is hard, all built of inorganic materials, bright with a myriad of lights. Suddenly, though, the organic lunar matter begins to drip and splatter, covering the Earth's surface. The City, as suddenly, appears fragile and vulnerable (54). Earth and Moon exchange each other's refuse, and the satellite moves away covered with trash: 'No trace was visible any more of our ancient earthly matter. The Moon was receding in the sky, pale and ... unrecognizable. If you looked very sharply, you could see it strewn with a thick covering of fragments, shards, and splinters, shining, sharp, and clean' ('Delle nostre antiche materie terrestri non era più visibile alcuna traccia. La Luna stava allontanandosi in cielo, pallida, irriconoscibile ...: aguzzando gli occhi la si scorgeva cosparsa d'una fitta coltre di cocci e schegge e frantumi, lucidi, taglienti, puliti'; 57). As for the Earth, it remains half drowned in organic filth, 'a matter made up of gelatin, and hair, and mould, and slaver' ('una materia fatta di gelatina e pelo e muffa e bava'; 55).

The cosmic upheaval causes terror and anxiety; and yet, as in an Ovidian metamorphosis, it is precisely because of that upheaval, and because of the disgusting deposit left by it, that life arises, mud, vegetation, and 'wriggling organisms' ('organismi sguscianti'; 58). The attempt to recapture the invulnerable hardness of a mineral world, 'plastic, and cement, and sheet metal, and glass, and enamel, and pegamoid' ('plastica e cemento e lamiera e vetro e smalto e pegamoide'; 58), goal and dream of our times, is bound to fail, as our lives can exist only among 'the Moon's excretions, dripping with chlorophyll, and gastric juices, and dew, and nitrogen fats, and cream, and tears' ('la deiezione lunare, fradicia di clorofilla e succhi gastrici e rugiada e grassi azotati e panna e lacrime'; 59). The chaotic enumeration underlines the paradox of the origin of life, in a playful rewriting of mythological geneses. It is from that cosmic 'soup' that earthly lives, with their obsession for precision, order, and hardness, have sprung. Earlier, in the story entitled 'La Luna come un fungo' (The Moon like a Mushroom), the narrator/observer had become aware that 'the fragile layer of objects that covered the world could be obliterated, and replaced by a moving desert whose passage would overrun and erase all living presence' ('il fragile strato delle cose che copriva il mondo poteva essere negato, sostituito da un deserto mobile al cui passaggio ogni presenza vivente era travolta ed esclusa'; 38). Qfwfq was more than a witness, when confronted by a phenomenon that disrupted his entire way of life, the birth of the Moon from the very womb of the Earth. The ambivalent feelings of the protagonist, uncertain between hope for a new equilibrium and a sense of utter dislocation, take the form of a mock epic struggle reminiscent of children's adventure stories. Change is fraught with danger, uncertainty, and doubt. Evil presences try to reassert themselves in the new order, untrustworthy prophets abound, and the voice of science turns into irresponsible technobabble, that of Rabelais's *science sans conscience* (*La memoria del mondo* 41–2). As for the nascent Moon, it is hardly a soothing sight: 'A stony mass of immense size floated in the sky, light as a leaf; on the top, it was washed-out and porous, and underneath it was still drenched with a sort of mucus from the earth's entrails, streaked with mineral fluids and lava, and bearded with entire colonies of earthworms' ('un macigno di grandezza smisurata – nella parte superiore dilavato e poroso, e sotto ancora intriso come del muco delle viscere terrestri, striato di fluidi minerali e lava, barbuto di colonie di lombrichi – si librò nel cielo, leggero come una foglia'; 44). What to do? The earthy birthing image that closes the short story is at the same time explicit and ambiguous. Qfwfq had to make a choice in fear and trembling and also under the impulsion of chance. He opted for Earth, and now he is stranded on the surface of the planet, while the Moon recedes in the distance. He carries within himself a new awareness, that he is 'indebted to the Moon for what I have on Earth, to what is not here for what is here' ('debitore alla Luna di quanto ho sulla Terra, a quello che non c'è di quel che c'è'; 45). This is a new version of the Calvinian leitmotif for which distance is full of significance and pathos.[7] In 1969, curtly discarding a dualistic vision of the human environment, a paragraph in *Tarocchi* would strip the Moon of its content, making of its emptiness and silence the alpha and omega of all discourse: the Moon is not 'the world full of sense, the opposite of the senseless Earth. No, the Moon is a desert ... From this arid space every discourse and every poem sets forth, and every journey ... brings us back here, to the centre of an empty horizon' ('il mondo pieno di senso, l'opposto della Terra insensata. No, la Luna è un deserto ... Da questa sfera arida parte ogni discorso e ogni poema; e ogni viaggio ... ci riporta qui, al centro d'un orizzonte vuoto'; *Il castello dei destini incrociati* 39). In a parallel way, Calvino's journalistic writings of later years stressed the vulnerability of the cosmos, the inevitable co-penetration of human and cosmic spaces, and the vanity of our yearning for a realm untouched by strife and ambivalence: 'Our societies, with their private and state capitalisms ... take their perplexities into the emptiness of space and the uninhabited planets' ('la società dei capitalismi privati e statali ... affaccia la sua incertezza su spazi vuoti e pianeti deserti'), stated the 1977 article 'Al di là della morte di von Braun' (Beyond von Braun's Death). No escape from our context is possible, no haven can open up for us: 'The sky becomes a mirror of the merciless struggle to attain hegemony among the nations, and an outlet for the problems that remain unresolved down here' ('Il cielo diventa lo specchio della lotta spietata per il predominio tra le nazioni, lo sfogo dei problemi non risolti quaggiù').

'The kernel of the world is empty, the beginning of what moves in the universe is the space of nothingness, around absence is constructed what exists' ('Il nocciolo del mondo è vuoto, il principio di ciò che si muove nell'universo è lo spazio del niente, attorno all'assenza si costruisce ciò che c'è'; *Il castello dei destini incrociati* 97). Absence, loss: the Calvinian discourse finds its origins in them, and at the same time defeats them. In 1972, the many elaborations of the theme of a duality negated culminate in the collection *Le città invisibili*, Calvino's 'last love poem to the city' ('The Written and the Unwritten World').

As we have seen, cityscapes had often returned as representations of the sum of human experience, with its constraints and suffering as well as its ambiguities, daydreams, creative urges, and moments of escape. What made them significant, though, was their hidden part, the 'perspectives of a city that had never been seen' ('le prospettive di una città mai vista'; *La giornata d'uno scrutatore* 95), a revelation of unforeseen complexity and unexpected promise. In 1949, Calvino had written a short story/report entitled 'Freddo a Napoli' (Cold Weather in Naples), in which the city was a 'city of glass' ('una città di vetro'; *Romanzi e racconti* III 869) that enclosed and at the same time displayed the harsh lives of its poorest inhabitants, and did so not with shame but with pride. Family scenes, humble daily gestures, and non-stereotypical characters appeared through open windows and doors, as if magically revealed, and the hidden Naples opened up to the watching eyes of the narrator. Thus the city made possible a double freedom, for the observer and for the observed. In the Marcovaldo stories, the city is the place where Marcovaldo's playful freedom is enacted, when the city of summer, that other city, is 'glimpsed for just an instant, or perhaps only dreamed' ('intravista solo per un momento, o forse solamente sognata'; *Marcovaldo* 115), or when in winter it is erased by snow. The eighteenth and nineteenth stories of the Marcovaldo collection also returned to the theme of the discovery of a hidden city. The city, in those stories, is present in its invisibility; it is a 'negative' of the visible city, and a geometric mosaic of empty spaces. 'Positive' and 'negative' mean themselves and their opposites: on the one hand, there is the 'città degli uomini,' 'città inabitabile,' 'città verticale,' 'città compressa' ('city of men,' 'uninhabitable city,' 'vertical city,' 'compressed city'); on the other hand, there is the 'città dei gatti,' the 'controcittà,' 'una città negativa,' the 'città di intercapedini, pozzi di luce, canali d'aerazione, passaggi carrabili, piazzole interne ... una rete di canali secchi' ('city of cats,' the 'counter-city,' 'a city in the negative,' 'a city of air spaces, light wells, air ducts, passageways, internal courtyards ... a network of dry canals'; *Marcovaldo* 118), a hidden labyrinth. As the seasons pass swiftly, the cats slyly enforce the survival of the city of disorder, with its trash, weeds, and decay, at the heart of the technological wonder-city, sterile and hard. The opposition between natural beauty and built environment had elicited bitter humour and disenchanted guilt in 'La speculazione edilizia' (Building for Profit) – in which the title refers to the huge and widespread illegal profits made during the building frenzy of the fifties and sixties in Italy, as at other times in other expanding economies. That concept of opposing realities gave way to the realization that, ultimately, nothing could be outside the city. In *Le città invisibili*, the City even became both the outer and the inner cosmos, at the same time ever present reality in Marco Polo's memory and lost object of desire in his fantasy.

Down Memory Lane

When Calvino wrote 'La strada di San Giovanni' (The Road to San Giovanni, 1964), he staged a moving but also humorous drama between two characters by then silenced, one by death (the father) and the other by maturity (the son). The reasons of the country contend with the reasons of the city, and yet country and city live on the page inextricably joined. From all we have said, it is obvious that the writer rehearsed for decades the realization of his most controlled and precariously perfect work, *Le città invisibili*. The City with a capital initial as Calvino wrote it in *La giornata d'uno scrutatore* underwent multiple metamorphoses, which gave birth to a wealth of possibilities for urban and narrative constructs. Architectural and sensorial images proliferated, but found lean and graceful ordering on the page thanks to the constraints of the text's structure. All potentialities are suggested by the narrator, although only a finite number find actualization, in a brilliant fictional mimesis of natural probability. Multiplicity, in which Calvino rejoiced,[8] contains all the opposites bound to each other, and so does his book of cities, from Isidora to Despina, from Isaura to Maurilia, Valdrada, Zemrude, Bauci, Laudomia, Perinzia, and Berenice, and to Raissa, 'the unhappy city [that] contains a happy city that is not even aware of its own existence' ('la città infelice [che] contiene una città felice che nemmeno sa d'esistere'; *Le città invisibili* 155). But it is Leonia of the proud name that embodies the images of the ecological nightmare that haunts our contemporary metropolis. Leonia's inhabitants enjoy the luxuries and comforts of a technologically advanced society. Paradoxically, the mountains of trash they accumulate testify to their opulence. Does their pleasure lie in consumption, or in discarding what is no longer new; 'expelling, discarding, cleansing [themselves] of a recurrent impurity' ('l'espellere, l'allontanare da sé, il mondarsi d'una ricorrente impurità'; 119)? No matter, since no one in the city cares to know what happens to the waste that is produced. And yet that wasting has become the identity of the city, which is now an erupting crater surrounded by mountains of refuse, encircled by a ring of other cities also in continuous eruption.

The vision of the city drowning in the landslide of the waste it does not wish to acknowledge is not apocalyptic, but deeply disturbing and repellent because so familiar. As in a fight between gigantic insects, other cities move onto the territory of Leonia, the rich city that has disappeared under its collapsing garbage: 'In the nearby cities they are already waiting with steamrollers to flatten the terrain, to push into the new territory, expand, and drive the new dumping grounds[9] still farther out' ('Già dalle città vicine sono pronti coi rulli compressori per spianare il suolo, estendersi nel nuovo territorio, ingrandire se stesse, allontanare i nuovi immondezzai'; 121). The wasting does not involve only the material world, but includes those human beings who make their homes in the garbage dumps ('Le figlie della Luna' [The Daughters of the Moon] in *La memoria del mondo*). Faced with the threat of the City's obliteration, the text renews a call for the necessary trust in 'constant vigilance and learning' ('attenzione e apprendimento continuo'; 170). Salvation from the nightmare of the cities 'that threaten ... in maledictions' ('che minacciano ... nelle maledizioni'; 169), rescue from the spiralling fall into the infernal city, is actually glimpsed at the end of the volume. A wilful, hope-against-hope determination enlivens the Calvinian text with a stubbornness that refuses despair: 'What matters is that the space where this development can take place be not suffocated' ('Quello che conta è che non sia soffocato lo spazio in cui questo sviluppo può avvenire'; *Coraggio e viltà degli intellettuali* 10). *Le città invisibili* is a love poem to the most complex construct of human imagination and know-how; a love poem to the place where is enacted what is most human, a combination of cooperation and strife. The City is, above all,[10] the analogue of language and storytelling, as *Le città invisibili* amply demonstrates. The very presence of the City reasserts that, although they are imperfect and perhaps unequal to the task, human reason, fantasy, and concern can provide the energy for the continuing possibility of a survival of the universe. Even the chaos of universal entropy may be a vital 'broth,' nourishing a cosmic renewal: 'These periods of great cultural accumulation and homogenization of many materials actually are like the biological soup from which, at the dawn of time, life originated' ('Questi periodi di grande accumulazione culturale, di centrifugazione di tanti materiali sono poi come quel brodo biologico in cui agli inizi dei tempi ha preso origine la vita'; *Saggi* II 1814).

In the seventies, Calvino wrote more explicit and lesser-known (because more abstract) meditations on the future of the environment, natural as well as human. In 1974, during his Parisian period, he published two essays with their opposite themes, 'Collezione di sabbia' (A Collection of Sand), which later became the title piece in a volume of articles, and 'La poubelle agréée' (The Certified Garbage Can). A reading of those meditations on collecting and discarding shows the direction in which Calvino was moving, and foreshadows the turn his works would take in the eighties. In those essays, 'the story is set in motion ... by a concern with a more essential and strict rigour, even though this may be hidden behind the playful irony of paradoxes' ('a mettere in moto il racconto ... [è] una lezione di rigore più essenziale e severa, sia pur dietro lo scherzo ironico del paradosso'; La memoria del mondo 8). In the first piece, the narrator, visiting an exhibition of unusual collections, is particularly drawn to a series of sand samples that a collector has brought back from the most disparate areas of the world. This 'anthology of sands' ('florilegio di sabbie') includes some very colourful items, but is made up mostly of material with minimal differences in colour and texture, which 'force a more and more focused attention, so that one imperceptibly enters a different dimension' ('obbligano a un'attenzione sempre più assorta, e così a poco a poco s'entra in un'altra dimensione'; Collezione di sabbia 10). Does this collection function as a description of the world, in the collector's intentions? muses the visitor. Or does it fulfil a need to transform the flowing away of one's life into a series of objects rescued from dispersion, just as the writer gathers a series of written lines, crystals subtracted from the incessant flux of thinking? Or is the collection useless and dead? The observer, after asking himself the questions, interprets positively what he sees: that collection is a stimulus for the imagination, an occasion for reconstructing the entire universe. The ultimate relics of a dehydrated world, those crystals that are the precipitates of all impurities suggest to the viewer the possibility of recapturing through what is visible – the grains of sand – that which is by now invisible – the multiplicity of being, 'the world crumbled and eroded' ('il mondo triturato ed eroso'; Collezione di sabbia 13).

'La poubelle agréée,' whose title refers to the garbage can authorized and approved by the Paris Sanitation Department, already belongs to the Palomar universe in tone and theme. The narrator, inept helper in household tasks, is entrusted – just as the frightened adolescent was in the 1945 short story – with the disposal of garbage. A subtle thread runs through the text: the protagonist is not only clumsy, but also very methodical and conscientious, and given to lengthy reflections only tenuously related to the matter at hand. He is a Marcovaldo who has somewhat grown up (or simply grown older) and has certainly changed social status, resembling – in his perplexity and concerned mood – Amerigo Ormea, the poll watcher. The ballet-like steps in the elaborate procedure that effects the 'distancing' of domestic waste are listed with painstaking and vivid precision. The man, 'a humble cog in the domestic mechanism' ('umile rotella del meccanismo domestico'), feels himself invested with a social role: 'I define myself as the first gear in a chain of operations that are fundamental for the existence of the community; I affirm my dependence upon the institutions, without which I would die buried by my own refuse in my own shell' ('mi costituisco primo ingranaggio d'una catena d'operazioni decisive per la convivenza collettiva, sancisco la mia dipendenza dalle istituzioni senza le quali morrei sepolto dai miei stessi rifiuti nel mio guscio'; *La strada di San Giovanni* 93).

Has a solution been found to the terror of ecological apocalypse? Probably not, but the many digressions in this text, the linguistic analyses, cultural comparisons, humorous self-deprecations, autobiographical vignettes, and chronological dislocations in the narrative flow, as well as the protagonist's consideration of the urgent need for a recycling program, lead to an important thematic simile: like eating what is edible and discarding the inedible, 'writing is to give up possession, not unlike throwing things away' ('scrivere è dispossessarsi non meno che il buttar via'; *La strada di San Giovanni* 115). The written pages and the pages crumpled in the wastebasket are equally expelled and eliminated by the writing subject, who labours to attain the utmost leanness, an elusive core. The narrator in *Ti con zero* had said that in order 'to plan a book ... the first thing to know is what to exclude' ('per progettare un libro ... la prima cosa è sapere cosa escludere'; 164). The domestic task now becomes a symbol of that fundamental human activity: defining oneself, which is done not only through the choices one makes and through 'collections,' but also through rejections and eliminations. The notes that the writer left as a pro-memoria for the preparation of the article being written thus acquire new significance as extant bits and pieces of a long reflection:

> *theme of purifying refuse   discarding is complementary to appropriation*
> *hellish world where nothing is thrown away   you are what you do not throw*
> *away   garbage as autobiography   autobiography as garbage ... living*
> *without carrying anything along ('tema di purificazione delle scorie   il buttar via è complementare dell'appropriazione   inferno d'un mondo in cui non fosse buttato via niente   si è quel che non si butta via identificazione di se*

stessi   *spazzatura come autobiografia*   *autobiografia come spazzatura*
... *il vivere senza portarsi dietro niente'*; *La strada di San Giovanni* 115. Spaces
and italic type in the text).

In 1980, Calvino turned to the implementation of those theoretical suggestions: he edited a volume of essays that constructed his intellectual
autobiography by excluding the texts he deemed useless and collecting
those he saw as valuable. He called that volume *Una pietra sopra* (literally, 'Put a Stone on It'), to confirm that the construction of the self is a
double process of elimination, by exclusion as well as by collection,[11] the
first step necessary in closing a career and beginning again from zero.
The season of fashionable games was over, and Calvino's protagonist
returned, more experienced and still searching, to a meditation on a fundamental epistemological issue: if the world's presence is entrusted to
our presence, however feeble,[12] and vice versa, then it is essential to
devise the manner by which we can focus on that connection, that
mutual quickening. From 'tide of residue ... garbage beaches of the
cemetery-continents' ('marea delle scorie ... spiagge-immondezzaio dei
continenti-cimiteri'; *Palomar* 19), the world turns into light, sea, vegetation, fauna, because of the human eye. From 'flotsam among the flotsam,
a corpse being rolled along' ('relitto tra i relitti, cadavere rotolato'; 19),
Mr Palomar is defined as a living consciousness by the splendour of sea
and sun: 'They were made for each other' ('Erano fatti l'uno per l'altro';
20). Mr Palomar consciously participates in the world's construction, in
his own conscientious and clumsy way; he 'takes responsibility for the
form the world takes around him, and feels a part of [the world's] image'
('sente la responsabilità della forma che il mondo prende intorno a lui, e
si sente parte di questa immagine'; *Saggi* II 1991-2). Much earlier in
Calvino's career, in 1964, the character speaking and reminiscing in 'La
strada di San Giovanni' had mentioned the nurturing function of human
beings vis-à-vis the universe,[13] where everything is threatened and precarious. That theme finds its confirmation and development in one of
Palomar's chapters, entitled 'Luna di pomeriggio' (Moon in the Afternoon 35-7). The protagonist, despite all his rationality, does empathize
with the rest of the universe, whether giraffes, gorillas, or a mute array of
objects. In his humorously calculated moments of abandon, he is sensitive to a woman's annoyance ('Il seno nudo' [The Naked Bosom]), floats
to the rhythm of sea waves ('La spada nel sole' [The Sword of the Sun]),
whistles in dialogue with a blackbird ('Il fischio del merlo' [The Blackbird's Whistle]), attempts visually to take possession of a planet

('L'occhio e i pianeti' [The Eye and the Planets]), imagines himself a bird ('Dal terrazzo' [From the Terrace]), participates vicariously in the hunting of insects by a gekco ('La pancia del geco' [The Gecko's Belly]), is seduced by exquisite foods in Parisian stores ('Il museo dei formaggi' [The Cheese Museum]), and is attracted by iguanas ('L'ordine degli squamati' [The Order Squamata]). But it is the Moon that elicits his most poetic and intense response. The hesitations and clumsiness of the Calvinian protagonists and the stylistic and linguistic tensions of the text are gone. The lexicon that served to establish the primacy of the Moon's presence in Italian literature lends its lightness to this excerpt of Calvinian prose. By now, the image of garbage has disappeared for Calvino; the only deposit left in the Calvinian universe is sand:[14]

> Between humankind–sand and world–boulder one can intuit a sense of possible harmony as if between two non-homogeneous harmonies: that of the non-human ... that seems not to correspond to any pattern, and that of human structures, which aspires to the rationality of a geometrical or musical composition, never definitive' ('tra umanità–sabbia e mondo–scoglio si intuisce un'armonia possibile come tra due armonie non omogenee: quella del non-umano che sembra non risponda a nessun disegno; quella delle strutture umane che aspira a una razionalità di composizione geometrica o musicale, mai definitiva'; 96).

At the very end of his life, still looking to the future, Calvino thus echoed the voices of his models, Ovid, Lucretius, Ariosto, Galileo, and Leopardi, as he wished for the utter comprehensiveness of writing: 'a work that would allow us to escape the limited perspective of the individual self, not only to enter into selves like our own, but to give a voice to that which has no language, to the bird ... the tree ... stone, cement, plastic' ('un'opera che ci permettesse d'uscire dalla prospettiva limitata d'un io individuale, non solo per entrare in altri io simili al nostro, ma per far parlare ciò che non ha parola, l'uccello ..., l'albero ..., la pietra, il cemento, la plastica'; *Lezioni americane* 120).

---

1 Gian Carlo Ferretti chose, as the title of his book on Calvino's career as a journalist, *Le capre di Bikini*, a phrase used by Calvino in a 1946 article. The topic of the article was the nuclear bombing of the Bikini atoll, where a number of domestic animals were sacrificed in nuclear experiments: 'Have you ever asked yourselves what the goats on Bikini must have thought? ... How they

must have judged us human beings, in those moments?' – 'Vi siete mai chiesto, wrote Calvino, cos'avranno pensato le capre di Bikini? ... come avranno giudicato noi uomini in quei momenti?' (Ferretti 9).

2 A children's word game, well known to most Italians, uses repetitively the expression 'È arrivato un bastimento carico di ...' ('A ship has arrived, full of ...'), followed by the name of some likely objects. Calvino's linking of the naïve rhyme with the hidden colonies of small but monstrous crustaceans suggests the presence of something disturbing below the luminous surface of the world.

3 In the Italian context in particular, even small communities (the *paesi*) tend to have something of an urban air, towns feel like cities, and small cities behave like capitals.

4 For Vittorini's ideas on the positive function of industrialization and technology in the future of the world, see *Il menabò* 5, and the posthumous *Le due tensioni*. For Calvino, see the interview he gave Ferdinando Camon in 1973 (Camon 1973, 187–90 and 195–6).

5 See the extensive quotations from a letter written by Anna Maria Ortese that Calvino used to introduce his essay entitled 'Il rapporto con la luna' (Our Relationship with the Moon, *Una pietra sopra* 183). The epistolary exchange first appeared in the *Corriere della sera* (24 December 1967) 11.

6 Kathryn Hume says that, by placing side by side various hypotheses on the Moon's origin, Calvino also 'exposes another weakness of the scientific narrative,' besides pointing to its potential dogmatism – 'the tenuous relationship between hypothesis and reality and ... the unstable and erratic development of scientific theory' (69).

7 For this Calvinian theme, see the previously mentioned Cases 1958, 'Il pathos della distanza.'

8 Chapter 5 of *Lezioni americane* is a *summa* of Calvino's many statements on multiplicity.

9 Here, the Weaver translation has 'street cleaners.'

10 Calvino himself mentioned in the jacket blurb his 'usual tone, ... his ethics of action, and his ironic and melancholy reserve, his aspiration to the fullness of life, to a human completeness' ('l'accento solito ..., la sua morale attiva e il suo ironico e malinconico riserbo, la sua aspirazione a una pienezza di vita, a un'umanità totale'; *Le città invisibili*). See also his article 'Con Macchia senza paura' (With Macchia without Fear, 1985).

11 See Jeannet 1989, 207–25.

12 'To look at itself the world needs the eyes (and the eyeglasses) of Mr Palomar' ('Per guardare se stesso il mondo ha bisogno degli occhi [e degli occhiali] del signor Palomar'; *Palomar* 116).

13 His father, whose figure looms large in Calvino's reconstruction of his own
   memories, was not so much concerned with making his land produce abundantly, as in a state of perpetual concern and activity 'to do what he could to
   help forward the tasks of nature that needed human help' ('il fare quanto
   poteva per portare avanti un compito della natura che aveva bisogno
   dell'aiuto umano'; *Romanzi e racconti* III 9).
14 See 'L'aiuola di sabbia' (The Sand Flowerbed) in *Palomar*.

6

Under the Crescent Moon[1]

But you,
O young immortal woman,
know all of this, for certain.

(Ma tu per certo,
giovinetta immortal, conosci il tutto.)

Giacomo Leopardi, Canto di un pastore errante dell'Asia

The *bambina*

Critics who have written about the feminine in the works of Italo
Calvino have concentrated almost exclusively on two characters, the
Amazon and the Reader. But the feminine takes more numerous and
complex configurations in Calvino's fiction, well before and after the
appearance of those two specific images. The transformations of that
essential component of Calvino's literary universe confirm the internal
coherence of the writer's work, its evolution, and its profound connection with the culture of which he was a critical, but faithful, heir.

The first short story published by Calvino, in 1946, entitled 'Paura sul
sentiero' (Fear on the Trail), had as its main character a very young man
who served as a courier in the Resistance. During his dangerous mis-
sions through the woods at night, he dreamed of Woman, such as an
adolescent might imagine her in his erotic fantasies. A reading of the
original version of the short story (*Romanzi e racconti* I 1275 and 1285–6)
confirms the naïvety of the young writer, and his dependence on the
models proposed by Moravia's and Pavese's fiction, where women are
all body and are usually designated by their lower parts, not their geni-

tals but their heavy legs and their *sedere* ('bottom'), often described in grotesque shapes and positions. On the other hand, the variants that contributed to the definitive version of the short story show Calvino's skill and awareness in finding his truest voice, even at that early stage. The most obvious attributes of the female physique, those the boy had originally daydreamed about, disappear; to assuage his fear, a 'wild animal ... reawakened from the depths of childhood realms' ('bestia ... svegliata dal fondo di regioni bambine'; *I racconti* 59), there remains the consoling image of a regal and vague feminine figure, Regina. The narrating voice elaborates and comments on the boy's fantasy, defining Regina as 'the young woman who lives within all of us, and for whom we all would like to dig a nest deep in the woods' ('la ragazza che è in tutti noi e per cui tutti noi vorremmo scavare una nicchia in fondo al bosco'; 61). For the male protagonist and for the male voice, woman is a powerful being, desired but distant, whose life is full and steady; she remains a stranger to the male universe, which is rich in adventure but tormented by fear, doubt, and longing. As a new Eve born out of the boy's loneliness, she embodies the male's awareness of his vulnerability and desire for tenderness, but evokes also the male's greatest anxiety, which is a recurring motif in the Italian cultural and literary tradition. Kim, the Resistance leader, expresses it in clearly masculine terms in the first version of *Il sentiero dei nidi di ragno*: 'All of us carry a secret impotence' ('tutti noi abbiamo un'impotenza segreta'; *Romanzi e racconti* I 1252).

Many other female silhouettes peek through the pages of the short stories written between 1946 and 1956, invariably patterned on Neorealist models. They have the usual traits of the stereotype: they are capricious, stubborn, mysterious, alien to the masculine universe, and deaf to man's concerns. A Pirandellian quality persists in Calvino's early works, as we can see in *La giornata d'uno scrutatore*, 'La nuvola di smog' (The Cloud of Smog), 'La formica argentina' (The Argentine Ant), and so on, and also in most early twentieth-century figurations of the feminine. The female is a disturbing element, animalistic in her needs, a placid yet unpredictable force of nature whose maternal pragmatism frustrates the male protagonist. She inevitably becomes the standard mature woman in Pirandello's plays, most clearly drawn in *Sei personaggi in cerca d'autore* (Six Characters in Search of an Author) as the Mother. This conventional image of femininity, however, is immediately contradicted, in Calvino's fiction, by the appearance of another character, the little girl, who is no less mysterious than Regina in her aloofness, but is endowed with different qualities. The Calvinian fantasy elaborates another image of the feminine that is autonomous in its reserve, sure of itself, and full of serene disdain for its male peer.

In 1947, this very young figure appears in two apparently dissimilar short stories. In the first, she is six years old and in the second she is about fifteen, but in both she is athletic and able to defend her independence in a firm and direct manner. In 'Un bastimento carico di granchi' (A Ship Full of Crabs), a band of young boys who are playing on a rusty old ship, offshore, under 'a resplendent spring sun' ('un sole allegro e giovane'; *I racconti* 25) are involved in the competitive games characteristic of their sex and age, with litigious, exhibitionistic, and somewhat clumsy exchanges. Suddenly the boys discover the presence of someone different, a little girl, who is clearly portrayed by the narrator as presexual and independent. Her almost magic apparition and her silence, as she concentrates on a mysterious activity of her own, isolate her. Her game is individual, serious, and gratuitous: she is trying to turn over a medusa that was stranded on the ship's bridge. The boys' surprise, as they make a circle around her 'with open mouths' ('a bocca aperta'; 27), contrasts with her indifference to their presence. The little band decides to take her hostage to spite a rival band of boys, because they wrongly assume that she is related to them; but they are beaten in a water fight with their rivals and abandon the ship, which is then occupied by the other band. The *bambina*, oblivious to the new arrivals and to their adolescent rituals, is still there; she succeeds in turning over the medusa and is trying to pick it up with a stick ('era sempre lí. Era riuscita a voltare la medusa e ora cercava di sollevarla sullo stecco'; 28). The leader of the new band, again wrongly assuming that she is the rivals' 'woman,' attempts to take her hostage, but the little girl surprises him by motioning him to lean down to watch and then picking the medusa up, and up and up, and slapping him in the face with it ('gli fece cenno di star fermo ... Mariassa si chinò a guardare. Allora la bambina tirò su lo stecco, con la medusa in bilico sopra. Lo tirò su, lo tirò su, sbatté la medusa in faccia a Mariassa'; 28–9). The reaction of the boys is minimal because of the rapidity of the event, while the reaction of the little girl is a statement made with irony and poise. She looks laughing at the boys, then calmly walks away, takes the classic position of the diver, dives, and swims away without looking back. After a moment of surprised immobility, the boys revert to their games. Yet they (and we) sense that something has changed, something is missing from their little universe, even though they are unable to reflect on its meaning, closed as they still are in the unripeness of childhood.

The episode perhaps could be viewed simply as a light-hearted look at the world of children's games, were it not for the attention the writer devoted to it as he selected very precise details for its description. Looking further in the collection of short stories, we discover that this early character has a small group of sisters. Sometimes they are not named but are presented as the *bambina* in absolute. The situations evoked in other stories also involve a tension or danger that causes the young female protagonists to become poised in a gesture of defence. We can take as an example the short story entitled 'Va' cosí che vai bene' (Keep Going Down That Road, Mate!), although it is certainly not one of Calvino's best, with its attempts at developing techniques, characters, and devices in a Neorealist style. The girl is older in this story and has acquired braids (*I racconti* 101). She is called a 'fragoletta' (little strawberry) and becomes the potential prey of an enterprising young boy, who attempts to sell her to some human wrecks who have survived the Second World War. The potential customers consider her an 'aperitivo,' fresh and wild as she is. However, the attempted sexual transaction, actually not pursued with great conviction by the would-be client, ends up unconsummated. First, the young girl resists and runs away in a gamelike chase, then she stops, picks up one sharp stone after another, and starts throwing them at him with the force and infallible aim of a country girl ('la forza e la mira di quella ragazzetta di campagna'; 111). The man retreats, assuring her that he is giving up: 'The girl with the braids *was still up there, immobile, looking at him,* still clutching a stone in her hand ... It looked as if she wanted to stop, but instead *she turned around* and *started on a run* along the highway; *she ran like a wild rabbit,* and *soon disappeared at a curve*' ('La ragazza con le trecce *era rimasta su, ferma a guardarlo,* sempre con un sasso stretto in mano ... sembrava volesse fermarsi, invece *si voltò, prese una corsa* per la carrozzabile, *correva come una lepre* e *presto sparí a una svolta*'; 111–12. Emphasis added).

The thematic similarities between the two short stories – the magical quality of the young girls' presence, the possessive assumptions made by the males, and the girls' finding themselves as items of exchange – are obvious. But they are perhaps less important than the scenes' iconic elements and linguistic choices, because these are less conscious and therefore reveal the persistence of a significant leitmotif. The girls are described as silent, immobile in their concentration on their own activities, serenely acting out their extraneity to the males' projects; they appear suddenly, are caught in the act of an efficient and elegant gesture; they are agile and fast in their flight, but calm and competent in

eluding their pursuers. Compared with the noisy and colourful population of male characters, they bring an aura of self-assuredness and determination to the narration as they succeed in protecting their own space.

Calvino's work between 1953 and 1956 with the dialectal versions of
fables from Italian folklore determined an interesting evolution in
everything he wrote during and after those years. Vaguely magical
objects and presences visit the stories with greater and greater fre-
quency, and the *bambina* also reappears as a central factor in the narration's resolution. In 'Paese infido' (Treacherous Village), one of the best
stories inspired by the Resistance, some villagers conspire to trap a
wounded Resistance fighter and hand him over to the Nazis, but in his
quasi-delirium he finds someone who shows him a magical passage to
safety:

> *And suddenly* Tom heard a *little voice* calling to him: 'Partisan, hey! parti-
> san!' and from a pile of hay *a little girl with braids* came out. She held *a red
> apple* in her hand. 'Here,' she said, '*have a bite and come with me*! ... *They sent
> me to show you the path* to run away,' said the little girl. 'Who?' went Tom,
> biting into the apple. *But he was already sure that he could trust that little girl,
> with his eyes shut* (Ed ecco Tom sentí *una vocetta* che lo chiamava: – Parti-
> giano! di,' partigiano! – e da un mucchio di fieno venne fuori *una bambina
> con le trecce.* Aveva in mano *una mela rossa.* – Tieni, – disse, – *mordila e vieni
> con me* ... M'hanno mandato a insegnarti la strada per scappare, – disse la
> bambina. Chi? – fece Tom mordendo la mela, *ma era già sicuro che di quella
> bambina poteva fidarsi a occhi chiusi'; I racconti* 87. Emphasis added).

The sense of mystery, the magical happy ending, the fairy-tale red of the
apple enchant us precisely because they are unexpected, and contradict
the harshness of the 'reality' from which the story has taken its departure. There is even a double magical gesture that brings the tale to closure: '*If I can throw the core of this apple in the stream, I am safe,* thought
Tom' ('*Se riesco a buttare il torsolo della mela nel torrente sono in salvo,* –
pensò Tom'; 88). Just then the point of view is reversed, as in a fairy tale,
and there is a reverse field effect to underline the second magical gesture: 'The little girl with the braids, *from high up in the untilled field, saw
Tom* cross the small bridge hunched down behind the parapet, and then
the apple core fall in a clear pool of the stream splashing all over the
reeds. *She clapped her hands,* and went away' ('La bambina con le trecce,
su dal campo incolto, vide Tom che traversava il ponticello, nascosto dietro

il muretto, e poi il torsolo cadere in un limpido laghetto del torrente alzando spruzzi sulle canne. *Batté le mani* e se ne andò'; 88. Emphasis added). Not only is the fighting man's safety entrusted to the little girl, but the very definition of human compassion acquires a fairy-like quality thanks to her, a lightness that a much older Calvino would praise above all the other qualities of literature. Telling the exploits of the Resistance, a historic turning-point and later the myth *par excellence* of the new Italy, paradoxically documents in Calvino the disappearance of the 'heroic' individual and the rise of a character that is a mixture of boy/*naïf*/poet, who lives perpetually bewildered in a world of great beauty but also of great treachery and cruelty. In the twilight of the icon of the Heroic Man, the *bambina* is the Other, who opens up the mystery of a universe desired but alien, while remaining distant in her serenity.[2]

The function of this character is evident also in 'La nuvola di smog.' The fifties had arrived, and for the protagonist, a man oppressed by a world tainted by pollution and ugliness, a man 'who was looking only for signs' ('cercava solo dei segni' *I racconti* 492), everything was losing meaning. The signs he saw referred only to one another, in a vicious circle. Disheartened and irresolute, he dragged himself here and there around the city, which was being suffocated by dirt, polluted air, and trash of all kinds. More and more frequently, though, he was surprised by the appearance of mysterious carts 'loaded with sacks ... and on top of the pile of white sacks a little girl' ('carichi di sacchi ... e in cima al mucchio di sacchi bianchi una bambina'; 949). They were laundry carts, and the girl was not just any girl, but 'a little girl with braids ... [sitting] on the white mound of sacks, reading a children's magazine' ('una bambina con le trecce ... in cima alla montagna bianca dei sacchi [che stava] leggendo un giornalino'; 493). During the entire pick-up operation, she was present but absorbed in her own activity: 'the little girl still up there who kept on reading' ('la bambina sempre in cima che continuava a leggere' 493). Her repeated appearances, her immobility, the recurring characteristics of her physical appearance, the mountain of white sacks, and the prominent position of the child all indicate that the little girl was something that finally *signified*. Precisely because of that apparition, the protagonist was led to a place he did not know about, where everything was cleansed. It was a world of meadows, river banks, sun and wind, the natural laundering place that no longer exists and probably never existed, the humble and concrete evidence of the possibility of purification. The protagonist observed the scene without indulging in excessive illusions: 'It wasn't much, but for me, who was looking only for images to keep in my mind's eye, perhaps that was enough' ('Non era molto, ma a me che non cercavo altro che immagini da tenermi negli occhi, forse bastava'; 495).

Duets under the Moon

As we have seen, when the Marcovaldo stories began to appear between 1952 and 1954, it was clear that a crucial shift in the Calvinian production was taking place. As far as the feminine is concerned, the character of Marcovaldo is immersed in total solitude: he has no mother, he has no companion, and there is no woman near him, if we except the occasional appearance of a caricature of a wife. There is not even a *bambina*, since his little daughters are simply names. The nostalgia for the feminine is entrusted to a being who lives farther and farther away, a source of tender humour and astonished contemplation – the moon girl ('la ragazza lunare').

It is no surprise that Marcovaldo should use a highly poetic language. Calvino knew that the subversion of cultural clichés such as the benignity of Nature, and of literary traditions such as the pastoral, must take place through the manipulation of prescribed and therefore very familiar models. But the premises and the consequences of the narrator's irony perhaps escaped Calvino himself. On the one hand, Marcovaldo searches for a good he has never known; on the other hand, Calvino quietly does away with everything, objects and delusions, around his lanky urban clown. Calvino's poetic language evokes the bourgeois myth of the individual in a world of his own construction; that language serves accurately to reveal the myth's illusoriness, since freedom and natural goodness certainly do not exist for the poet/labourer Marcovaldo, nor for those who live in his world. The feminine has no place here either, except as a poetic construct.

Logically, first we find a couple of lovers, an entity that can be conceived of only as a One binding two components. The lovers serve as obstacle to the realization of Marcovaldo's desires in 'La panchina' (The Park Bench). Then we find the impossible idyll of Marcovaldo's magicomic moonlit nights: the lovers recite their scene in strict obedience to the codes of the pastoral and the theatre. In fact, Calvino wrote 'La panchina' also as a text for a chamber opera.[3] Words and gestures underline what is essential in the cliché of the couple of lovers, that is to say, the total immersion of the characters in a private labyrinth defined by language. The two, in deference to convention, can only coo and fight. Their duet, using all the variations of the word *ammettere* (to admit), winds upon itself like the steps of the impatient Marcovaldo, who wants to stretch out on the park bench the lovers occupy (*I racconti* 167). But the episode includes an important and by now famous incidental component, a comparison Marcovaldo makes between two shades of yellow, the amber of a nearby traffic light and the pale nuance of the moonlight. It is doubtful that what we hear at this point is Marcovaldo's voice. The narrator selects for the comparison a highly specific language, whose poetic quality suggests that there has been a shift in register, a leap toward greater intensity and lightness of writing. The moon first appears in a rapid Leopardian quotation (from 'La sera del dí di festa' 2–3): 'He went to look at the moon, which *was full, large above the roofs and trees*' ('Andò a guardare la luna, che era *piena, grande sugli alberi e i tetti*'; *I racconti* 167. Emphasis added). With the quotation there opens a brief lyrical passage. The amber yellow of the traffic light, intermittent, abstract, and mechanical like the lovers' dialogue, is, in spite of its pretended brightness, 'tired and enslaved' ('falsamente vivace, stanco e schiavo'; 167); it is evidence of a world without freedom. Compared to it, the moon has a delicate hue, a 'mysterious pallor, yellow as well, but with an undertone of green and sky blue, ... serenely calm, irradiating her light without hurry, veined with the passing tracery of wisps of clouds that she majestically let fall from her shoulders' ('pallore misterioso, giallo anch'esso, ma in fondo verde e anche azzurro ... tutta calma, irradiante la sua luce senza fretta, venata ogni tanto di sottili resti di nubi, che lei con maestà si lasciava cadere alle spalle'; 167). Far away and autonomous, not subject to the misery of Marcovaldo's world, the moon is again the 'immortal young girl' of the Leopardian poems. Her distance suggests but does not make explicit the dichotomy to which the poetic consciousness is by now condemned, divided as it is between the unattainable myths of the past and the wretched mechanisms of the present. 'La panchina' recounts the nostalgia for problematic possibilities, the illusion of 'a nature rediscovered in the thick of civilization, the anxious awareness of a difficult and unusual felicity' ('una natura ritrovata nel folto della civiltà, la trepidante coscienza d'un bene difficile e inconsueto'; 'Gli amanti' [The Lovers] 193).

At the same time, the other short stories inform us that even the persistent memory of the concept of a benign Nature is the consequence of a cultural dysfunction. 'Luna e Gnac' (Moon and Gnac), which originally was placed right after 'La panchina' as closure to the Marcovaldo series of short stories, asserts by reiterating its modules that the pastoral manner is by now archaic. In that famous short story, the narrating voice uses two opposite linguistic levels to create an alternance between the contemplation of a moonlit night and the syncopated rhythm of a blinking neon sign. The description of the latter is as energy-laden as the former is subtle in its melodious precision. The light of the moon reveals to fifteen-year-old Fiordaligi a heart-melting presence: 'the barely lit small window of a mansard. And behind the window pane the face of a young girl the *colour of the moon,* the colour of neon, *the colour of light in the darkness,* and *a mouth, still almost childish,* that, when he smiled at her, imperceptibly parted and seemed about to open up into a smile' ('la finestrina appena illuminata di un abbaino. E dietro il vetro un viso di ragazza *color di luna,* color di neon, *color di luce nella notte, una bocca ancor quasi da bambina* che appena lui le sorrideva si schiudeva impercettibilmente e già pareva aprirsi in un sorriso'; 174. Emphasis added). Marcovaldo is excluded from the young people's 'storm of passions,' but he too can abandon himself to the enchantment of the cosmos that the narrating voice amorously evokes. The moon, in its double identity as inhabitant of the sky and pubescent girl, is the object of desire for all the characters, Isolina, Marcovaldo, and Fiordaligi. Because of that, the disappearance of the moon behind the neon-lit publicity is at the same time the disappearance of the moon girl, the shock of desire denied, and the last blow to the universe of the idyll.

The years during which Calvino wrote the first Marcovaldo stories were also the years during which he was about to retire from the more explicit forms of political activity, among them membership in the Communist party. It was then that the writer became aware of the complexity and immanence of the political dimension in its widest definition. The implicitly political quality of the Calvinian fiction would from then on testify to the most profound malaise of his society, a malaise that is certainly connected with economics and classism, but also with the lies a culture nurtures, even those 'beautiful' lies that perpetuate our illusions about a universe that never existed. It is significant that the power of those 'illusions' – to quote Leopardi once again – suggested to Calvino these words full of hope, which served as his commentary on an exhibition of paintings by a friend:

> These silent figures of lovers are ... the image of a yearning born in a world of estrangement and incompleteness. Carlo Levi, with the perfect lines of these embraces, expresses the awareness that we live in a historical situation utterly precarious, always at the edge of violence and massacres, and

at the same time the awareness of a happiness that human arms can reach ('queste silenziose figure d'amanti sono ... l'immagine d'un'aspirazione nata da un mondo d'estraniamento e d'incompletezza. Nel giro perfetto di questi abbracci, Carlo Levi esprime la coscienza di vivere in una condizione storica d'estrema precarietà, sempre sull'orlo dell'arbitrio e del massacro, e insieme la coscienza d'una felicità raggiungibile dalle braccia dell'uomo'; 'Gli amanti' 153–4).

The Cloven Amazon

Ordinarily, in fables and fairy tales the little girl suddenly becomes a woman, introducing into the story an image of big sister or mother or godmother; and then she disappears as suddenly, after accomplishing her mission as facilitator in the maturation of the male or female protagonist. In the late Renaissance epic tradition, the little girl blossomed into a virgin warrior, proud and disdainful of the passion of love, a virgin who was ultimately redeemed by Love from her abnormal condition. With the Enlightenment, the Amazon and the woman endowed with a 'virile' soul coexisted with the Prisoner, who first inhabited the Castle and then moved to the bourgeois Home; they all disappeared in time, leaving the field open to the tearful Beauty of Romantic fantasies.

In the Calvinian fiction of the second half of the fifties, that *sign*, the *bambina* with her braids and a red apple or a children's book in her hand, undergoes a metamorphosis inspired by various older iconographies. The athletic young girl accentuates her imperiousness, as she gallops on her pony and establishes her authority over the little boys of the neighborhood, as a budding Amazon in the magic world of childhood (*Il barone rampante*). Then, as temporal strata and literary reminiscences shift, she becomes a young Amazon part aristocrat and part anarchist, a Viola or a Bradamant (*Il barone rampante* and *Il cavaliere inesistente*). In Pirandello's vast production, female characters were either virginal or tarnished (by sex and/or maternity); in Moravia and Pavese, the female was sex, dark and mostly repellent. Calvino's young women are ambivalent; they engage in equestrian and sexual feats that tickle and amuse the readers' imagination, evoking a frank sexuality that is aggressive and capricious, but they remain, paradoxically, chaste. One trait is constant in these characters, as Claudio Milanini has aptly observed: 'Pamela, Viola, and Bradamant certainly do not defend their virginity; they defend their autonomy' ('Pamela, Viola, Bradamante non difendono certo la loro verginità: difendono la loro autonomia'; *Romanzi e racconti* I liv).

Yet things are not as simple as they seem. Viola's transformation from little girl to blond Amazon riding a white horse is still the prototypical image of the free woman who satisfies the (male) dream of a (female) vital energy that is not bound by the imperatives of a vaguely Kantian ethics, which Cosimo di Rondò on the contrary seemed to follow.[4] Cosimo's and Viola's encounter as adults marks the moment of passion shared, but also the discovery of an unbridgeable gulf between man and woman. And that gulf looms even more worrisome when the cloven femininity of Sophronia and Bradamant appears in *Il cavaliere inesistente*, almost as a double of the dimidiated pair formed by Agilulf and Gurduloo. There is another surprise for the readers: Bradamant the warrior turns out to be the writer Sister Dorothea, who, in a faraway convent, is filling pages with a chronicle of her own past active life. It is a female voice, then, that narrates female exploits, even though the narrative perspective, if we look carefully, reveals that what we have here is an unconvincing ruse.[5] Bradamant's story is paradigmatic of the ambiguous function of the feminine in Calvino's fiction. Having been told by the abbess to write, Sister Dorothea is not satisfied with that task, and sets to performing it with humorously expressed misgivings. Around her, stories and history wind their exciting events, but she must deal with pen and ink and paper, which leaves her frustrated; until the sound of active life calls her back to fight and to love, away from writing, toward the silence of her narrating voice. The 'virile' half of the pair Bradamant–Sister Dorothea abandons her authority, loses her voice, or, as Jean Starobinski says, appears to us 'in the process of remaining mute forever' ('in procinto di ammutolire per sempre'; *Romanzi e racconti* I xvii). The same thing happens to the other more 'feminine' half of the female pair in the same novel, Sophronia, a Giorgione-like figure contemplated in her soft, erotic physicality. Her patience in meeting life's adversities, which always derive for her from the attractiveness of her voluptuous femininity, captivates Torrismund, one of the novel's young knights in search of their identities; and so brings the knight's quest to a happy ending.[6] The text, in short, tells us that it is not only males who are insecure and uncertain of their function in the human community, at the time of the crisis of patriarchal ethics (Milanini lv). The feminine also dissolves and is reabsorbed by silence, once the characters caught in the tumult of incomprehensible events find rest in heterosexual bonding. Through the female characters also, Calvino documents and explores the situation of the bourgeoisie in a world full of turmoil and disappointments. His was a world of many losses: political, since the Resistance had not given life to a new world; cultural, because the centre, as Montale had said, 'did not hold,' or simply did not exist, and human beings doubted themselves; and literary, since the Author seemed to be losing authority, or at least creativity, and roamed nervously without compass among the relics of the past and the emptiness of the present.

Toward a New Woman?

The written text, in spite of it all, remains for Calvino the place where hope and doubt meet, and his writing contains more than playful battles and mythical loves. There is another current in Calvino's fiction, thoughtful and empathetic, that carries some of his texts in different directions from those of most of his other works, allowing him to weave together with seamless ease the fantastic and the realistic. Reflecting the ambivalence shown by twentieth-century Italian literature toward the female body (and here again, Pirandello, D'Annunzio, Svevo, Moravia, and Pavese are apt examples), the Calvinian text repeatedly focused on the image of a woman's nudity, usually against the backdrop of the sea. That image was a promise of repose and a source of silent contemplation and sense of mystery for the male protagonist. But the mature Calvino had become aware of the contradictions inherent in the female experience of the world, and his characters' emotions reflect those contradictions. In several scenes, a man playfully adorns a woman's body, with deft hands and admiring eye ('Desiderio in novembre' [Desire in November], *Ultimo viene il corvo* 218–19; *Il cavaliere inesistente* 118–20). In other scenes, the body of a naked swimmer, not muscular but endowed with 'a sweet plumpness' ('una dolce pinguedine'; *I racconti* 297), appears almost as a mirage, a revelation of the beauty and the vulnerability of the world. In 'L'avventura di un poeta' (The Adventure of a Poet), the woman's naked body swimming is a vision of lunar whiteness in the multicoloured water, enveloped by a silence that includes the man's wordless contemplation. In *La giornata d'uno scrutatore*, the image of Lia, the protagonist's lover, is evoked as the only certainty that a world of beauty still exists outside the walls of the home for incurables: 'Amerigo swam on and on toward the mirage, to touch again that distant shore, and could see in front of him Lia swimming, her back skimming the surface of the sea' ('Amerigo nuotava nuotava verso il miraggio, per riguadagnare questa riva irreale, e davanti a sé vedeva Lia nuotare, il dorso a filo del mare'; 33). Marilyn Schneider, commenting on this novella, rightly observes that in Calvino's universe love is inescapably the male's desire for the female; and her evaluation of Lia's character is rather negative because of the characteristics that tie her to a stereotypical literary image of woman: she is capricious, all physicality, irrational, and so on. However, a different note is sounded when Amerigo, dimly aware of his own limitations and hypocrisies and of the incomprehension evoked in him by Lia's concerns and attitudes, catches a sudden glimpse of another aspect of his confused and contradictory relationship with her: he sees her as a vulnerable but fierce being, with a shadow of sadness in her eyes, at times defenceless in her resistance against the world (86–8).

Woman as refuge, woman as mirage and puzzle, woman as the motive for tenderness and compassion: these three components mesh into an image that is the source of man's hope in the midst of chaos, and in the midst of his sense of ineptitude. But again, Calvino was concerned with the complexities of the concept of femaleness, its images in literature, and its situation in a society undergoing great changes. During those years, he made a remark that deserves close attention: 'The few examples of resoluteness, whether intellectual or moral or in action, are to be found in the female characters drawn by some of our writers' ('i pochi esempi di risolutezza o intellettuale o morale o d'azione li troviamo nei personaggi femminili di alcuni nostri scrittori'; *Una pietra sopra* 7).[7] While existence was veering toward a universal bourgeois system of values, Calvino's own female characters brought to some of his most unusual short stories if not resoluteness, then certainly awareness and doleful lucidity. These characters recognized and acknowledged the wounds that neither new prosperity nor ancient traditions could heal, as well as the pleasure still to be found in the world. Calvino's imagination and his attention to the world of people and things were firmly anchored in ordinary life by his insistence on linguistic precision. In 1950, in 'Pesci grossi, pesci piccoli' (Big Fish, Little Fish), a young boy in love with fishing attempted to distract, by showing her his dazzling specimens of the deep, a woman to whom the natural world kept revealing only violence and suffering.[8] The personal pain caused in the ungainly female character by an unlucky love history acquired a gently humorous cosmic dimension. In 1951 'L'avventura di una bagnante' (The Adventure of a Swimmer) analysed in a sensitive and lively way a situation, embarrassing as it was trite, that made a young bourgeois woman aware of her complex relationship to her own body and to the world, which until then she had left unexamined. The world imagined from a 'female' perspective in Calvino turns out to be a mirror image of the world in its 'male' version, but also highlights a sense of what exclusion and community can mean from a 'female' perspective. Interestingly, in 'Pesci grossi, pesci piccoli' and 'L'avventura di una bagnante,' the male presence is divided between two characters, a middle-aged man and his young son, who in both instances are sensitive but simple and taciturn people quietly absorbed in everyday occupations. In 1958, two other short stories proposed original images of the feminine, which were convincing in the authenticity of their portrayal of women dealing with the contradictions of modern life. 'L'avventura di una moglie' (The Adventure of a Wife) explores the desire for autonomy experienced by a young bourgeois woman. Her adventure is defined not in the tiresome terms of conventional fiction, even the kind of fiction that wanted to be 'modern' (an adulterous night, an escape), but as the simple desire for the freedom to see the world at an unusual hour, to experience one's aloneness, and to mingle and talk with other human beings as a self-contained person. 'L'avventura di due sposi' (The Adventure of Two Spouses) is the development of a mere two-sentence exchange found in 'La panchina' (1955), which was eliminated in the 1963 version of the same short story. That image of conjugal love, with its authentic human sharing and discrete sensuality, evidently was dear to Calvino. He had not found before, and would not find again, the same note of mature and genuine man-to-woman love.[9]

Meanwhile, the sixties had arrived, and with them profound shifts in a tormented Italian society, shifts that took place in the context of a cultural upheaval of planetary dimensions. As if in syntony with the world's events, Calvino's fiction turned to exploring the realms of fear and conflict. The tone had changed: 'The crossing of the forest had cost ... the loss of speech' ('La traversata del bosco era costata ... la perdita della favella'; *Il castello dei destini incrociati* 5), as a Calvinian narrator put it. The unsteady balance achieved by Calvino's fictional universe was broken. Mythical, one-dimensional images of women thirsting for vengeance pursued young knights who abandoned them after a brief season of love, as in 'Storia dell'ingrato punito' (The Punishment of the Faithless Knight). Horror of a resurgent feminism that threatened to compromise thousands of years of social order brought to the Calvinian page a different sort of Amazon. Ferocious giantesses look out from the flat surface of playing cards, and the encounter of male and female is described as a confrontation without mercy in which he is the betrayer and she the betrayed, or he the victim and she a diabolical incubus. In order to stress the power of inclusiveness possessed by the tarots thanks to their innumerable permutations, the mute narrator borrows details from previous Calvinian texts, such as the modest eroticism of Amazons like Bradamant and Viola. But the narration is burdened with nightmarish conflicts and ends with an apocalyptic finale: 'For the man who believed he was the Man there is no redemption. Punishing queens will govern for the coming millennia' ('Per l'uomo che credeva d'essere l'Uomo non c'è riscatto. Regine punitrici governeranno per i prossimi millenni'; 'La taverna dei destini incrociati' [The Tavern of Crossed Destinies] 77). Regina has come back, how different from what she was! The Amazon has split in two, and what rages now is the Mean half.

The Reading Game

The narrating voice in Calvino is without doubt a masculine voice. Its metaphors for everything that is pursued and unattainable are invariably feminine in form.[10] The Cities that live in memory and desire have women's names, seductive and mysterious. The archetypal City, the queen of cities, is the one the narrator left when a child, Venice. Absence is woman, and in her place a precious residue is left, and is entrusted to the only presences possible: man's imagination and the authority of the written word. But if imagination and writing are to come to life, somebody must be there to read and reflect. Unfortunately, a male reader's aspiration is to take power, and he tends to be devious, a hypocrite: 'He is brother and double of a hypocritical I' ('è fratello e sosia di un io ipocrita'; *Se una notte d'inverno un viaggiatore* 142), as Baudelaire had already said; in other words, the male reader resembles the author too closely. What is needed is a female reader, someone who truly enjoys reading, who serves as its mirror, someone who is seduced by it. First, there was the little girl atop a laundry cart, lost in the reading of her children's magazine; later, there was the adolescent girl, nursing her cold and mesmerized by 'fumetti,' a sort of written soap-opera ('Il gatto e il poliziotto' [The Cat and the Policeman] in *I racconti*); now, in *Se una notte d'inverno*, there is the *Lettrice*, the female reader, with a capital L. Even if the story is continually interrupted and the reading pleasure is perversely made problematical, the Writer can now establish with the *Lettore* (the male reader) the traditional man-to-man rapport, which – as anthropology has taught us – takes place through woman's body. Here, the *Lettrice* serves that purpose, literally, if one may use such a term in this strange case.[11]

Everything seems to have re-entered the centuries-old order according to which the feminine is container, mirror, and means of exchange – or almost everything. This is the Calvinian game, but what is a game if not a rehearsal of the actual show? A lot of ink has flowed in the debate about the question of the reader's power, and Calvino provided multiple replies to it. Still, the controlling presence of the one who writes is declared in several ways, some of them quite unambiguous: 'I say "I" and this is the only thing you know about me' ('io mi chiamo "io" e questa è l'unica cosa che sai di me'; *Se una notte d'inverno un viaggiatore* 15). The Writer is the subject, he sets the rules, he decides what the phases of the game are, and he teases the hapless Reader, sure as he is of the seductive superiority of his position vis-à-vis the Female Reader, whom he ends up by 'reading' through the Book's, and the Reader's, intermediary.

Given this setting, the only real danger, a thorn in the side of the narrator, is for the female reader to escape the writing's control and begin a revolt. Sure enough, in the Calvinian bookstore there is a first warning about just that feared challenge. There is a second female reader, another *lettrice*, this time with a lower-case *l*, and she is as Bad as the other is Good. The Bad One is a feminist Amazon, called nothing less than Lotharia, and she does not behave like a good girl, a facilitator in the textual game. As a matter of fact, she deconstructs books, literally tearing them to pieces, in a readers' collective organized as a zap action group. And lo! the devious retribution handed out by the text is not long in coming. Lotharia is shown as a plain and pedantic woman; her provocations are useless, and she is so unperceptive that she takes seriously the literary theories expounded by some new Trissotin; she is a true great-granddaughter of the *femmes savantes*. We realize at this point that our jovial author has ended up by retrieving from Renaissance fantasies and Enlightenment irony the true roots of a so-called bourgeois common sense; his text exhumes the centralizing passion of a European culture that remains profoundly in love with its own established Order. Reading may be said to come first, but the Author, even when filled with self-doubt, is still the Author-ity. The irony in Calvino's playing games with the concepts and devices of postmodernity resides perhaps exactly in that paradox.

Under the Crescent Moon

If City and Reading are metaphors of the feminine, perhaps the reverse is also true: the feminine is City and Creation, the point of encounter and discovery. New ambiguities and old themes mix in the texts Calvino wrote in the sixties, years that mark another turning-point in his writing. The magical presence of a mythical being returns in 1964 from the depths of the Western tradition with the first 'cosmicomic' tale, entitled 'La distanza della Luna' (The Distance from the Moon). That return is once again at the centre of the first four tales of *La memoria del mondo*.[12]

When Regina was born, in 'Paura sul sentiero,' she was born 'with the moon' ('assieme alla luna'; *I racconti* 57). Later, at the time of the first Marcovaldo stories, the setting of the moon, due not to a natural rhythm but to a technological interference, took on a wider significance in the Calvinian poetic universe. When the moon reappears, it is synonymous with a distance both inevitable and desired, the metaphor for a human condition constructed on the basis of a perspective attributed to the male. For him, according to the Calvinian texts, 'to be' implies the pain of separation, and carries only the bitter comfort of an awareness that has been reached on the other side of loss. In the cosmicomic universe, what is most evidently stressed is the continuous changing of the Moon, whose name is now spelled with a capital letter to indicate her having become a legitimate character in the fictional world. In the first short story, she is the remote object of desire, clearly female in her appearance and in her bond with a seductive and aloof female character. The story tells us of a double assertion of otherness from the male characters. Then, in 'La Luna come un fungo' (The Moon like a Mushroom), the Moon is a cold and empty desert, a pale sphere that is the negative of the Earth's splendour. Later, by moving closer, she reveals a marred and oozing surface, becoming an image of something alien and producing on humans 'an effect of fascinated disgust' ('un effetto d'affascinato disgusto'; 'La molle Luna' [The Soft Moon]).

And what about 'la ragazza lunare' of Marcovaldian memory, absorbed in the contemplation of the magic of moonlight? She returns in the fourth story of the sub-series, 'Le figlie della Luna' (The Daughters of the Moon), multiplied into a little horde of action-oriented 'ragazze lunari.' The Moon is decrepit and empty: 'She is old ... riddled with holes, worn ... naked in the sky' ('è vecchia ... bucherellata, consumata ... nuda per il cielo'; *La memoria del mondo* 63). And she is not unique; as other Moons before her, she is condemned to 'nascere e correre il cielo e morire' ('to be born, run through the sky, and die'; 63), in a modified citation of Leopardi's nomadic shepherd, for whom the Moon was an immortal young goddess, moving forever across the sky. The deaths of earlier Moons paralleled the growth of a world given to frantic consumerism, and this latter-day Moon hovers above a sci-fi New York. She is now attempting to flee the polluted Earth as she drags helplessly on its surface. Only a mythical Diana with her companions can free the dying celestial body from the city dump. A metamorphosis again takes place: the Moon rises, pulled with long ribbons by the young women, as a crowd of people from 'the throw-away city' ('la città da buttar via') look on. The happy ending comes with the successful ascent of the Moon, which floats away, free again, soaring with its cargo of young girls, who are the protagonists of the moon-rescue expedition. The girls leave with her, indifferent to terrestrial appeals, into an elsewhere that is denied the narrator, who refuses to climb aboard the cosmic ship. Yet he immediately feels nostalgia for what he has lost, while in his perplexity he remains bound to his hapless planet (as he did in 'La distanza della Luna'). City dump and Moon have briefly coexisted, and only a fable-like event has succeeded in restoring their distinct identities. As for the Earth's inhabitants, they are left with the characteristic feelings Calvino had already evoked in 'La distanza della Luna': 'The happiness of having found them again [the moon girls] was already undermined by the torment of having ended up by losing them forever' ('la felicità d'averle ritrovate [le ragazze lunari] già vibrava dello strazio d'averle ormai perdute'; 77). Desire, ultimately, is and will always remain a matter of distance and yearning, inherent in the restless spirit of all Calvinian protagonists. It is not surprising that, when Calvino playfully attempted to say the unsayable, how the primeval One became Two through love in a new genesis with scientific parameters, he would define falling in love as 'being torn from oneself' ('uno strappo da se stesso'; *Ti con zero* 69–81). In the one-celled universe, when the (female) Other appears, Eve of the biological world, her presence carries the weight of a condition that a dimidiated culture makes inevitable. It is the persistence of that duality that Calvino never ceased to explore and to attempt to exorcise, with melancholy and humour.

The years went by and the texts accumulated, but the dilemma remained, and the obstinacy to observe and speak lived on as well. The lunar metaphor triumphed in the later Calvino writings. With 'Luna di pomeriggio' (Moon in the Afternoon), Calvino wrote his most lyrical homage to the cosmic presence that is the sign of the feminine. Mr Palomar, just like Marcovaldo, is a man alone, without a woman, even though a solicitous wife is glimpsed once or twice in the wings. Like Marcovaldo, Mr Palomar also scrutinizes the universe in order to understand it and understand himself. And suddenly his eye discovers that it is his task to help what is absent to become present; more specifically, that his gaze must help the moon to be born in the afternoon sky. The moon needs us, says the text, it needs 'our concern, since its existence is still in doubt' ('il nostro interessamento, dato che la sua esistenza è ancora in forse'; *Palomar* 35), in the bright blue expanse of an afternoon sky. The poetic voice sustains her, almost draws her out of the depths of the heavens. Lights and colours shift, the very weight of the celestial body varies as the words describe with precision the viewer's perception of the moon's volume and shape. Tenderness and Mr Palomar's comical sense of importance alternate and even coexist in these pages: 'She is so fragile [the moon] pale and thin ... still all drenched with sky-blue. She is like a transparent host' ('È così fragile [la luna] e pallida e sottile ... ancora tutt[a] imbevut[a] di celeste. È come un'ostia trasparente' 35). Because the moon looks flat, a doubt that has not yet become terror emerges: the moon, is it a form, or an emptiness? Is it 'a breach that opens onto the void behind it' ('una breccia che s'apre sul nulla retrostante')? Only Mr Palomar's eye and the written word can serve as midwives to the world, and exorcise the nightmare of the disappearance of that privileged object from the world, the transformation of the moon into void. Is it the sky that recedes in the darkening of the evening, or is it the moon that moves imperceptibly forward, 'gathering the previously diffused light and depriving the sky of it, concentrating it all in the round mouth of its funnel' ('raccogliendo la luce prima dispersa intorno e privandone il cielo e concentrandola tutta nella tonda bocca del suo imbuto'; *Palomar* 37)?[13] The periwinkle colour of Bradamant and the violet colour of Viola are back. No, it's not a ghost of a moon that is coming into view, but a very solid body, however bruised and made imperfect by flaws. As soon as she has found her place in the evening sky, the moon, 'the most mutable among the visible heavenly bodies, and the most regular in her complicated habits ... imperceptibly is beginning to escape you' ('il più mutevole dei corpi dell'universo visibile, e il più regolare nelle sue complicate abitudini ... impercettibilmente ti sta sfuggendo'; *Palomar* 37). That 'ti' (singular 'you') unexpectedly reveals that Mr Palomar has split into two, perhaps in complicity with the ever present (male) Reader. The alter ego seems to witness with wonderment and satisfaction the firming up and moving away of the lunar body. In fact, there is now a resplendent celestial body ascending in the sky: 'The moon is a great blinding mirror flying in the sky' ('La luna è un grande specchio abbagliante che vola'; 37). As the moon triumphs in the night darkness, he can return to being the clumsy, perplexed Mr Palomar, 'now that *he* is sure that the moon no longer needs *him*' ('assicuratosi che la luna non ha più bisogno di *lui*'; 37. Emphasis added). The hypocrite! She is far away, he is freed of anxiety for her mutability, he thinks that he has placed her solidly in the sky, and can peacefully go back home ...[14] The effort has succeeded not because we believe in the power of Mr Palomar's will or eyes (the narrator has told us that he doesn't see well at all, and sees barely enough with various seeing aids), but because the writing, in its precision and elegance, has condensed in three pages the style, themes, and passion of a whole tradition, and has done so not heavy-handedly but with a touch of humour. As Calvino himself commented in a more pedestrian moment, 'Love for the moon is often doubled by love for its reflection, as if that reflected light pointed to a passion for the hall of mirrors' ('L'amore per la luna si sdoppia spesso in amore per il suo riflesso, come a sottolineare in quel lume riflesso la vocazione per il giuoco di specchi'; *Collezione di sabbia* 179).

Through the years, melancholy, humour, fear, and desire for distance mark Calvino's discourse about the feminine. That is why Calvino surprises us when he writes a story in which the encounter between man and woman opens up the possibility of a completely reciprocal rapport, and he allows that potential to be played out in an extraordinary moment of surrender to sensuality. The short story is 'Sotto il sole giaguaro' (Under the Jaguar Sun), and a 'spasm of suppressed suffering' ('uno spasimo di sofferenza contenuta'; *Sotto il sole giaguaro* 29) announces the theme. Now the female character is the one who speaks first. She is the one who guides the hesitant male into the erotic trance of biting into, and devouring, fiery and aromatic Mexican dishes.[15] Do we see here, fleetingly, a complicity between the sexes that replaces the habitual disparity? True, the only possible union of male and female is in 'the agonies of devouring each other, in the process of ingestion and digestion of universal cannibalism' ('lo spasimo d'inghiottirci a vicenda nel processo d'ingestione e digestione del cannibalismo universale'; 56–7). And yet, in this next-to-last fictional effort, Calvino's old metaphor returns. Perhaps 'the sun has tired of rising' ('il sole s'è stancato di sorgere'; 49); and in the two other pieces that form the incomplete collection of prose poems devoted to the five senses, the feminine reasserts its absence, which is both painful and inevitable. The phantom Other returns, and it is in her that Man searches for a reciprocity that is supposed to be impossible, since our culture in all its forms denies it. What remains to be captured by the senses is the perfume of a woman fleeing and the voice of an invisible woman. Calvino's decision to have his protagonists rediscover the world through all the senses leads to a text that proclaims once again the necessity for the concurrent absence and presence of the feminine. In 'Un re in ascolto' (A King Listening), the text speaks of language, of stories being told: 'Is there a story that binds one noise to the other? You cannot avoid searching for a meaning, which perhaps hides not in the single, discrete noises, but in the pauses that separate them' ('C'è una storia che lega un rumore all'altro? Non puoi fare a meno di cercare un senso, che forse si nasconde non nei singoli rumori isolati ma in mezzo, nelle pause che li separano'; 71). The king says that he has the situation firmly in hand. Or does he? As the Writer did before him, the king senses the precariousness of his control. Outside, beyond the lonely palace, is the City, 'varied and multicoloured, full of clamour and a thousand voices' ('la città varia e screziata, strepitante, dalle mille voci'; 78–9). But it is not fear of a revolt brewing nor fear of death that causes the king to listen intently to all sounds; he is beguiled away from his fears by 'a woman's voice ... in the summer nights ... a voice that came from the shadows ... from the dark' ('una voce di donna ... nella notte d'estate ... che veniva dall'ombra ... dal buio'; 86). That voice is like a bridge toward all the other presences; it is unique, impossible to reproduce, rooted in the body, in history, and in pleasure, exactly as writing is. It is also communication, and a love duet returns to charm the intent ear of the king, just before a dawn of Marcovaldian freshness: 'If you raise your eyes, you'll see a faint light. Above your head, the rising morning is brightening the sky ... Somewhere, in a fold of the earth, the city is awakening' ('Se alzi gli occhi vedrai un chiarore. Sopra la tua testa il mattino imminente sta rischiarando il cielo ... Da qualche parte, in una piega della terra, la città si risveglia'; 92–3).[16]

Bambina, Amazon, ragazza lunare, Moon – their common traits, within the metaphor of gender, describe what is the writer's true desire, what eludes and forever enchants and haunts him: language. Throughout his career, Calvino pursued what Dante once called 'the scented wild quarry,' a written medium that Calvino tirelessly described with the same attributes he used for the moonlight: clear, simple, sober, sharp, dry, and luminous. This is the message for the next millennium that is contained in the 'six memos' of the Lezioni americane, where the name of Leopardi returns more often than that of any other author: literature lives, and the feminine is the inseparable companion of literature, with the moon as its privileged sign. Calvino asserted that at first he had wanted to devote the entire lesson on 'Lightness' to the moon, because 'as soon as the moon has risen in the poets' verses, it has always had the power to communicate a sense of weightlessness, of suspension, of mute and calm enchantment ... unburdening language until it comes to resemble moonlight' ('la luna appena s'affaccia nei versi dei poeti, ha avuto sempre il potere di comunicare una sensazione di levità, di sospensione, di silenzioso e calmo incantesimo ... di togliere al linguaggio ogni peso fino a farlo assomigliare alla luce lunare'; *Lezioni americane* 26). The shadow of the absence of a feminine that evokes a contradictory desire for total possession and complete reciprocity, 'l'ombra della sua assenza' (26), is at the heart of the Calvinian universe, not only as an image of the feminine itself, but as a metaphor for the search for style, that is to say, the search for language, also totally possessed and completely transparent. So much so, that for Calvino the memory of his first encounter with style, a never forgotten example of exactness in simplicity, was a pen-and-ink drawing filled with magic: 'the black shape of Felix the Cat on a road that disappears in the landscape, over which hovers a full moon in the black sky' ('la sagoma nera di Felix the Cat su una strada che si perde nel paesaggio sormontato da una luna piena nel cielo nero'; 'Visibilità,' *Lezioni americane* 94).

Calvino's ability to seduce even those who are aware of the precariousness and the conservative aspects of his enterprise is due above all to his integrity as a writer who reflects on our society's hypocrisies and predicaments: 'Mr. Palomar laments the fact that it is impossible for him to look at woman with "enlightened intentions" ... for the customary way of looking and the customary response to that look seem too ingrained in society to accommodate good readings on man's part ... No look can ever be innocent' Finucci 255–6). We find in Calvino no pretence at having escaped the bonds imposed on everyone through the centuries, or at giving the definition for what one does not know. His project is a search for harmony (perhaps impossible) and for a convergence (perhaps only desired), and a never quenched curiosity for everything in the world that is other than oneself. He also dared to be honest, in his late portion of the twentieth century, in affirming the value of pleasure and playfulness, in exploring ambivalence, and in acknowledging fear without giving in to despair, or guilt, or ponderous seriousness. Calvino's passion for writing is the witness and sign of a certain culture that is also ours, imperfect and embattled, with its undeniable riches and crushing weights. He spoke dryly and clearly of a universe that was on its way to transformation – or perhaps to disappearance – and he was the rare author who chose to speak to our future, in spite of his perplexity and doubt as to the fate awaiting us.

1   This article is based on a much shorter version read at the symposium on Italo Calvino held at Universidad de Castilla–La Mancha in Almagro, Spain, in 1995.

2   As a matter of fact, a little girl in the short story entitled 'Il giardino incantato' (The Enchanted Garden) is called Serenella.

3   See Corti 'Un modello' 1978.

4   For this motif, I wish I were able to transcribe the very witty spoof written by Francesca Sanvitale for *La Stampa*, in which Cosimo meets Moll Flanders and is so entranced with her that he climbs down from his trees.

5   For the contradictions in the narrator's perspective, see the episode in which Raimbaut sees Bradamant peeing (*Il cavaliere inesistente* 58–9), and also Finucci 299 n24.

6   For this topic, see Schneider.

7   Calvino was alluding in particular to Cesare Pavese and his novel *Tra donne sole*, seeing in Clelia the key character of that novel. I would add that Clelia is the 'free' woman such as a conventional male imagination constructs her, that is to say, a copy of a subject seen as a predator, dry and without illusions. Not surprisingly, homosexuality, even in its less threatening female form, is barely hinted at, and remains the gnawing secret of a masculinism torn by anxiety. How can we avoid thinking, in this context, of the tormented artistic existence of Pavese's true disciple, Pier Paolo Pasolini?

8   A Leopardian note sounds again in this short story.

9   This short story unfortunately is not well known; even though collected in *I racconti* and in *Gli amori difficili*, for instance, it does not appear in the American volume *Difficult Loves*. It would be interesting to speculate on the reasons for such a glaring exclusion. For 'L'avventura di due sposi,' see the comments of two women readers, de Lauretis 1989 and Gabriele.

10 For this topic, see de Lauretis's articles.

11 For this topic, see Garboli and Schneider.

12 The reordering of the 'cosmicomic' series of short stories in ever new collections went on incessantly, almost obsessively. See the edition of 1975, and then the totally revised *Cosmicomiche vecchie e nuove* of 1984.

13 This is an image that returns at least twice in a prominent position in Calvino's fiction. Significantly, the other occurrence is in the last story in the volume *Marcovaldo*, 'I figli di Babbo Natale' (Santa's Children), twenty years earlier.

14 An interesting comparison could be made between this short story and the one entitled 'Il seno nudo' (The Bare Breast), for which one can usefully read Greimas's comment, and Finucci's 'Afterword' to her book *The Lady Vanishes*.

15 The terms used to describe this experience are seductive: 'fiery hot, biting
   sourness, a touch of bitter, creamy and sweetish smoothness, elaborate and
   daring cuisine, indelicate secrets' ('piccantissimo, asprezza pungente, fondo
   amaro, arrendevolezza cremosa e dolcigna, cucina elaborata e audace, se-
   greti indelicati'; *Sotto il sole giaguaro* 31). As for the women for whom the
   foods are expression and metaphor, the are called 'refined, and fiery, and
   introverted, and complicated,' etc. ('raffinate, e accese, e introverse, e complicate'; 32–3).

16 This luminous ending, as the narrator again addresses an elusive 'you' ('tu'),
   seems to contradict Ginzburg's view of Calvino's darkening vision in her
   1985 book review.

Bibliographical Information

Works Cited

Italo Calvino's works have the dubious privilege of being hot commercial property in Italy at the present moment, at least as distinguished literary works go. This means that several editions of most of his writings now exist, including the shorter pieces that previously were dispersed in innumerable daily and weekly publications, which often were difficult to retrieve. For today's reader, on the one hand there is the advantage of finding the majority of what is interesting in Calvino's writing career in just two or three collections; but there is also the annoying problem of wondering whether or not the texts that appear over and over again in different volumes are identical. A list of the Calvino works I consulted follows, in the chronological order of their writing, or in some instances according to their date of publication; they are accompanied by information about the translations available in the United States. The dates of the editions consulted appear in parentheses. The volumes available in English, unfortunately, often do not correspond exactly to their supposed counterparts in Italian, owing to decisions made by their curators. Other texts consulted are listed under individual chapter headings. Unless otherwise indicated, all the translations in this volume are mine.

Il sentiero dei nidi di ragno. Turin: Einaudi, 1949 (1964). *The Path to the Nests of Spiders*. Trans. Archibald Colquhoun. Boston: Beacon, 1957.
Ultimo viene il corvo. Turin: Einaudi, 1949 and 1969 (1976, 'Nuovi coralli' edition, almost identical to the one published in 1949).
Il visconte dimezzato. Turin: Einaudi, 1952 (1980). *The Nonexistent Knight and The Cloven Viscount*. Trans. Archibald Colquhoun. New York: Random, 1962.

Fiabe italiane. Turin: Einaudi, 1956. *Italian Folktales*. Trans. George Martin and
Catherine Hill. New York: Harcourt Brace Jovanovich, 1980.

Il barone rampante. Turin: Einaudi, 1957 (1960). *The Baron in the Trees*. Trans.
Archibald Colquhoun. New York: Harcourt Brace, 1959.

I racconti. Turin: Einaudi, 1958 (1983).

Gli amori difficili. Turin: Einaudi, 1958 (1970). *Difficult Loves*. Trans. William
Weaver, Archibald Colquhoun, and Peggy Wright. New York: Harcourt Brace
Jovanovich, 1984.

Il cavaliere inesistente. Turin: Einaudi, 1959. *The Nonexistent Knight and The Cloven
Viscount*. Trans. Archibald Colquhoun. New York: Random, 1962.

'I racconti che non ho scritto.' *Marsia* January–April 1959, 11–13.

I quaderni di San Gersolè. Turin: Einaudi, 1959.

I nostri antenati. Turin: Einaudi, 1960.

'La strada di San Giovanni' (January 1962). In *Questo e altro* 1:1; then in *I maestri
del racconto italiano* (Milan: Rizzoli, 1964) and in *La strada di San Giovanni*; now
in *Romanzi e racconti* III 7–26.

La giornata d'uno scrutatore. Turin: Einaudi, 1963. *The Watcher and Other Stories*.
Trans. William Weaver ('The Watcher' and 'Smog') and Archibald Colquhoun
('The Argentine Ant'). New York: Harcourt Brace Jovanovich, 1971.

Marcovaldo. Turin: Einaudi, 1963 ('Nuovi coralli' edition, 1973). *Marcovaldo, or
The Seasons in the City*. Trans. William Weaver. New York: Harcourt Brace
Jovanovich, 1983.

'Italo Calvino a Mario Boselli' (1964). *Nuova corrente* 109 (1992): 90–8.

'Gli amanti' (Presentazione a una mostra, 1964). In *Carlo Levi. Autoritratto*. Roma:
Edizioni Carte segrete, n.d. [1970?]. Now 'Litografie di Levi,' in *Saggi* II 1961–
2.

Le cosmicomiche. Turin: Einaudi, 1965. *Cosmicomics*. Trans. William Weaver. New
York: Harcourt Brace Jovanovich, 1968.

Ti con zero. Turin: Einaudi, 1967. *t-zero*. Trans. William Weaver. New York:
Harcourt Brace Jovanovich, 1969.

'Cibernetica e fantasmi' (1967). In *Una pietra sopra* 164—81.

La memoria del mondo e altre storie cosmicomiche. Milan: Club degli editori, 1968.

Tarocchi – Il mazzo visconteo di Bergamo e New York. Parma: FMR, 1969.

Italo Calvino racconta l'Orlando Furioso. Turin: Einaudi, 1970 (1988).

'Dall'opaco.' First published in *Adelphiana* (Milan: Adelphi, 1971); now in
Romanzi e racconti III 89–101.

Le città invisibili. Turin: Einaudi, 1972. *Invisible Cities*. Trans. William Weaver.
New York: Harcourt Brace Jovanovich, 1974.

Il castello dei destini incrociati. Turin: Einaudi, 1973. *The Castle of Crossed Destinies*.
Trans. William Weaver. New York: Harcourt Brace Jovanovich, 1976–7.

'Liguria.' In *Liguria*, ed. Italo Calvino and Folco Quilici (Rome: Esso italiana, 1973); now in *Saggi* II 2376–89.

'Il terzo lato è il mare.' In *Monumenti d'Italia. Le piazze*, ed. Franco Borsi and Geno Pampaloni (Novara, Istituto Geografico De Agostini 1975); now in *Saggi* II 2403–6.

'La squadratura.' Preface to *Idem* by Giulio Paolini (Turin: Einaudi, 1975); now in *Saggi* II 1981–90.

'Forse un mattino andando' (1976). In *Letture montaliane* (Genoa: Bozzi, 1977); then in *Perché leggere i classici*.

'I nostri prossimi 500 anni.' *Corriere della sera* 10 April 1977; now in *Saggi* II 2294–9.

'La poubelle agréée.' *Paragone* 324 (February 1977); then in *La strada di San Giovanni*; now in *Romanzi e racconti* 7–26.

'Al di là della morte di von Braun. Il tramonto della luna.' *Corriere della sera* 102, 139 (19 June 1977) 1. Now 'Il tramonto della luna,' in *Saggi* II 2316.

'Al di là dell'autore' (1978). In *Creatività, educazione e cultura*. Venice: Fondazione Cini, 1980. 125–32.

Se una notte d'inverno un viaggiatore. Turin: Einaudi, 1979. *If on a Winter's Night a Traveller*. Trans. William Weaver. New York: Harcourt Brace Jovanovich, 1981.

Una pietra sopra. Discorsi di letteratura e società. Turin: Einaudi, 1980. Most of these essays appeared in *La machine littérature* (Paris: Seuil, 1984) and then in *The Uses of Literature*.

'Montale's Rock' (1981). In *The Uses of Literature*.

'Poche chiacchiere!' *La Repubblica* 22 October 1982.

Palomar. Turin: Einaudi, 1983. *Mr. Palomar*. Trans. William Weaver. New York: Harcourt Brace Jovanovich, 1985.

'La coda di Minosse.' *La Repubblica* 10 March 1983; now in *Saggi* II 1735–8.

'The Written and the Unwritten Word [*sic*].' *New York Review of Books* 12 May 1983. 'Mendo scritto e mondo non scritto.' *Saggi* II 1865–75.

'Lo scrittore? E' un idiota come Flaubert' (1983). *L'Unità* 17 August 1986, 1.

'Cecchi e i pesci-drago.' *La Repubblica* 14 July 1984, 16–17; now in *Saggi* I 1034–9.

'Il gatto e il topo.' *La Repubblica* 24–5 June 1984; now in *Saggi* I 844–9.

Collezione di sabbia. Milan: Garzanti, 1984.

'Con Macchia senza paura.' *La Repubblica* 19 June 1985, 24–5.

Sotto il sole giaguaro. Milan: Garzanti, 1986. *Under the Jaguar Sun*. Trans. William Weaver. New York: Harcourt Brace Jovanovich, 1988.

The Uses of Literature. Trans. Patrick Kreagh. New York: Harcourt Brace Jovanovich, 1986.

Lezioni americane. Sei proposte per il prossimo millennio. Milan: Garzanti, 1988. *Six Memos for the Next Millennium.* Trans. Patrick Creagh. Cambridge: Harvard University Press, 1988.

La strada di San Giovanni. Milan: Mondadori, 1990. *The Road to San Giovanni.* Trans. Tim Parks. New York: Random, 1993.

I libri degli altri. Turin: Einaudi, 1991.

Perché leggere i classici. Milan: Mondadori, 1991.

Prima che tu dica pronto. Milan: Mondadori, 1993. *Numbers in the Dark.* Trans. Tim Parks. New York: Random, 1995.

Eremita a Parigi. Milan: Mondadori, 1994.

Romanzi e racconti. 3 vols. Milan: Mondadori, 1993–4. The appendices are particularly useful.

Saggi. 2 vols. Milan: Mondadori, 1995. The appendices are particularly useful.

Album Calvino. Milan: Mondadori, 1995.

The most complete treatment in English of Calvino's life and works is Beno Weiss's *Understanding Italo Calvino* (Columbia, SC: University of South Carolina Press, 1993).

References

Monographs on Calvino are not numerous, but articles and reviews abound. This selection lists only works relevant to the discussion in this book. Titles are listed only once, under the heading for the chapter in which first reference is made.

Introduction

Benedetti, Carla. *Pasolini contro Calvino. Per una letteratura impura.* Turin: Bollati Boringhieri, 1998.

Hewitt, Andrew. *Fascist Modernism.* Stanford: Stanford University Press, 1993.

Gobetti, Piero. *La rivoluzione liberale.* Turin: Einaudi, 1995.

Kocka, Jürgen, ed. *Borghesie europee dell'Ottocento.* Venice: Marsilio, 1989.

Il menabò 6 (1963).

Spriano, Paolo. *Le passioni di un decennio (1946–1956).* Milan: Garzanti, 1986.

Chapter 1

Ahern, John. 'Out of Montale's Cavern: A Reading of Calvino's *Gli amori difficili*.' *Modern Language Studies* 12:1 (Winter 1982): 3–19.

Almansi, Guido. *Eugenio Montale – The Private Language*. Edinburgh: Edinburgh University Press, 1977.

Arbasino, Alberto. *L'anonimo lombardo*. Turin: Einaudi, 1959 (1973).

Avalle, D'Arco Silvio. 'Cosmografia montaliana.' In *Tre saggi su Montale*. Turin: Einaudi, 1970. 101–14.

Bàrberi-Squarotti, Giorgio. 'La storia.' In *Letture montaliane*. Genoa. Bozzi, 1977. 283–96.

Becker, Jared. *Eugenio Montale*. New York: Twayne, 1986.

Biasin, Gian Paolo. *Il vento di Debussy: La poesia di Montale nella cultura del Novecento*. Bologna: Il Mulino, 1985. *Montale, Debussy, and Modernism*. Princeton: Princeton University Press, 1989.

Calinescu, Matei. *Five Faces of Modernity: Modernism, Avant-Garde, Decadence, Kitsch, Postmodernism*. Durham: Duke University Press, 1987.

Camon, Ferdinando. 'Giovanni Raboni su Montale' and 'L'editore a Italo Calvino.' In *Il santo assassino*. Milan: Garzanti, 1991. 111–14 and 115–19.

Cé, Sergio. 'Montale e Debussy: Verso l'uniformità di suoni e strutture.' *Strumenti critici* 16:1 (January 1992): 129–56.

Contini, Gianfranco. *Una lunga fedeltà. Scritti su Eugenio Montale*. Turin: Einaudi, 1974.

Coraggio e viltà degli intellettuali. Ed. Domenico Porzio. Milan: Mondadori, 1977.

Corti, Maria. 'Intervista. Italo Calvino.' *Autografo* 2:6 (1985): 47–53.

Falaschi, Giovanni. 'Ritratti critici di contemporanei. Italo Calvino.' *Belfagor* 27:5 (September 1972): 530–58.

Frye, Northrop. *Anatomy of Criticism*. Princeton: Princeton University Press, 1957 (1971).

– *The Critical Path: An Essay on the Social Context of Literary Criticism*. Bloomington: Indiana University Press, 1971.

de Lauretis, Teresa. 'Narrative Discourse in Calvino: Praxis or Poiesis?' *PMLA* 90:3 (May 1975): 414–25.

Letture montaliane. Genoa: Bozzi, 1977.

Luperini, Romano. *Storia di Montale*. Bari: Laterza, 1986.

Manzoni, Alessandro. *I promessi sposi*. Milan: Feltrinelli, 1965.

Mengaldo, Pier Vincenzo. *La tradizione del Novecento. Da D'Annunzio a Montale*. Milan: Feltrinelli, 1975.

– 'La lingua di Calvino.' In *La tradizione del Novecento*. Turin: Einaudi, 1991. 3rd series, 227–91.

Montale, Eugenio. *Sulla poesia*. Ed. Giorgio Zampa. Milan: Mondadori, 1976.

– *L'opera in versi*. Critical ed. by Rosanna Bettarini and Gianfranco Contini. Turin: Einaudi, 1980.

Pasolini, Pier Paolo. 'In morte del realismo' (1960). In *Le poesie*. Milan: Garzanti, 1975. 281–9.

Paulicelli, Eugenia. 'Natalia Ginzburg and the Craft of Writing.' In *Natalia Ginzburg: A Voice of the Twentieth Century*, ed. Angela M. Jeannet and Giuliana Sanguinetti Katz. Toronto: University of Toronto Press, forthcoming.

Pavese, Cesare. *La letteratura americana ed altre cose*. Turin: Einaudi, 1959.

Pirandello, Luigi. *Uno, nessuno e centomila*. In *Tutti i romanzi* II. Milan: Mondadori, 1990. *One, No One, and One Hundred Thousand*. Trans. and with an introduction by William Weaver. Boston: Eridanos, 1990.

Re, Lucia. *Calvino and the Age of Neorealism: Fables of Estrangement*. Stanford: Stanford University Press, 1990.

Savoca, Giuseppe. *Concordanza di tutte le poesie di Eugenio Montale*. Florence: Leo S. Olschki, 1987.

West, Rebecca. *Eugenio Montale: Poet on the Edge*. Cambridge: Harvard University Press, 1981.

Chapter 2

Alinovi, Francesca. '"Natura" impossibile del postmoderno.' *Il Verri*, 7th series, 1–2 (March–June 1984): 110–21.

Almansi, Guido. 'Il mondo binario di Italo Calvino.' *Paragone* August 1971, 95–100.

Barilli, Renato. 'I racconti di Calvino' (1959). In *La barriera del naturalismo*. Milano: Mursia, 1964. 210–20.

Belpoliti, Marco. *L'occhio di Calvino*. Turin: Einaudi, 1996.

Bernardini Napolitano, Francesca. 'Letteratura e scienza. Linguaggio poetico e linguaggio scientifico ne *Le cosmicomiche* e in *Ti con zero* di Italo Calvino.' In *Letteratura e scienza nella storia della cultura italiana*. Atti del IX congresso AISLLI, 1976. Palermo: Manfredi, 1978. 852–9.

Biasin, Gian Paolo. '*4/3 r (spazio scientifico, spazio letterario)*.' In *Letteratura e scienza nella storia della cultura italiana*. Atti del IX congresso AISLLI, 1976. Palermo: Manfredi, 1978. 860–72.

– *Icone italiane*. Rome: Bulzoni, 1983.

Cases, Cesare. 'Il pathos della distanza' (1958). In *Patrie lettere*. Turin: Einaudi, 1987. 160–6.

Frasson-Marin, Aurore. 'Structures, signes et images dans *Les villes invisibles* de Italo Calvino.' *Revue des études italiennes* 23 (1977): 23–48.

de Lauretis, Teresa. 'Italo Calvino e la dialettica dei massimi sistemi.' *Italica* 53:1 (Spring 1975): 57–74.

– 'Semiotic Models, *Invisible Cities*.' *Yale Italian Studies* 2:1 (Winter 1978): 13–37.

Marietti, Marina. 'L'uso dell'antilogia nelle *Istorie fiorentine*.' In *Culture et société en Italie du Moyen Age à la Renaissance*. Paris: Centre Interuniversitaire de Recherche sur la Renaissance italienne (CIRRI), 1985. 187–98.

Mengaldo, Pier Vincenzo. 'L'arco e le pietre.' In *La tradizione del Novecento*. Milan: Feltrinelli, 1975. 406–26.

Ossola, Carlo. 'L'invisibile e il suo 'dove': Geografia interiore di Italo Calvino.' *Lettere italiane* 39:2 (April–June 1987): 220–51.

Sartre, Jean-Paul. *La nausée*. Paris: Gallimard, 1938.

Tamburri, Anthony J. 'La "Nevicata" di Italo Calvino: Una ri-lettura di "Marcovaldo."' *L'asino d'oro* 5:10 (1994): 35–62.

Valesio, Paolo. *The Practice of Literary Semiotics: A Theoretical Proposal*. Working Paper series D, 71. Urbino: University of Urbino, February 1978.

Vergilius Maro, Publius. *Eclogues*. Ed. Robert Coleman. Cambridge: Cambridge University Press, 1977.

Chapter 3

Alpers, Paul. 'What Is the Pastoral?' *Critical Inquiry* 8:3 (Spring 1982): 437–60.

Asor Rosa, Alberto. 'Lo Stato democratico e i partiti politici.' In *Letteratura italiana I: Il letterato e le istituzioni*. Turin: Einaudi, 1982. 614.

Bakhtin, Mikhail. *Problems of Dostojevsky's Poetics*. Minneapolis: Minnesota University Press, 1984.

Bakhtin, Mikhail M., and P.N. Medvedev. *The Formal Method in Literary Scholarship*. Cambridge: Harvard University Press, 1985.

Bàrberi-Squarotti, Giorgio. *Fine dell'idillio*. Genoa: Il Melangolo, 1978.

Barilli, Renato. *La barriera del naturalismo. Studi sulla narrativa italiana contemporanea*. Milan: Mursia, 1970.

Battaglia, Salvatore. *Grande dizionario della lingua italiana*. Turin: UTT, 1961– .

Bonura, Giuseppe. *Invito alla lettura di Calvino*. Milan: Mursia, 1972–4.

Calvino, Italo. *Marcovaldo ovvero Le stagioni in città. Libri per l'infanzia e la gioventù*. Turin: Einaudi, 1963.

– *Marcovaldo ovvero Le stagioni in città. Letture per la scuola media*. Turin: Einaudi, 1966.

– *Marcovaldo ovvero Le stagioni in città. Coralli*. Turin: Einaudi, 1969.

– *Marcovaldo ovvero Le stagioni in città. Nuovi Coralli*. Turin: Einaudi, 1973.

Collodi (Lorenzini), Carlo. *Pinocchio [sic]*. Ed. Ferdinando Tempesti. Milan: Feltrinelli, 1972.

Cortelazzo, Manlio. *Dizionario etimologico della lingua italiana*. Bologna: Zanichelli, 1979–88.

Corti, Maria. 'I generi letterari in prospettiva semiologica.' *Strumenti critici* 6 (February 1972): 1–18.

– 'Testi o macrotesto? I racconti di Marcovaldo di I. Calvino.' *Strumenti critici* 9 (1975): 182–97.

– 'Testi o macrotesto? I racconti di Marcovaldo' and 'Un modello per tre testi: Le tre "Panchine" di Italo Calvino.' In 'Trittico per Calvino,' in *Il viaggio testuale*. Turin: Einaudi, 1978. 167–220.

– 'Nel laboratorio di Italo Calvino (da lettere inedite).' *Strumenti critici* 5:2 (1990): 137–46.

De Federicis, Lidia. *Italo Calvino e La giornata d'uno scrutatore*. Turin: Loescher, 1989.

Ettin, Andrew. *Literature and the Pastoral*. New Haven: Yale University Press, 1984.

Falaschi, Giovanni. *La resistenza armata nella narrativa italiana*. Turin: Einaudi, 1976.

Ferretti, Gian Carlo. *Le capre di Bikini. Calvino giornalista e saggista, 1945–1985*. Roma: Editori Riuniti, 1989.

Garber, Frederick. 'Pastoral Space.' *Texas Studies in Language and Literature* 30:3 (Fall 1988): 431–60.

Genette, Gérard. *Palimpsestes*. Paris: Gallimard, 1982.

Ginzburg, Natalia. *Mai devi domandarmi. Opere*. Milan: Mondadori, 1987.

Guglielmi, Angelo. 'Una "sfida" senza avversari.' *Il menabò* 6 (1963): 259–67.

Jeannet, Angela M. 'Collodi's Grandchildren: Reading *Marcovaldo*.' *Italica* 71:1 (Spring 1994): 56–77.

Jehenson, Myriam Y. *The Golden World of the Pastoral*. Ravenna: Longo, 1981.

Milanini, Claudio. 'Natura e storia nel "*Sentiero*" di Italo Calvino.' *Belfagor* 40:5 (30 September 1985): 529–46.

Poggioli, Renato. *The Oaten Flute*. Cambridge: Harvard University Press, 1975.

Ricci, Franco. *Difficult Games. A Reading of 'I racconti' by Italo Calvino*. Waterloo, ON: Wilfrid Laurier University Press, 1990.

Riffaterre, Michael. 'Système d'un genre descriptif.' *Poétique* 9 (1972): 15–30.

Thomson, Clive. 'Bakhtin's Theory of Genre.' *Studies in Twentieth Century Literature* 9:1 (Fall 1984): 29–40.

Todorov, Tzvetan. *Les genres du discours*. Paris: Seuil, 1978.

Vološinov, V.N., and M.M. Bakhtin. *Il linguaggio come pratica sociale*. Bari: Dedalo, 1980.

Chapter 4

Balice, Michele. 'La città di Calvino.' *Paragone* 37:438 (August 1986): 73–88.

Bàrberi-Squarotti, Giorgio. 'Gli schemi narrativi di Collodi.' In *Studi collodiani*. Pescia: Cassa di Risparmio Pistoia e Pescia, 1976. 87–108.

Barenghi, Mario. 'Italo Calvino e i sentieri che s'interrompono.' *Quaderni piacentini* 15 (1984): 127–50.

Bryce, Judith. 'Rousseau and Calvino: An Unexplored Ideological Perspective in *Il barone rampante.*' In *Moving in Measure*, ed. Judith Bryce and Doug Thompson. Hull: Hull University Press, 1989. 201–14.

Calvino Revisited. Ed. Franco Ricci. Toronto: Dovehouse, 1989.

Camon, Ferdinando. *Il mestiere di scrittore*. Milan: Garzanti, 1973.

Catalano, Antonella. 'Le mappe dell'esilio. Sulle *Città invisibili* di Italo Calvino.' In *La torre abolita. Saggi sul romanzo italiano del Novecento*, ed. Ferdinando Pappalardo. Bari: Dedalo, 1988. 291–324.

Corriere dei piccoli. Weekly illustrated supplement of *Corriere della sera*. Milan, 27 December 1908 – . Nos 22:1 to 41:3 (1930–49) consulted.

Darnton, Robert. *The Great Cat Massacre and Other Episodes in French Cultural History*. New York: Basic, 1984.

Diderot, Denis. *Jacques le fataliste et son maître*. Critical ed. by Simone Lecointre and Jean Le Galliot. Geneva: Droz, 1976.

Eco, Umberto. 'Elogio del riassunto.' *L'Espresso* 20 October 1982, 90.

Gatt-Rutter, John. 'Calvino Ludens: Literary Play and Its Political Implications.' *Journal of European Studies* 5 (1975): 319–40.

Hassan, Ihab. *The Dismemberment of Orpheus: Toward a Postmodern Literature*. New York: Oxford University Press, 1971.

Horatius Flaccus, Quintus. *Opera*. Ed. S. Borzsak. Leipzig: Teubner, 1984.

Huizinga, Johan. *Homo Ludens: A Study of the Play Element in Culture* (1938). Boston: Beacon, 1950.

Hutcheon, Linda. *A Poetics of Postmodernism: History, Theory, Fiction*. New York: Routledge, 1988.

Huyssen, Andreas. *After the Great Divide: Modernism, Mass Culture, Postmodernism*. Bloomington: Indiana University Press, 1986.

Inchiesta sulle fate. Ed. Delia Frigessi. Bergamo: Pierluigi Lubrina, 1988.

Jeannet, Angela M. 'A Writer's Project: Cornerstones, Milestones, and Headstones.' In *Calvino Revisited*, ed. Franco Ricci. Toronto: Dovehouse, 1989. 207–25

Jonard, Norbert. 'Calvino et le siècle des lumières.' *Forum Italicum* 18:1 (Spring 1984): 93–116.

Kaplan, E. Ann, ed. *Postmodernism and Its Discontents*. London: Verso, 1988.

Kipling, Rudyard K. *The Collected Works*, vol. 16. New York: Doubleday, 1941.

de Lauretis, Teresa. 'Reading the (Post)Modern Text: *If on a Winter's Night a*

Traveler.' In *Calvino Revisited*, ed. Franco Ricci. Toronto: Dovehouse, 1989. 131–
45.

Lévi-Strauss, Claude. *La pensée sauvage*. Paris: Plon, 1962.

Lyotard, Jean-François. *La condition postmoderne. Rapport sur le savoir*. Paris:
Minuit, 1979. *The Postmodern Condition*. Minneapolis: University of Minnesota
Press, 1984.

Petrignani, Sandra. 'Italo Calvino.' In *Fantasia e fantastico*. Brescia: Camunia,
1985. 13–22.

Pirandello, Luigi. *Maschere nude*. Milan: Mondadori, 1967.

– *Novelle per un anno*. Florence: Giunti, 1994.

Rodari, Gianni. *Favole al telefono*. Turin: Einaudi, 1962 (1980).

Scalise, Gregorio. 'The Game of Palomar.' *Review of Contemporary Fiction* 6:2
(Summer 1986): 138–45.

Stevenson, Robert Louis. *Treasure Island*. New York: Random, 1949.

Suleiman, Susan. *Subversive Intent: Gender, Politics, and the Avant-Garde*.
Cambridge: Harvard University Press, 1990.

Valéry, Paul. 'Monsieur Teste.' In *Oeuvres II*. Paris: Gallimard, 1960. 11–75.

Xenophon. *Anabasis*. Biblioteca Universale Rizzoli. Milan: Rizzoli, 1978.

Chapter 5

Asor Rosa, Alberto. 'Il cuore duro di Calvino.' *La Repubblica* 1 December 1985,
22.

Boselli, Mario. 'Italo Calvino: L'immaginazione logica.' *Nuova corrente* 78 (1979):
137–50.

Cases, Cesare. 'Calvino al bando' (1973). Now in *Patrie lettere*. Turin, Einandi,
1987. 167–71.

Hume, Kathryn. *Calvino's Fictions: Cogito and Cosmos*. Oxford: Clarendon, and
New York: Oxford University Press, 1992.

Il menabò 4 and 5 (1961 and 1962).

Pasolini, Pier Paolo. *Descrizioni di descrizioni*. Turin: Einaudi, 1979

Vittorini, Elio. *Le due tensioni*. Milan: Il Saggiatore, 1967.

Chapter 6

Finucci, Valeria. *The Lady Vanishes: Subjectivity and Representation in Castiglione
and Ariosto*. Stanford: Stanford University Press, 1992.

Gabriele, Tommasina. *Italo Calvino: Eros and Language*. Teaneck, NJ: Fairleigh
Dickinson University Press, 1994.

Garboli, Cesare. 'Come sei, Lettrice?' *Paragone* 366 (1980): 63–71.

Ginzburg, Natalia. 'Il sole e la luna.' *L'indice dei libri del mese* 2:8 (September–October 1985): 26–7.

Greimas, Algirdas. 'Le guizzo.' In *De l'imperfection*. Paris: Fanlac, 1987. 23–33.

de Lauretis, Teresa. 'Through the Looking-Glass: Woman, Cinema, and Language.' In *Alice Doesn't: Feminism, Semiotics, Cinema*. Bloomington: Indiana University Press, 1984.

Sanvitale, Francesca. 'Moll Flanders fa scendere Cosimo dagli alberi.' *La Stampa* February 1993, Tuttolibri 3.

Schneider, Marilyn. 'Calvino's Erotic Metaphor and the Hermaphroditic Solution.' *Stanford Italian Review* 2 (Spring 1981): 93–118.

Index

absence, 145; the feminine and, 174, 176

Agilulf, 23, 24, 43, 44, 51, 137, 138, 165

Amazon, the, 155, 164, 168, 170

ambiguity, 22; the world's, 21

Amori difficili, Gli (Difficult Loves), 26, 32

animals, in Calvino, 37, 43, 52, 65, 68, 75, 81, 114–15, 135, 152 n1

antithesis, 36, 57, 58, 71, 73, 75, 80, 82

antithetical, 52, 58, 60, 66; in Pirandello, 58

Arbasino, Alberto, 8

Author, the, 88, 120, 123–4, 166, 170

avant-garde, xix, 15, 61 n2

Bakhtin, Mikhail, 72, 95 n8

Bakhtinian, 69, 112

Barone rampante, Il (The Baron in the Trees), 15, 83

bourgeois, 80, 161

bourgeoisie (also *borghesia*), xv, xvi, xvii, xviii, 40, 56, 110, 128, 165. *See also* middle class

Bradamant, 24, 44, 164, 165

Calvino, Italo: childhood of, xv; death of, xiii; family of, xvi, 6, 41; and ecology, xv; and literary tradition, xiv, xv, xix, 4, 5, 57, 77, 89, 104, 118, 134; and the Masons, xvi, 40; and politics, xv, xvii, 29, 104, 125; and Protestantism, xv, xvi; and rationalism, xv

Capre di Bikini, Le, 152 n1

Castello dei destini incrociati, Il (The Castle of Crossed Destinies), 138, 168

Cavaliere inesistente, Il (The Nonexistent Knight), 23, 43

Cecchi, Emilio, 129

Chaplin, Charlie, 76, 77

Chiron, the centaur, 107

Città invisibili, Le (Invisible Cities), 28, 50, 145, 147, 148

city, the, 12, 20, 25, 27, 39, 45, 46, 50, 146–8; in the background, 138; as cosmos, 142, 147; as dream machine, 89; duplicity of, 44; emblematic, 12, 66; ; fragile, 143; as freedom, 146; geometric, 44; invisible, 50, 93, 139; as labyrinth, 71, 146; as language, 148; as maze, 25; metamorphosis of, 92; as metaphor of the feminine, 170; and nature, 85; as place of contradictions, 140; as prison, 89; as storytelling, 148; of today, 77

clown, the, 16, 31, 40, 58, 161

collections, 49, 60, 82, 83, 85, 111, 115

'Collezione di sabbia' (A Collection of Sand), in *Collezione di sabbia*, 128, 149

Collodi, Carlo (Lorenzini), 88, 91, 97 n24, 102

Collodian, 91

comic strip, 75, 76, 77, 86, 100 n39, 104–6; American, 105

Communist party, Italian, xvi, 9, 83, 163; character of, 136

contaminazione, 74, 75, 77

Conversazione in Sicilia (Conversation in Sicily), 9, 10

Corriere dei piccoli, 105

Corti, Maria, 84, 94 n3, 117

Cosimo di Rondò, 104

Cosmicomiche, Le (Cosmicomics), 103, 142; 'I cristalli' (Crystals), 21; 'La distanza della Luna' (The Distance from the Moon), 171

crystal, the, 17, 20, 41, 47, 62 n16. *See also* glass; lens

'Dall'opaco' (From the Shady Side), 49

De Amicis, Edmondo, 110

death, 42, 48, 56, 58; in Pirandello, 31, 58; as ruse, 127; simulation of, 127

Diderot, Denis, 124–5

dilemma, 36, 37, 39, 45, 172

Don Quixote, 61 n5, 73; the character, 79

doubt, xvi, xviii, 18, 25, 29, 57, 59, 166, 176

duality, 37, 137, 145, 172; as cloven-ness (*dimidiamento*), xix, 134; also dichotomy, dyad, dualism, 23, 36, 53, 81, 86, 162

duplicity, 45, 52, 53; of the city, 44; of the world, 89

eighteenth century, 66, 67, 107, 108

Enlightenment, xvi, xix, 124, 132 n5, 164, 170

Eremita a Parigi (A Hermit in Paris), xiii, xvi, xix, 13

escape, 25, 26, 40, 46, 64 n24, 76, 83, 89, 92, 93; disappearance as, 128. *See also* flight

ethics, 12, 30, 32, 124; of action, 153 n10; literary, 129; patriarchal, 165; of writing, 112

existentialist, 19

eye, the, 21, 35, 46, 49, 52–3, 56, 57, 59, 60, 61, 127, 151, 172; as metaphor, 52, 55; Mr Palomar's, 172–3; of the surveyor, 41

fable, 18, 38, 159, 164

Fascism, xv, xvi, 6, 7

Fascist, xv, xvi, 3, 136

feminine, the, xx, 155, 161, 165, 169; as City and reading, 170; and distance, 174; and literature, 175; and the moon, 172, 175

Fiabe italiane (Italian Folktales), 108–11, 119

flight, 25, 33, 60, 90, 93, 158. *See also* escape

folk-tale, 108–11

'Formica argentina, La' (The Argentine Ant), in *Racconti*, 22, 42, 137

Frye, Northrop, 28

game, the, 92, 116, 124, 169

geometric, 43, 46, 50, 51; as obsession, 40

geometry: plane, 41, 45, 49, 54, 60, 109; solid, 47

Giornata d'uno scrutatore, La (The Day of the Watcher), 39, 84, 139, 166

glass, 20, 27, 41, 47, 48, 146. *See also* crystal; lens

Gobetti, Piero, xx, 6

Gurduloo, 24, 137, 138, 165

Hermeticism, 9

hermetic man, 4, 23

'Idilli difficili, Gli' (Difficult Idylls), in *Racconti*, 66, 85

idyll, 66, 74, 82, 90, 161

idyllic, 72

ink, 29, 88, 165

invisible, the, 49–50, 93, 149

Jacques le fataliste et son maître (*Jacques the Fatalist and His Master*), 124

Kim, xvii, 103

Kipling, Rudyard, 4, 103, 104

labyrinth, 25, 41, 46, 59, 89, 146; challenge to the, 93; love as a, 161

language, xv, 15, 31, 41; and antithesis, 76; choice of, 69, 162; as clue, 88; crisis of, xviii, 15; and culture, xiv, xviii, xix; poetic, 162; as tool, 29; usefulness of, 31; as value, 131; and the world, 41; and writing, 102

lens, 22, 53, 57, 109. *See also* crystal; glass

Leopardi, Giacomo, 53, 55, 163, 171, 175

Leopardian, 79, 82, 83, 162, 177 n8

Lévi-Strauss, Claude, 117–18

Lezioni americane (*Six Memos for the Next Millennium*), 28, 130, 152

Liguria, xv, 27, 46, 49

literature, xix, 13, 28, 29, 31, 130; castle of, 101, 102; as communication, 33; as dialogue, 19, 107; as endurance, 128; as existential function, 130; and the feminine, 175; as a form of truth, 109; future of, 125, 131; and history, 107, 131; as joy, 33; as a means to knowledge, 24; and the moon, 175; as resistance, 33; as search for understanding, 130; and society, 28; sustenance in, 107; usefulness of, 31; as value, 131

magic(al), 120, 159, 176

Marcovaldo (the character), 15, 69–71, 81, 85, 88, 89, 149, 162; city-bound, 87; loneliness of, 172; as mediating presence, 80; new avatar of, 127; the poet, 74, 142, 161; the proletarian, 59, 74, 76

Marcovaldo ovvero Le stagioni in città (*Marcovaldo, or The Seasons in the City*), 46, 77, 83–96, 127, 141; 'La città smarrita nella neve' (The City Hidden in the Snow), 88, 142; 'La città tutta per lui' (The City All to Himself), 142; 'Dov'è più azzurro il fiume' (Where the River Is More Blue), 90, 141; 'La fermata sbagliata' (The Wrong Stop), 46, 90; 'I figli di Babbo Natale' (Santa's Children), 88, 90, 142; 'Fumo, vento e bolle de sapone' (Smoke, Wind, and Soap Bubbles), 141; 'Il giardino dei gatti ostinati' (The Garden of Stubborn Cats), 90, 142; Luna e

Gnac' (Moon and Gnac), 88, 90, 162; 'Marcovaldo al supermarket' (Marcovaldo at the Supermarket), 142; 'La pioggia e le foglie' (The Rain and the Leaves), 90, 142; 'Un sabato di sole, sabbia e sonno' (A Saturday with Sun, Sand, and Sleep), 90; 'La villeggiatura in panchina' (Vacation on a Park Bench), 87, 90, 140

Marcovaldo stories, first cycle, 66–83, 141, 161; 'Il coniglio velenoso' (The Poisonous Rabbit), 68; 'I figli di Babbo Natale' (Santa's Children), 91–2; 'Funghi in città' (Mushrooms in the City), 67; 'Luna e Gnac' (Moon and Gnac), 68, 78–80, 162; 'La panchina' (The Park Bench), 68, 74, 78–80, 82, 161; 'La pietanziera' (The Lunch-Pail), 67–8; 'Il piccione comunale' (The City Pigeon), 68

masculine, 156, 169

Mediterranean sea, 27, 55

Memoria del mondo, La (The Memory of the World), 46, 143, 171; 'Le figlie della Luna' (The Daughters of the Moon), 148, 171; 'La Luna come un fungo' (The Moon like a Mushroom), 171; 'La molle Luna' (The Soft Moon), 171

'Memorie difficili, Le' (Difficult Memories), in Racconti, xvii, 11

Menabò, Il, xv

Metamorphoses (Ovid), 115

metamorphosis, 49, 68, 90, 92, 121, 144, 164, 172

middle class, xv, xvi, 3, 4, 5, 30, 31. See also bourgeoisie

Modernism, xv, xix, 4, 5, 6

Monsieur Teste, 58

Montale, Eugenio, 4–7, 12–33, 131; 'Arsenio,' 26; Bufera, La (The Storm), 24; Occasioni, Le (Occasional Poems), 13; Ossi di seppia (Cuttlefish Bones), 12, 13; Satura, 26

moon, the, 80, 98 n30, 140, 142, 152, 162; as character, 171; as girl, 163; latter-day Moon, 171; Leopardian, 79; moon girl(s), 80, 88, 161, 162, 163; moonlight, 176; moonlit, 79, 161; as organic body, 142; origins of, 143–5

Moravia, Alberto, 7–9, 155

Mr Palomar, 30, 31, 51, 52–60, 176; loneliness of, 172; as older Marcovaldo, 149

narrator, 52, 69, 135; comments and interventions of, 95 n10; extradiegetic, 69, 127; irony of, 161; as mediator, 57; position of, 74; and protagonist, 78, 80; as voice, 70, 88, 162

natural, 25, 71, 82, 160

nature, 20, 56, 68, 70, 82, 136; benign, 66, 161, 162; as construct, 65; disappearance of, 20; as ghostly presence, 69; as haven, 78; and history, 89; as literary memory, 71; as topos, 73

Neorealism, 33 n6

Neorealist(ic), 9, 67, 71, 106

Nostri antenati, I (Our Ancestors), 105

nothingness, 28, 145

nouveau roman, 41, 84

'Nuvola di smog, La' (The Cloud of Smog), in Racconti, 137, 160

obstinacy, 25, 42, 43, 53, 81, 99 n35, 172; without illusions, 84, 91

oral expression, 13; storytelling, 110

Ortese, Anna Maria, 98 n30, 141
Ovid, 115

Palomar (Mr. Palomar), 21, 52–60, 127,
130; 'Luna di pomeriggio,' (Moon
in the Afternoon), 151
Parini, Giuseppe, 107
Paris, city of, 50, 84
Pasolini, Pier Paolo, xx
Passioni di un decennio, Le (The Passions of a Decade), xv
pastoral, tradition of, 71–6, 79, 80, 161;
dream, 78, 89, 93; overtones, 85;
universe, 80, 81, 82
Pavese, Cesare, 9, 10–12, 30, 65, 155,
177 n7
pedagogic(al), 110, 121, 129; ideal,
113
pedagogy, 77, 124, 131
Pensée sauvage, La (The Savage Mind),
117
Perché leggere i classici (Why Read
Canonical Authors?), 20, 21
perplexity, xix, 13, 18, 29, 36, 131, 141,
150, 172, 176
Pietra sopra, Una (Burying the Past),
xvii, 9, 12, 13, 29, 51, 52, 151; 'Il
midollo del leone' (The Lion's Marrow), 4, 107
Pin, 103, 138
Pinocchio, Le avventure di (The Adventures of Pinocchio), 4, 88, 97 n24,
102, 105
Pirandello, Luigi, 19, 30–1, 58, 156;
bourgeois drama in, 128; death
theme in, 63 n23
playful(ly), 16, 23, 31, 38, 102
playfulness, xix, 83, 90, 137
poetic modes, 14, 15, 79
poetics, xix

postmodern, 54, 114, 121, 123; hyper-
reality, 128
postmodernism, postmodernity, xvi,
xix, 122–3, 170
'Poubelle agréée, La' (The Certified
Garbage Can), 149
proletariat, xvii

Qfwfq, 103, 142, 144, 145

Racconti, I (Short Stories), xvii, 8, 13,
14, 22, 37, 66, 72, 83, 84; 'Andato al
comando' (Sent to Headquarters),
10; 'L'avventura di due sposi' (The
Adventure of Two Spouses), 79, 87,
168; 'L'avventura di una bagnante'
(The Adventure of a Swimmer), 22,
167; 'L'avventura di una moglie'
(The Adventure of a Wife), 168;
'L'avventura di una poeta' (The
Adventure of a Poet), 22, 166; 'Un
bastimento carico di granchi' (A
Ship Full of Crabs), 157; 'Il bosco
degli animali' (The Animals'
Woods), 114; 'L'entrata in guerra'
(The War's Beginning), 38; 'I fratelli
Bagnasco' (The Bagnasco Brothers),
11; 'Il gatto e il poliziotto' (The Cat
and the Policeman), 15, 44, 114, 169;
'Paese infido,' (Treacherous Vil-
lage), 138, 159; 'Paura sul sentiero'
(Fear on the Trail), 155, 171; 'Pesci
grossi, pesci piccoli' (Big Fish, Little
Fish), 22, 36, 137, 167; 'Ultimo viene
il corvo' (The Crow Comes Last),
15, 16, 42, 48; 'Uno dei tre è ancora
vivo' (One of the Three Is Still
Alive), 138; 'Va' cosí che vai bene'
(Keep Going Down That Road,
Mate!), 158

Raimbaut, 23, 24, 43, 44, 62
reader, the, 52, 69, 70, 112; reader's
    response, 112
reader, the female, 155, 169, 170; the
    second female reader, 170
reader, the male, 169, 170, 173
reception, 77, 86, 104
Resistance, the, xv, xvii, 6, 106, 107,
    138, 159
rhetorical devices, 14, 24, 30, 57, 71,
    72, 79, 106; figures, 70, 111
Rimbaud, Arthur, 100 n41
Robinson Crusoe, 126
Roquentin, 54, 57, 59

sand, 41, 47, 56, 60, 149, 152
Sarraute, Nathalie, 107
Sartre, Jean-Paul, 54, 59, 107
sea, 27, 46, 50, 52, 55, 151
senses, the, 17, 54, 135, 174; as part of
    totality, 128
Sentiero dei nidi di ragno , Il (The Path to
    the Nests of Spiders), xvii, 7, 103
Se una notte d'inverno un viaggiatore (If
    on a Winter's Night a Traveller), 123,
    169
silence, 57, 60, 90, 145; the feminine
    and, 165, 166; Mr Palomar's, 56; as
    tool, 127
snow(fall), 17, 45, 88, 90, 91, 92
Sophronia, 165
Sotto il sole giaguaro (Under the Jaguar
    Sun), 16, 128; 'Un re in ascolto' (A
    King Listening), 33, 175; 'Sotto il
    sole giaguaro,' 174
soup, the, 138, 139, 140, 144, 148
'Speculazione edilizia, La' (Building
    for Profit), in Racconti, 40, 146
spiral, 46, 48
Spriano, Paolo, xv

Stevenson, Robert Louis, 4, 103, 104
storytelling, 26, 69, 102, 119; function
    of, xx, 116; image and, 114; rational
    element of, 109; style of, 69, 105;
    tradition of, 86
'Strada di San Giovanni, La' (The
    Road to San Giovanni), 65, 147, 151
stubborn(ly), 21, 27, 119, 156
stubbornness, 59, 137, 148
style, 30, 104, 125; devices of, 117; and
    the feminine, 176; of folk-tales, 108
Symbolism, 5, 6

Tarocchi (Tarots), 3, 46, 49
tarots, the, 49, 119; and history, 119;
    inclusiveness of, 168
'Taverna dei destini incrociati, La'
    (The Tavern of Crossed Destinies),
    in Il castello dei destini incrociati, 138,
    169
thread, as metaphor, 17, 26, 29, 51, 92,
    120
three, the number, 41, 50, 52, 54, 57,
    60
Ti con zero (t-zero), 47–8
Tofano, Sergio, 86, 105, 123
triangle (geometric form), 39–41, 43,
    45, 46, 49, 50, 51, 55, 61
triangular, 40, 113
Turin, 9, 12, 44–5, 50, 139
Tuscanisms, 78, 91

Ultimo viene il corvo (The Crow Comes
    Last): 'Angoscia in caserma'
    (Anguish in the Barracks), 136;
    'Desiderio in novembre' (Desire in
    November), 166; 'La stessa cosa del
    sangue' (Like Your Own Blood),
    136; 'Ricordo di una battaglia'
    (Memories of a Battle), 56

urban, 20, 21, 44, 68, 76, 89, 91, 139. *See also* city

Visconte dimezzato, Il (*The Cloven Viscount*), 38, 40
'Vita difficile, La' (Living Is Hard), in *Racconti,* 137
Vittorini, Elio, 7, 9, 10–12, 30, 107, 141, 153 n4
void, the, 18, 24, 27, 48, 53, 57, 59, 126. *See also* nothingness

waste, 134, 136, 139, 140, 147, 148
watcher, the, 35, 55, 128
writing, 12, 17, 26, 101, 104; characteristics of, 28; as discipline, 126; as elimination, 150; as game, 116, 127; as impulse to learn, 141; as magic, 89; as obstinacy, 91; organic quality of, 17; as salvation, 126; as thread, 93, 120; as trade, 130; woman's voice and, 175